PEACE BY REVOLUTION

AN INTERPRETATION OF MEXICO

PEACE BY REVOLUTION

AN INTERPRETATION OF MEXICO

BY

FRANK TANNENBAUM

DRAWINGS BY

MIGUEL COVARRUBIAS

BOOKS FOR LIBRARIES PRESS

FREEPORT, NEW YORK

INTERNATIONAL STANDARD BOOK NUMBER:
0-8369-5996-5

LIBRARY OF CONGRESS CATALOG CARD NUMBER:
72-169776

PRINTED IN THE UNITED STATES OF AMERICA
BY
NEW WORLD BOOK MANUFACTURING CO., INC.
HALLANDALE, FLORIDA 33009

TO

DIEGO RIVERA

WHO, MORE THAN ANY ONE ELSE,
HAS REVEALED TO THE WORLD THE PROFOUND
DIGNITY OF THE MEXICAN PEOPLE

ACKNOWLEDGMENTS

I wish to express my profound gratitude to Moises Saenz, Rafael Ramirez and Juan de Diós Bojórquez, whose help and coöperation were indispensable in gathering material for this book, and to Professors Milton David Marx and Arthur Preston Whitaker of Cornell; to Miss Marguerite Owen and Dr. Fred D. Powell of Washington for reading and improving the manuscript; to Professor Carlton J. H. Hayes and Father R. A. McGowan for reading the chapters on religion; to Homer Dodge for his kindness in reading proof; to Glenore Fisk Horne for editorial help; to Dr. Marjorie Clark for making the index; to the Social Science Research Council for a stipend to finish the book; and to the Brookings Institution for the hospitality which provided a place where the work could be done.

It is needless to add that the author alone is responsible for errors of judgment or fact the book may contain.

WASHINGTON, D.C.   FRANK TANNENBAUM
August 1, 1933

CONTENTS

CONTENTS

LABOR

EDUCATION

DRAWINGS

MAPS

PART ONE

FLINT AND STEEL

CHAPTER I

THE INDIAN AND THE SPANIARD

THE social revolution that has intermittently torn Mexico during the last twenty years may be best understood as an attempt to liquidate finally the consequence of the Spanish Conquest. This explanation of the Revolution is at the same time the best key to Mexican history.

No history has a unitary principle. The influences that shape human destiny are too subtle, and the threads out of which history is woven are too numerous to be expressed by a formula. Such contradictory and conflicting trends go on at the same time, that even a complete description would not explain, nor a detailed enumeration give direction or meaning. But, looked at from the outside, with an eye for explanation, meaning, and direction, the answer for Mexico seems clear enough: to undo, as far as can be, the effects of the Spanish Conquest. "Undo" is perhaps too strong a word. But strong or not, the current of Mexican life during four hundred years seems bent to absorb, to subdue, to liquidate, to destroy as a visible and conscious influence the institutions rooted in the Conquest.

It is not suggested that this undoing of the Conquest has, as a conscious principle, supported Mexican social, political, and economic history. That would be too simple an explanation. Though there were isolated rebellions, like those of Lozada in Nayarit and the War of the Castes in Yucatan, which declared that their objective was to destroy, root and branch, all that the white man brought to Mexico, these had, however, little direct influence. Yet, these rebellions must be taken as outcroppings, as an unconscious pushing upward of the underlying social structure against the foreign body injected by the Spanish Conquest.

3

In 1519, suddenly and without warning, a small group of Spaniards, with coats of mail and gunpowder, injected themselves into the Mexican body politic. By force the Spaniards grafted a totally unfamiliar political, economic, religious, and cultural pattern upon the conquered area totally strange to the population that occupied it. This band of soldiers, adventurers, and priests were too few to exterminate the Indians they had subdued; the Indians were too divided and inadequately armed to eject the foreigners; so they have lived for the last four hundred years—one like a parasite, too small a body to destroy its victim, the other too weak internally either to absorb or cast off the parasite.

Mexican history for the last four centuries is the history of the relationship between the parasitical body and the body politic, between the conqueror and the conquered, between the victor and the defeated. The conquerors and the conquered lived lives peculiar to themselves, with their special interests, problems, conflicts, and passions. More important in the long run was the institutional by-product that grew out of this enforced relationship. The larger meaning of the Conquest has found expression in the partial blending of the two races, of their institutions, of their culture, and in the gradual absorption of the Spaniard by the Indian. Not that the Indian is reverting to his past, but the Spaniard with all of his institutional set-up is being frittered away by slow attrition.

It is interesting and worthy of contemplation by all students of culture in Mexico, where a system of institutions was implanted by one race upon another, implanted by force, fear and fraud, by cruelty, murder, and robbery, that such a system, after four hundred years, should have practically disintegrated—and that with it the race responsible for the imposition should also have largely disintegrated. This may seem extravagant language; but, when clearly seen, the facts apparently indicate that although the Spaniards succeeded in conquering Mexico, succeeded in imposing a political, economic, and cultural system to their own liking, that although they apparently succeeded in winning the Indians over to the new order, in spite of all that, as the centuries have passed, the foreign politics, economics, belief, culture, even race itself, has, in an increasing degree, been submerged to such an extent that it is now possible to speak of the liquidation of the Conquest and its institutional outcome.

Not that the older pre-Spanish Mexico is returning; but that the Mexico of Spain is disappearing, and a new Mexico, a new race, a new religion, a new economy, a new politics, a new culture, in all of which the Indian pattern looms large and the Spanish pattern small, is emerging. Underlying Mexican history, therefore, is a conflict between two races with sharply divergent cultures. To speak of race war, except during the conquest, or, at best, during the first half century of Spanish domination, would be misleading. It was not war between the races—it was attrition—an attrition that still goes on. It was a system of behavior that had hate, fear, and suspicion on one side, with power, cruelty, and lust on the other.

At the bottom was the Indian. He was the pariah, the slave, the forced mine laborer, the beast of burden who, for hundreds of years, carried on his back the ore, the goods, even the masters themselves. One can still find traces of this subjection in certain isolated places in Mexico. I saw it in 1926 in Chiapas, where the Chamula Indian is still the beast of burden. The lack of roads, the poor wages, and the scarcity of animals make the Chamula Indian the natural carrier for the white community. He carries from the railroad station to Tuxtla Gutiérrez, and from there to San Cristóbal and to Comitán, a large part of the merchandise consumed in these communities. I have seen him carry sewing machines, bags of flour, crates of canned foods, pottery, cloth, bottles of all sorts (wine, oil and kerosene), and, on one occasion, automobile tires, on another, a piano. This position of the Indian as burden bearer, modified somewhat by the increase of animals, the construction of roads, the introduction of new foods, and, very recently, by the development of steam transportation and automobile roads in some parts of Mexico, persisted until 1910, and may still be found in some localities.

Attrition, tinctured by the passions that emerge wherever the defeated and the victorious, the helpless and the arrogant live side by side, has marked the relations of the two races century after century. In this relationship each little struggle over land, over power, over "rights," over prerogatives, over possession of the Indians' women, over possession of their land, over possession of their toil, of their wealth, was an individual note in the larger composition. The Indian yielded or died; usually he yielded. The white man took all that he wanted—and he wanted all that he could take and absorb. In the end he was himself taken in; he was himself absorbed.

First, he was absorbed physically. The children of the Indian mother were also his children, but they belonged to her. The first generation of Mexicans born of Indian women was the knell that sounded the ultimate physical extinction of the Spanish conqueror, and, because the mother rather than the father brought up the children, they were to carry with them through life her hatred, not merely of an unwelcome and uninvited mate, but of all his works. The process was slow and time-consuming, and is only partially completed, but the end is in sight. Mexico is returning to the children of the Indian mother and will be colored largely by her blood and by her cultural patterns.

The conquest of Mexico by the Spaniards was facilitated by the diversity of Indian groups that inhabited the Mexican territory. Molina Enríquez quotes from Orozco y Bara, mentioning some 700 different "races," or tribes separately identified by name. The census of 1921 enumerated 51 separate languages and dialects, and Wissler notes 29 linguistic stocks for Mexico and Central America, and some 71 sub-classifications. For our purposes the number of races does not matter. It would have made little difference if they had been half as many or twice as numerous. The divergence in type among these Indians could be compared to the racial differentiation of Europeans. In the only sense that the term "race" has any meaning, differences in stature, pigmentation, and social institutions, were so wide as to be incomparable in important respects. The Spaniards found in the territory they conquered sedentary agricultural nations with elaborate arts and crafts, complex institutions of government, and broad ideas of social policy; and at the same time found small, isolated, wandering tribes, living by hunting and war, having little or no agriculture.

Cultural divergence was sharpened by the conflict that raged between the separate groups in Mexico. The most powerful, the Aztecs, were at war with their neighbors and were spreading dominion and conquest far beyond their immediate confines, making themselves felt as far as Central America. The persistent enmities among the Indians favored the invaders. Those recently subdued by the Aztecs, in their desire to avenge themselves upon their oppressors, welcomed the Spaniards as allies, and the Indians of Tlaxcala became a major military aid in carrying the conquest to early completion. The speed of the victory was in itself ominous. It was too easy to be permanent. A long-drawn-out struggle might have destroyed the Indians; the easy conquest left them where they had been found, to reassert slowly, over the centuries, their earlier prerogative to the soil. Because of the sharp cultural and racial divergence between the Indians the conquest was never fully achieved, for some, and will now have to be accomplished through cultural assimilation rather than through military force. The Yaquis, the Tarahumaras, the Lacandones, the Chamulas, the Miji were conquered in name only; and these are but a few examples.

Differentiation of race and culture among the nations delayed and prevented assimilation. It is conceivable that a single race with a unified culture, a common language, and a centralized government might, if conquered, have yielded more readily to assimilation, might more easily have patterned itself upon its conquerors; but the Indians were not unified, and the conquest, the cultural conquest, of each group had to be made separately, in a new language, and with different methods. The *misiones* of northern Mexico differed from the village groups in southern Mexico, and from the convents and churches built among the sedentary populations of the Aztec Empire.

For all practical purposes the struggle in central Mexico was over within the first 25 years of the Spanish invasion; but in the outlying regions, among the northern tribes of wandering Apaches, for instance, it was not over until they were virtually exterminated, long after the Spaniards had ceased to govern "New Spain." Even in central Mexico the mountain regions were but partially conquered. The Indians of the *Malinche* were famous for their irascibility; so were, and still are, the Yaquis on the west coast. A Yaqui Indian, even today, when he goes to work for hire on a plantation, carries his rifle on his back.

On the outskirts of Spanish power, war, conquest, and "civilization," went on for three hundred years. The assimilation of the Indians was never complete; their pacification was never complete; their civilization was never complete; their conversion was never complete. The Huichols, for example, still worship the sun and the fire, although some of them have learned to speak Spanish. In spite, therefore, of four hundred years of domination by Spanish language and Spanish custom, the cultural, linguistic, and economic complexity of the country is perhaps as great as before. Some of the smaller racial groups have probably disappeared. But

A RURAL SCHOOL

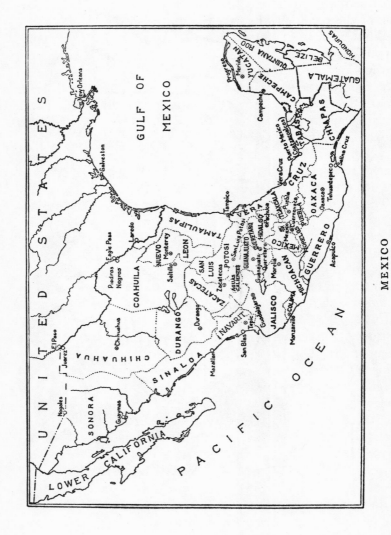

MEXICO

Map showing state boundaries and large cities.

even this is a matter of doubt. There are still in Mexico almost as many racial stocks, though each smaller in proportion of the total, as when the Spaniards came.

What is true of race is true of language. Undoubtedly, Spanish is now more widely used than any other language; or than any one language spoken at the time of the conquest; but the linguistic variety which persists does not differ greatly from that existing at the time of the invasion. There are still languages like Miji, Zapotec, Maya, and Mexicano spoken by hundreds of thousands of human beings, some of whom use Spanish in addition to their own tongue. The men generally speak both languages; the women and children are usually limited to their native tongue.

The older pattern persisted in economy as well as in language and race. Certainly the Spaniards added to the types of economy in Mexico, especially the economy organized about mining, and the economy of export and import; but they did not reduce the number they found—they persist even in the face of modern civilization. Railroads and airplanes vie with human burden carriers, with neolithic agriculture, with communal organization, with wandering possession, with no notion of private ownership in land. The ideas of the whites may have a wider acceptance than any previous system, but they have merely been superimposed upon the previous forms. This is also true of religion, of family customs, of art, and of music. The Spaniards have not succeeded in making a uniform culture area out of Mexico; they have merely complicated the previous culture types and introduced features which have a wider acceptance. This failure of Spain to substitute in Mexico a culture for a series of cultures (not even in religion has it completely succeeded in doing that) helps to explain the tension and conflict that has persisted. As has been suggested, there are, perhaps, as many different races, languages, types of economy, and forms of social organization as when the Spaniards first touched the shores of Mexico.

The pervasiveness of Spanish influence, therefore, varied in different areas and in different racial groups. The conquerors succeeded best in the valleys where large plantations were readily organized, and where a sedentary population, dependent exclusively upon agriculture, found escape from domination difficult. On the great plateaus about Mexico City, Puebla, Guadalajara, the invaders subdued the Indians most completely. Here the Indian became a slave, and later a serf. The plantation peon absorbed much of the white man's blood, acquired a little of his language, something of his habits of clothing, the outward forms of his religion, and a meager use of tools and animals. The Indian on the plantations became more nearly a *mestizo*, more nearly a Mexican, in the sense of a new race mixture, a cross between Spaniard and Indian. The results were not edifying spiritually. While the Indian lost much of his native *mores*, he took on but little of the Spaniard's, even if that little may be said to have been a great deal in comparison with what was absorbed by other Indian groups. The plantation Indian, with his bowed head, his fear of a white man, his complete abnegation, a conquered human being speaking a poor Spanish, tied to the soil, became proverbial in Mexico, and may still be found in places where the revolution has been slow in making itself felt.

In other parts of Mexico where for topographical reasons the Indian could not be easily subdued, nor estates carved out of his holdings, in the more mountainous regions of Vera Cruz, Puebla, Oaxaca, Morelos, Tlaxcala, everywhere, in fact, where broken lands, high mountains, the persistence of forest, or the absence of regular water supply made large-scale plantations difficult to achieve, there the Indian has continued to live in communities. Some of the communities had their origin in the Laws of the Indies, but most of them (the *pueblos viejos*, as they are called in the Valley of Oaxaca), seem to have antedated the coming of the Spaniards.

In these communities Spanish is less frequently spoken, the older ways in the use of land have continued more nearly as they were before; the use of tools has been less affected by the white man's methods; the use of animals is less general; the dress shows greater traces of precolonial influence; weaving is still done on looms of the type used before the Conquest; the internal unity of the village is greater; the sense of freedom is greater.

Spiritually, the Indian in these "free communities" has retained much of his original strength and sense of personality. Still higher in the mountains, or in the depths of the tropical forests, the Indian has even more completely escaped the cultural impact of the Spanish Conquest. The Huichols, the Coras, the Tarahumaras, the Chamulas, are typical mountain Indians who have largely kept their cultural integrity in spite of four hundred years of contact with the white man. Their numbers may not be large in proportion to the total, but they reflect the outside radius, and intensity of the Spanish authority. All along the mountain tops in Mexico, from the border of the United States to Guatemala, in more or less close contact, are tribes of Indians who live as they lived before the Conquest. They have little or no Christian belief; they retain an economic order comparable to the one they knew before the invasion; they have a non-monetary economy, a neolithic agriculture, and they hold on to small tribal organizations as instruments of power and self-defense. Their relations with the whites have most often been warlike; occasional depredation, and escape again into the mountains.

High mountain regions are very much like precolonial America. Lower on the mountain sides are the thousands of congregate communites, such as those of the Indians in Tlaxcala about Malinche, of the Miji Indians and the Otomi Indians, who have, to a large extent, retained their own language as well as much of their ancient way of life, and who have shielded themselves from too complete violation by the outsiders. Below these villages are the people of the plains, living on the plantations, especially where Indian villages have been destroyed or absorbed by the haciendas. Here the imprint of the conqueror is the deepest, and the spiritual and cultural denuding the greatest. So sharply defined are these three groups that Mexicans who have had occasion to see them closely recognize the distinctions. A friend of mine, who has traveled widely, described them in the following terms:

There are three classes of Indian in Mexico; those on the plantation who feel themselves the white man's inferior and look down on the ground while talking to a stranger, those in the villages who feel themselves a white man's equal and look straight at him while addressing him, and those in the mountain tops who consider themselves a white man's superior and look down upon him while addressing him.

That reflection is as descriptive of the quality of the Conquest as of its distribution. When speaking, therefore, of the influence of the Spaniard, of the mixing of the races, of transforming Mexico into a *mestizo* country, all of this difference must be taken into consideration. It is not merely a difference in space relationship, but in quality. If all of Mexico were like the Indian on the plantation, where Spanish influence was greatest, then there would be little hope for Mexico. If all had succeeded in being like the Indians of the mountain tops, then the conquerors could never have settled down even to the comparative security they have enjoyed during four centuries. It is out of the villages where the Indian has retained something of his morale, but achieved a contact with the whites, that the best influence for the Mexico of today and tomorrow is to be expected.

CHAPTER 2

THE DECLINE OF THE SPANIARD

ANOTHER phase of the racial impingement of the Spaniards upon Mexico is related to the development of mining in northern Mexico. In the main, the northern area was carved out and settled chiefly for two purposes: to set a line of defense against marauding Indians, and to exploit the mines. It was about the mines that the larger cities grew. San Luis Potosí, Guanajuato, and Zacatecas are good examples. It was to feed the miners that the early agriculture in the region was developed. It was to carry the ore away and to bring in supplies that roads were constructed to these areas; and it was along these roads that way stations grew into trading and marketing communities. Towns developed near watering stations, and petty agricultural enterprises grew with the increase of population, near the springs, the rivers, or other sources of irrigation. We therefore find here a demarcation of three distinct types of community: the *misiones*, defenses against the savage and unconquered Indian; the mining towns, which became great cities; and the way stations which became small commercial centers. Around all of these communities there developed a little agriculture. These areas were settled by Spaniards with elements brought up from the south, Indians from Tlaxcala, for example. It was in these centers that the mixture between the Indians and the whites became easiest. This, properly speaking, is the *mestizo* part of Mexico. Even here, of course, there are portions of the states, especially in the mountains, that have remained Indian. In the mountains of Sonora, Chihuahua, the eastern slope of San Luis Potosí, the mountain tops of Jalisco and Nayarit, even in the mountains of Coahuila, the Indian has held his own. But on the whole, the *mestizo* dominates in the north. Here Spanish is the dominant language; here *mestizo* costumes are more in evidence; here the community established by the Spanish Crown, with the *fundo legal* (community site) as a base, is most common.

In the south the *mestizo* is a minor element in the population. Generalization is difficult. In order to generalize, one would have to take the states by districts and specify definitely that certain areas are less Indian than others. Such cities as Mexico City, Puebla, Orizaba, Vera Cruz, Córdoba, Tehuacán; commercial cities, industrial cities, and the capitals of states (Chilpancingo, Cuernavaca, Tlaxcala); mining towns like Pachuca—these are white and *mestizo*. In the country, in the mountains of Guerrero, Morelos, Puebla (except in valleys like the one that stretches from Peubla to Tehuacan), in the mountainous parts of Tlaxcala, Hidalgo, Mexico, Vera Cruz, and in the greater part of Tabasco—in all of these regions the population is largely Indian, and in some states, such as Yucatan and Oaxaca, the great mass of the people are Indian, with few *mestizo* and white. The cities tend to loom large in the eyes of foreigners and Mexicans who travel little outside their own sections, and give a misleading impression. The rural districts in the south are dominantly Indian with a small percentage of *mestizo;* the rural districts in the north are dominantly *mestizo* with a small percentage of Indian. In other words, the racial distribution in Mexico has a sharp geographical line dividing the northern *mestizo* from the southern Indian. In the valleys, where the Indian is the dominant factor, the cities are *mestizo;* the villages on the mountainside, less so, and the Indians on the mountain tops, still less. It is to be noted that, leaving out the states of Jalisco and Guanajuato, the *mestizo* is dominant in states where population is sparse and, if we except mining districts, in the less favored regions of Mexico. *The white man and the mestizo have not displaced the Indian in his native habitat;* they have influenced him, they have filtered in, they have modified him; but the Indian has remained as he was and where he was —the most important element in the population except where large cities have grown up. The Indian dominates the rural districts in all sections that were densely populated before the Conquest.

In the north the *mestizo* has lost a large share of his Indian heritage; with it have gone the arts and crafts of the older tradition; with it, too, has gone the social cohesion of the Indian community; with it have gone the mores of the commune. The individualism which is a by-product of the *mestizaje*, because it is a hybrid with no basic culture or tradition, has developed disunity, suspicion, distrust, but it has also developed self-reliance which the older Indian has not. The Indian communities are more integrated, more cohesive; the tradition of leadership and obedience, of moral responsibility, is greater than among the *mestizo* groups. What the *mestizo* has gained in freedom he has lost in morale. He lacks the Indian's sense of permanence, security, and cultural integrity which makes a home something that binds in a way that no outsider can appreciate or understand.

The *mestizo*, having lost his community, has become a miner (the number of pure Indians who work in the mines is negligible), an industrial worker, a city employee, a clerk, an *aparcero* (share cropper), or a plantation laborer. The Indian, on the other hand, has retained his residence within the village, even though most of the village land was lost in the centuries of conflict with the plantation. He has striven to retain his communal ownership of the pasture and wood lands at least. Even today among the *mestizo* and Indian villages that retained their lands at least 80 per cent have some form of communal holdings. Only occasionally does the Indian work for a season on a neighboring *hacienda* or in the mines. The Indian high up in the mountains is still nomadic; the plantation laborer is still largely a serf; the difference in race is reflected in social and economic organization.

It must by now be clear that the Indian has surprisingly held to his older traditions and culture. Why has the process of assimilation been so slow? In the first place, the Indians, except when forcibly carried off to the mines, taken as soldiers to the frontiers, brought as servants into the towns, or harried to work upon distant plantations, have remained in their own communities. These communities have, during hundreds of years, certainly until the revolution of 1910, lost in wealth, in population, in land, and in prestige. In spite of that, they retained a measure of their older unity and tradition, even where there was an infiltration of white blood. The past was against change, and as long as the village succeeded in retaining a semblance of community life, it succeeded in continuing the pattern of its culture, even when it became bilingual. The white man was an isolated individual in opposition to an organic group that lived on after the white man went away, died, or was killed. If the Indian's internal unity had been disintegrated, and especially if he had been driven from his communal moorings, the mixture of the races would have been more complete and more devastating.

The limited penetration of Spanish culture into the mountain communities is explained in part by the fact that after the mining towns were developed, mainly by forced labor brought up for that purpose, and the plantations were laid out, frequently with the workers already upon them, there was no economic urge to break up the villages. After the best lands were taken by the conquerors, the villages remained as a labor reserve called upon during planting and harvesting seasons, or in other times of special need. Beyond that it was easier to leave the Indians to their own way of life. Those torn from their moorings, therefore, became *mestizos* even if their fraction of white blood was no greater than that of the brothers they left behind. The Indians that stayed in the villages remained Indians in fact as well as in name; Indians, in spite of the white blood in their veins. The absence of rapid economic development, which would have put great pressure upon the mountain groups, saved the natives and helped preserve their scheme of life.

This preservation of the Indian community was made easier by the stationary character of the rural population. There is little movement from one altitude to another, or from one village to another. In his own community the Indian has a place and a home; he has prerogatives, rights, privileges, and a future. Outside of his community he is a stranger, a stranger often with a different language, and with no property rights. Continuance at home has been customary for the rural population that retained even a semblance of its older communal tradition. We have already indicated that something like eighty per cent of the villages still have some elements of communal life.

The fact, too, that the Spaniard was not a colonist, but a conqueror and a gold seeker, helps to explain why the Indian population was allowed to retain so much of its older ways of life. Except in the mining districts or where plantations developed, the Spaniard was content to exact from the communities a payment in kind, without interfering, except for some special occasion, with the internal economy and *mores* of the communities. The Spaniard's greed, cupidity, and indifference saved the Indians from too much supervision, and, in so doing, saved for them their way of life and, with it, the promise of fulfillment which the recent revolution has opened up.

The colonial policy which for three centuries restricted migration to a limited number of Spaniards, and the persistent turmoil following independence were other factors that kept foreigners out. The white population was always a small evanescent group in the total population. The second generation either changed to *mestizo* or returned to Spain, after garnering such fruits as ambition and power had made possible.

The small Spanish immigration was motivated by both political and economic aims. Aside from the *entrepreneur* there is little room for foreigners. They cannot survive the low standard of living upon which the Indian and *mestizo* prosper and breed. That is one of the reasons for the very small immigration of Europeans or Americans to Mexico, except as investors and directors. Even the Chinese and Japanese in Mexico became petty merchants and not laborers. They could not compete with the native laboring population in the rural districts. The basic food of the Indian is maize, salt, and water, upon which he can live, work, and survive with remarkable energy. The Indian who has not only maize, salt, and water, but also pulque and beans, is a fortunate and well-fed Indian. Meat and wheat are luxuries which are rarely eaten, except on festive occasions.

With a few *tortillas* (thin pancakes made of corn meal) and a little salt, an Indian will outstrip a horse on a long day's march. He will travel forty miles and carry twenty-five kilos on his back. Anyone who has seen the Chamula Indians trot hour after hour with heavy loads on their backs, will understand that no white man can compete with the Indian upon his own level. All of Mexico's wars have been fought by the *mestizo*, mainly on a diet of *tortillas* and salt. A few half-dried corn pancakes, a little salt and water, and some morale, and the army will march and fight for months, aye, for years. The campaigns of the war of independence lasted years, as did the recent revolution; the armies of the revolution were not provisioned, nor were those of the war of independence. What is true of food is true also of clothing; and what is true of clothing is true of housing. The Indian can stand the sharp climatic changes and the difficult physical labor under conditions in which no white man can survive.

To this interlacing of factors should be added the land system developed under Spanish colonial administration. The large tracts with the Indians upon them given to individuals, made the Spaniard a master over the natives and left them at his mercy. It served, however, another purpose not foreseen. It made the new owners guardians of their own lands, and, therefore, guardians of the Indians who lived upon them against a too rapid intrusion from the outside. The lack of immigration, combined with the fact that the greater part of the area was early distributed among a few conquering favorites, saved their native places for a large portion of the Indians. The owners did not welcome strangers, even if they were Spaniards. In their attempt to keep the fruits of the Conquest to themselves, the few favored Spaniards laid the foundation of their own ultimate undoing. There were simply too few Spaniards to destroy completely the Indian *mores*.

This combination of circumstances helped to keep the Indians in southern Mexico bound to their older traditions despite four centuries of Spanish domination. Since the Spanish conquest, wandering military bands that have continuously ravaged Mexico have been the greatest source of racial mixture. Military turbulence, more than any other phenomenon, has spread the *mestizo* throughout Mexico. Armed bands went into every region of Mexico, and their seed sprouted in some proportion wherever they went.

It has thus come about that, although the percentage of mixed blood has increased, there has been no proportionate change in culture. The *mestizo* within an Indian community has remained an Indian in all but blood. Out of the 7,800,000 people in Mexico who are described as living in a primitive civilization, 4,300,000 are considered *mestizos*. Even the *mestizo* outside the Indian village (where racial change is gradual, as it is on the plantations), has retained to a surprising degree the Indian way of life. Entire areas have, therefore, remained almost completely Indian in culture, race, and even in language. It is not easy to give statistics for these facts. The Indians are always underestimated in any counting. They fear the census taker, because they are

ignorant of his aims, which they suspect to be higher taxation; formerly they also feared forced service in the army.
Also, who is there who will go and count the Chamula Indians
in their mountain recesses? Certainly no representatives of
the census office, certainly no one from the city of San Cristóbal, the nearest white community. The secretary of the Chamula *municipio*, who lives at the little village where the
Indians gather for their holidays, will not go because he is
afraid; because he has no time; because he would not know
where to go; because, in fact, the Indians are so scattered in
barrancas and mountains that no one really knows where to
find them. So any guess is a good guess, and if any counting
is done, it is limited to a small portion of the entire Indian
population.

The Indian in Mexico is, therefore, underestimated; by the
same token the white man is overestimated. Many a *mestizo*
prefers to pass for a white man, and does so, if he can by
grace of the census. In spite of this the present unfair figures
show almost four Indians to every white man. But that is
not the whole story. In 1921, there were in Mexico, according
to the census, ten people with Indian blood to every white
man; we have already indicated that the white population
is considerably overestimated. There are very few people
of Spanish descent in Mexico who have not also some
Indian blood. The white population which was one out of
ten inhabitants in 1921 by the most favorable estimate, was
probably one out of eleven in 1930, after four hundred years
of residence. But the story is only half told; it is also true
that the white population is decreasing in proportion to the
total. The number of whites has not varied for a hundred
years; the other races have increased, more than tripled their
numbers. The white man is at present possibly one out of
every eleven inhabitants; in 1800 he was approximately one
out of every four. In other words the white man, the conqueror of Mexico, is tending to lose his status as a numerically

dominant element in the population. This is made clear by some simple figures. In 1810 it is estimated that there were 1,097,928 Spaniards out of a total of 4,774,219; twenty-three per cent of the whole population. In 1823 there were, according to Humboldt, 1,230,000 whites out of 6,800,000 inhabitants; eighteen per cent of the whole. The census of 1921 gives 1,474,057 whites out of 14,344,700; ten per cent of the total. The census figures for 1930 on race are not yet available, but certainly the percentage of whites will not have increased.

Although there is no agreement on the number of Indians in Mexico, partly because of the difficulty of enumerating and defining them (most Indians pass as *mestizos* soon after they settle in larger cities), it is clear that they are increasing more rapidly than the whites. There were approximately three million Indians both in 1810 and in 1823. The census of 1910 gave the Indians 6,573,000, and the census of 1921, 4,179,499, showing a decrease which, in spite of the decline in the population between 1910 and 1921, seems altogether too large an estimate, and may be explained by the conditions of civil strife during which the 1921 census was taken, leaving the population of the remoter and more inaccessible areas uncounted. Whatever the relative growth of the Indians in comparison with the total population, they have shown an increase in comparison with the whites, while the number of whites has remained practically stationary. The great gains, as was to be expected, have been among the *mestizo* element of the population. The picture, from whatever angle it is drawn, indicates that the pure white strain in the Mexican population has so declined in importance that its future disappearance may be predicted.

Racial change thus reveals a definite tendency. The white element is declining in proportion to the total; the Indian is gaining in proportion to the white; the *mestizo* is gaining in proportion to both. The ultimate outcome seems clear enough: Mexico will become a *mestizo* country in which the Indian element will be greater than the white. The declining proportion of whites and the general tendency of the *mestizos* to be absorbed within the more stationary environment is sufficient explanation for that.

With the passing centuries, the *mestizo* has become increasingly significant, and has supplied Mexico with its leaders, its soldiers, its artists, and its politicians. In spite of his better cultural, social, and political status, the *mestizo* has been close to the Indian. In the days of the Spanish colony, the only occupation open to him was the Church, in which he was only eligible to the lower ranks of the clergy. With independence the *mestizo* has more nearly come into his own. For three centuries he had remained a social exile from both the pure white, and the pure Indian, groups, especially if he was born and raised outside an Indian village. His increase in number and the decline of the whites has made the *mestizo* the only really unified racial element in Mexico, with a uniform heritage in the soil. From his Indian mother he acquires his capacity for resistance, and the cultural content that separates the Indian from the whites. He has a common language; he has a more nearly common religion, and he is more nearly of the same type. He has a common social position between the top and the bottom of the ladder; he is Mexican: his horizon is broader than the Indian's; his aspirations more active. He wishes to conquer a place for himself in the scheme of things; whereas the Indian is content to stay in the little village of his birth.

To the white Spaniards, Mexico has been, and is, essentially a colony. The white man in Mexico has never surrendered the tradition that he is conqueror. Anyone who has seen the attitude toward, and the treatment of, the Indians and the *mestizos* by the foreigner (*criollo* or Spaniard), will understand what is meant. The stranger in Mexico is there to exploit, to enrich himself, and then to depart. He knows it is not his country.

The Indian on the other hand has no sense of the Great Society. He is local in tradition, education, and ambitions. Only the *mestizo* can fully understand and feel the future of Mexico as a nation. He alone shares in both the native roots of his mother and the exotic culture of the conqueror. The future belongs to the brown *mestizo*, true child of his mother and his mother's race, steeped in her environment, nurtured and cradled by her songs and her language. The white man is here a stranger; his contribution is accidental and incidental.

The problem of racial unification, however, is more complex than is here suggested. The large areas in southern Mexico, almost completely Indian, make racial mergence difficult. The cultural integrity of the Indian areas makes them resistant to change. The stubborn Indian villages surrounding a *mestizo* community, such as San Cristóbal in Chiapas, or Actopan in Hidalgo, which for hundreds of years have remained immune to outside influence, have refused to mix, retaining both racially and culturally their own pattern, are significant. These illustrations may be duplicated from almost every part of the country. The story of Xochimilco on the outskirts of Mexico City, for four hundred years the center of the most powerful forces in Spanish culture and economy, cannot be overlooked. Contemporary tendencies, however, are toward greater mixture of the races. The Revolution has given this fusion impetus. Thousands of soldiers wandering for years over every part of the republic have left the imprint of race mixture and race unity everywhere.

Racially, the trend is clearly enough toward unification and the disappearance of the white man. Culturally, however, unification is not so easy nor so evident. The assumption that cultural unity would follow the disappearance of the white man is not at all obvious. Although it is true that the cultural and economic gap between the Indian and the white man, is very great indeed, the gap between the Indian and the *mestizo* is still so profound that an easy fusion is not possible. Evidence upon this problem is not easily available, but the picture may be made out from some studies which we have made, and summarize here. The information obtained indicates that there are in rural Mexico two sharp economic and cultural classes: the Indian and the *mestizo*. This difference is confused by the fact that the *mestizo* predominates in the north, the Indian in the south. But the evidence is clear enough and shows the following: the Indian villages are more communal in character, more isolated; the wages of Indian laborers, for work done outside their own communities, are considerably lower than those of the *mestizo*; on the average, the Indians till less land per individual; they are considerably poorer in mechanical and animal power; they have fewer contacts with the outside world by means of railroads, automobiles, horses, telephones, and telegraph: the Indians carry their burdens to market upon their own backs more frequently than do the *mestizos*; they have fewer agricultural implements; their villages have fewer horses, cows, burros and mules, sheep, goats, pigs, and chickens; they more frequently use barter; they have fewer good roads; their villages are more poorly served by doctors. As an example of the last statement, it was found in our study that there was one doctor for every 10,231 *mestizos*, whereas there was only one doctor for every 48,270 Indians.

The position of the Indian with regard to the services of lawyers, engineers, teachers, druggists, *parteras, curanderos,* even of priests, is poorer than the *mestizo's*. Nor is the Indian as well served by skilled craftsmen. There are fewer carpenters, masons, plumbers, blacksmiths, tinsmiths, shoemakers, saddle makers, leather workers in Indian villages than in *mestizo* villages. The Indian communities tend to be poorer than those of the *mestizos* in everything but weavers. The difficulties of a statistical study, such as constituted the basis of these statements, are very great, and much is left that needs investigation. But careful students of Mexico have long known the substance of the findings: the Indian is poorer than the *mestizo* when measured by any test that indicates possession of modern skills, tools, or goods; very often the Indian community is so much more primitive as to be on a lower cultural level. As long as such broad distinctions separate the rural districts, as long as there is so marked a difference in the economic equipment and well-being of the people, and as long as this difference runs along racial lines, it is useless to speak of a unified race in Mexico. Race integration will be not only difficult, but it must even remain a chimera till the Indian is brought more nearly abreast of the *mestizo* in social and economic well-being.

We may now draw this part of our discussion to a conclusion by pointing again to the fact that the Spanish Conquest of Mexico left neither a unified race, nor a unified culture. The cultural and racial diversification is probably as great as, if not greater than, it was before the Conquest. In so far as the Spaniards have contributed to racial unification, it has been at their own expense as a race. The whites are declining in relation to both the Indians and the *mestizos*. The *mestizo* has mainly settled in those sections of Mexico where it was necessary to populate the country in order to guard against wandering and non-conquered Indians, and where the mines were developed. In the south, the real Indian area, there has been comparatively little direct influence upon the composition of the population. What change has occurred in the south is to be seen in the cities, the centers of districts, the commercial communities. The *mestizo* element tends to be more important in the valleys than in the mountains. There is a sharp line of demarcation between the *mestizo* and the Indian in the rural districts—the Indian being always the poorer. The *mestizo* and white man are always better equipped than the Indian. In regions where the three elements live side by side, as in Tlapa, Guerrero and San Cristóbal in Chiapas, or Batopilas in Chihuahua, the *mestizo* and white continue to exploit the Indian by every means at their disposal, and with little power of resistance on the part of the Indian. The centuries-old process, not of war, but of attrition, continues.

No general statements, therefore, concerning the racial distribution of Mexico, the cultural divergence between the races, or the strife between the whites, the *mestizos*, and the Indians, give an idea of the persistent conflict that has shaped the relationships between these groups. It is only upon examination of details, the little things, in attitudes, and physical bearing, that the depth of the separation can be sensed. The white man has exploited; the *mestizo* has played a double game when he could, having been now partner of the white man, and now of the Indian. The Indian has retired into the mountains when he could, otherwise into himself. He has kept himself apart, isolated, separate in every way. He has refused to learn the Spanish language; refused to take over the conquerors' customs; refused to share in the white man's interests; refused to be a part of the game as it was being played. In part, he could not participate, because he was not allowed to. He did not understand what it was all about. Values were different; purposes of life and living were different. It was partly fear, a fear of betrayal, of abuse, of denial, of death. The Indian has been at the mercy of his white master so long, he has been exploited so long, that he does not believe the outsider, who has always proved an enemy in the end, a self-seeker, a person of no trust, a liar, a cheat, a *gachupin* who, in the eyes of the primitive Tarahumara Indian, is worse than a pig, and in the opinion of some of the Puebla Indians, is a thief. The Indian has lost much of his self-respect, much of his confidence, much of his sense of worth. He has been beaten every time he has attempted to rise in rebellion, so he has retreated into apathy listlessness, drunkenness, fear, humility, subjection, silence.

His retreat has served to conserve and to protect him. Wherever he could, he has held on to his old values, his old culture, his old government, becoming poorer in every way (economically, culturally, spiritually) than he was before. He is, as Gamio has said, not as he was before the Conquest, but poorer.

CHAPTER 3

CONTINUED FRICTION BETWEEN THE RACES

FOUR HUNDRED YEARS of racial oppression have left a mark upon the Indian which even the Revolution has not completely eradicated. The superior power of the white man, his social prestige, his economic prerogatives, the ease with which he can use political and military agencies to sustain and maintain his position, tended to make the Indian submissive, obedient, suspicious, and revengeful. In his relations with the white man, the Indian, especially the plantation Indian, is exceedingly docile. From Michoacán, one teacher writes that the Indians of Pueblo Nuevo are slow to comprehend, and fearful. They approach a white man with lowered head and a vague look, seeming barely to listen. If they are forced to answer, their replies are in monosyllables. From Xocoyocán, Tlaxcala, the reports are that the women are so timid that the *agente municipal* had to go to bring them to a meeting of the social worker. They were afraid to approach a stranger. While traveling in Chiapas in 1926, it was my common experience to find, on reaching a village, that all of the women had fled into the mountains when the dogs announced the coming of strangers—and there were only three of us. Similar incidents occurred in the isolated sections of Nayarit in 1931. Excessive drunkenness is one form which the retreat from the white man has taken among many Indian groups. Drunkenness has become their one source of self-expression. In Tacanhuitz, San Luis Potosí, drunkenness is wide-spread among both the men and the women. In fact it seems to be so in the whole region of Huasteca. Drunkenness is fomented by the *gente de razón*, who pay in part in *aguardiente*, not merely wages, but also for products that the Indians bring to market.

In the city of Acayucán, Vera Cruz, the whites and the *mestizos* live in the center of a large Indian community, but the separation between the three groups is as great as if they lived "leagues" apart. The whites are called *gente de razón* (men of reason), by the Indians. The Indians are called, contemptuously, *los naturales*. Between the two a conflict over land has gone on for centuries, and is still in progress. Feeling runs high, and class distinctions are sharp. The city of Izucar de Matamoros, in Puebla, is surrounded by fourteen Indian villages (*barrios*). They have retained their original costumes and mores, and from time immemorial have "opposed having any social bonds with the inhabitants of the city." In Teteles, Puebla, the Indians "are haughty and look with dislike and suspicion upon the *mestizos* and strangers whom they call *gente de razón*." Between the Indians and the *mestizos* there is a profound division. Among the *mestizos* themselves there is conflict, for they have divided themselves into two parties, the "soldiers," and the "peasants."

Among the Indians, the *mestizos* and the whites, there is frequently extreme hostility. Anyone who has visited Tlapa, Guerrero, will be able to testify to that. Wherever there is a large Indian section in Mexico, with a *mestizo* or white city as a center of marketing or commerce, there exists an almost rancorous sense of conflict between them. Typical of such a district is the city of San Cristóbal in Chiapas. In the neighborhood are large groups of Chamulas, and the city lives by their labors. Here, there is a system of *enganchaderos* that is explained as follows:

The people here live largely by supplying labor to the coffee plantations in the southern part of the State. They send out agents to the villages who advance some money to the Indians for which they make a cross on paper. These Indians are brought to town where they are collected in certain houses, each of which has an *aguardiente* shope. Here they are fed all of the drink they want. They use up what has been advanced to them and are allowed to have all of the drink they wish on credit. When they come to themselves they have used up not only the cash that was advanced to them, but their credit for the future. In debt, they start for the coffee plantations where they are allowed food on credit to be worked off. After many months and years of labor an Indian may succeed in working off his debt, but not always.

This was in 1927. So dependent is the city upon the sale of *aguardiente* to the Indians, and upon the exploitation of them that an attempt by the Federal School Director to initiate an anti-alcoholic campaign among the Chamula Indians led to such violent protests and difficulties (including the murder of two teachers by members of the white community), that the Director was forced to leave the State. In more than one instance, teachers who have been educating the Indians to a sense of their rights have been murdered. What is true of the Chamulas in the southern state of Chiapas is true of the Tarahumaras in the northern state of Chihuahua. Here the *scabochis* (the Tarahumara's name for the *mestizo*) have almost always sided against the Indian "even if the Tarahumara had right and justice on his side."

The conflict between the Indian and the white man continues in various ways, especially the conflicts over land. In one place there is a conflict over an *ejido*; in another, a large landowner is burning houses of Indians settled upon his land, an act still customary in Nayarit to keep the Indians from developing a community; in another it is the paying of wages in pulque; in another, the Indians must accept their wages in corn, in goods, in the right to till a piece of land. In Zitácuaro, Michoacán, the local authorities, as well as the landowners, refused the school authorities all aid in 1926 because they looked upon the school as an undesirable influence upon the Indians. In Querétaro the village of San Juan del Río is reported to be in the same condition as before the revolution.

In spite of all this, the *mestizo* is gradually supplanting the white man and the Indian, becoming largely himself an Indian, because the stream of white blood, when it is ultimately disseminated throughout the whole population, will be very thin indeed. From one point of view, however, this is going to be of great importance in Mexico. The Spaniards, having conquered Mexico, will in time have given to the races of the country the contribution of their own physical heritage, and will thereby have made a race out of the races in Mexico—a race at least in the sense that each group will have a common relationship to the conqueror, who will have disappeared in the process. Perhaps this will be a sort of atonement for the sins committed during and after the Conquest. These sins were not merely physical, but spiritual: a denial of the essential dignity of the Indian as a human being. For centuries there was a well-defined attitude in Mexico toward the lower classes. This attitude was such as to make any sympathetic understanding between the whites and the Indians impossible.

It is difficult to exploit a race without finding a moral justification for the policies of suppression and denial. We have seen this everywhere. Our own southern attitude toward the Negro during, and after, slavery is illustrative of this point. It is also to be seen in our attitude toward other races, in the attitude of the Turk toward the Armenian, or the attitude of the English aristocrat toward the Irish, over many centuries; all of these examples illustrate the moral embellishment of acts that need moral bolstering; they represent a species of self-justification. If one can justify one's iniquitous acts by a moral doctrine of superiority, of greater cultural value, of serving better gods, then the evil one does may finally appear as good; if one does this long enough the act always tends to take on an appearance of virtue.

In Mexico, the doctrine of superiority took the form of an assertion that the Indians stood in the way of national progress. That the Indian was incapable of cultural achievement was repeated until believed; that he was an impediment, a "sterile field" in which no germ could flourish; that he must perish and pass out of existence to make a place for a better and more competent people. That was the doctrine. On this doctrine was postulated and justified all that was done against the Indian; all was justified on the grounds of justice, progress, and culture. It was all at the expense of the Indian and for the benefit of his master; but since his master both made the law and preached the theory, and as he was the only one who read it, he was also, perhaps, the only one who believed it. When there arose a great figure like Juárez, who was pure Indian, he was considered an exception, an accident. The truth of the doctrine was not impeached for those who believed it. It was left ultimately to be destroyed by the defeat of those who upheld it. It took a long and blood-soaked revolution to convince Mexico of the contrary, and there are still some who cling to their old notions.

Writing as late as 1904 Bulnes said:

... The Mexican Indian did not exist nor exists at present. He is an imaginary creature, an official creation, oratorical, fantastic. What does exist are Zapotec Indians, Mixteco Indians, Yaqui Indians, Maya Indians, Tarasco Indians, Tarahumara Indians, etc., etc. In Mexico there are nations of Indians, within the nation, that are unknown to each other or are enemies. To ask an Indian to defend Mexico is like asking a Japanese to defend the island of Cuba.

A thoughtful comment by Agustin Aragón says:

The contempt with which the Indian is viewed in Mexico is very marked. There are educated people in Mexico who consider themselves polluted by the mere fact of having to think of the Indian and his position.

That was in 1900; at an earlier date, Pimentel in listing the causes of the moral defeat of the Indians in Mexico, says: "The contempt with which they have been viewed, humiliated and dejected them." Probably in no other respect has the social upheaval of the last 22 years been so fruitful as in the dissipation of this attitude toward the Indian. This change has not yet affected all parts of Mexico, but as never before there is a growing feeling of a common race among all classes.

The Mexican people may look forward to a common race, in the sense we have indicated, a common participation in the conqueror's blood. What significance this blending of the races has, or will have in the long run, may be a matter of dispute. Clearly enough, it will provide an easier basis for a common language; that, in turn, will certainly favor mutual understanding and growth. It may be that a common language, the conqueror's tongue, is an essential element in liquidating ultimately the bad results of the conquest. In the process of racial unification, there must be an elevation of the Indian communities to meet the economic level and position of the *mestizos*, and the *mestizo's* communities must be integrated to be able to achieve again something which they lost during the last four centuries: the morale of an organized community, and the internal unity and harmony that can come only from common interests and from a common culture. The Revolution is working toward that goal: the achievement of national unity and racial homogeneity by providing the means for reasserting the village homogeneity through thousands of small but internally unified communities. It is along that road that a solution of the race problems of Mexico will have to be worked out. There are other roads, but they lead in different directions, away from what seems to be the special genius of the Mexican rural population.

CHAPTER 4

THE WORK OF THE CHURCH

THE Spanish Conquest brought to Mexico a new race, a new economic and political system, and a new religion. The Catholic Church, coming with the conquerors, intimately bound with them spiritually, serving them in their effort to subdue and pacify the Indians, becoming in a short time a great power, and gathering under its influence millions of new converts, has, during the last four centuries, had a history so closely entwined with that of Mexico that no consideration of that country is possible without an insight into the peculiar rôle and position of that institution. The passing of the Catholic Church—no other term will describe its changed position—is one of the most striking by-products of the general liquidation of the Spanish Conquest occurring in Mexico. That the Catholic Church should suffer this decline is perhaps the most surprising of the results of the last four hundred years of Mexican history. For though the Church was part of the Conquest, and served the Crown as an instrument of peace, it had an independent claim upon the population which should have given it a place in the life of the people that would have saved it from defeat. The Church sought to absorb the people of Mexico within its spiritual folds, to convert them into good Catholics, to bring to them the gift of a common fatherhood with their conquerors, to establish in Mexico an eternal faith, and a Church beyond and above the vicissitudes that rule and govern the material passions of man. Yet the Church has resisted the common disintegration of the Spanish heritage no better than, and perhaps not so well as, the political and economic institutions derived from the Conquest.

The Church was weakened even before the power of the

Crown was repudiated. The expulsion of the Society of Jesus in 1767, 54 years before Mexican independence, was a body blow to the Church from which it never recovered. No sooner was Mexican nationality achieved than an attack upon the Church began which by 1833, only twelve years after the consummation of freedom, took on that serious form which, with minor changes, has continued to this date, and, in the process, has destroyed its wealth, its power, and much of its influence.

This is the more striking as the attack upon the Church has been aimed against an organization rather than a system of belief. In the hundred years of conflict, there has been no important native Protestant movement. No significant group of Mexicans has sought to change the theology or modify the practices of the Catholic faith. It is not as a religion that the Catholic Church has been assailed, but as an organized power. The attack upon the Church has been carried out in a country where the people continued to call themselves Catholics and continued to be baptized and buried under Catholic auspices and Catholic ritual.

Coming with the Conquest, the Church served that enterprise by exerting its influence to secure submission, obedience, and acceptance of the new rulers. The hold that the priest and friar secured over the Indians accounts in part for the great weight the Church had in the colonial government. The Crown frequently called the bishops and archbishops to serve it as chiefs of the civil power. The strength which the Crown derived from the prestige of the Church redounded to the benefit of the Church. The two institutions, one serving the interests of this world, and the other of the next, found a common footing in conquering the Indian, converting him, and civilizing him. While the *encomendero* used the Indian in the mines and in the fields, the Church used him to build temples and churches. While the Spaniard as soldier established internal peace and a common government, the Spaniard as priest established a common faith, and brought to the Indians the benefits of Christianity in addition to the arts and crafts then known in Spain, taught many of them how to read and write, and imparted to them the use of new and unknown tools, domestic animals and plants. Here we have a unified effort, under the control of the Crown and the blessing of the Pope, serving the great end of enhancing the power and prestige of Spain in the New World, one dedicated to economic and the other to spiritual enterprise, each seemingly rooted deep in the soil of Mexico, each living in comparative peace for three hundred years, and each leaving an imprint upon the country and its people, which even today, though largely deteriorated, can still be counted as of great significance.

Whatever his future, the Mexican Indian, looking back upon the history of his race, must count it a good fortune that the Catholic Church came with the Spanish conqueror. Had the invader been bent only on gold and riches, upon the exploitation of mines and the collection of tribute, then the fortune of the Indian, hard and bitter as it has been, might have proved still less bearable, still less amenable to the elementary demands of ordinary justice. The Catholic Church, representing as it did the non-material elements in the Conquest and the interests of the Spanish Crown as a Christian power, the priest representing as he did the spiritual aspiration of the Most Catholic Nation in Europe and the ideal interest of the Catholic Church, contributed in large measure to the development of those laws, practices, and attitudes which made possible the saving of the Indian as a race. That the Indian has a future in Mexico is in no small measure due to the saving influences of the Catholic Church and the Catholic religion.

The insistence that the Indian was a human being, that he had a soul, that he could be saved, that he could become a Christian—that he had become one—saved the Indian in

36

Mexico from the fate of that state of mind among the *conquistadores* that for so long was current in the United States: "The only good Indian is a dead Indian." The Indian was abused, misused, enslaved, branded, worked against his will in the mines, robbed. Everything evil that one human being can do to another was done to him. This need not be denied— it cannot be. But the cruelty, the brutality, the harshness, is not the whole story. The Indian woman was taken as a wife; her children were given a place in the household. Indian princes were accepted as allies. The influence of the Church was used to help the Indian achieve a medium of defense in the Crown against the *conquistadores*. Land was set aside for him. Special laws were passed in his favor. Special exemptions were developed for him. A community, a church, a law, a body of rights—all these were given to him, largely because he was considered a human being possessed of a soul and capable of redemption. The argument that the Spanish gold seeker needed miners, carriers, servants, that the adventurer needed women, that the *encomendero* needed laborers is true, of course; but men like Las Casas, Quiroga, Zumárraga, and Fuenleal labored, fought, and defended the Indian against the rapacity of the white man, and in that defense initiated a series of currents, ideals, ideas, laws, and practices, within which the Indian has the more easily saved his race from extermination, and, by saving his race, has saved his genius for the world.

One need not deny that in their fanaticism the early clergy, friars, monks, and priests, destroyed idols, burned temples and obliterated records that might have helped explain the heritage of a past that may now forever have disappeared from human cognizance and understanding. But when one remembers the cruelty of the religious strife that then raged in Europe, in a Church divided against itself; when one remembers the massacres, the murders, the burnings, the bloody civil wars within nations of the same race and language; when one recalls that a difference in religious allegiance represented so great a difference in moral status as to make the cruel annihilation of one group by another seem a great virtue; when one remembers these things, it must be considered an act of kindness and generosity for the Spaniards under the Church not only to have spared the Indians, but to have attempted to bring them to the faith that identified the conquered with the conqueror as children of the same Father.

The Church achieved more than it planned. It saved the Indian's status as a human being in the eyes of his conquerors. He became not merely a Christian and a Catholic, but one who might ultimately become an equal. Certainly this was the result of a much kinder view than the one that has so long passed current among so-called scientifically-minded people, who declare the Indian an inferior race, permanently inferior, never to be fitted for anything other than a beast of burden, only a little above a domesticated beast, as one of those scientifically-minded people expressed it to me recently. Certainly the Catholic doctrine which gave the Indian a soul gave him a moral hold upon the imaginations of pious people, and perhaps saved enough of his own self-respect to make his lot tolerable.

The Church did more than that. It gave the Indian an opportunity not merely to save his life, but also to save his faith in his own gods—the Indian gods. It is true that the friars and priests destroyed the temples and the idols. But they built churches upon the very spots—Cholula, for example—where the old gods had ruled so long, and they filled the churches with saints, not unlike the old idols that had stood in the very same places. The Indians easily adorned the new saints with the virtues the old gods possessed, prayed to them in the same language, sang the same songs to them, danced the same dances, and even to this day occasionally sacrifice a chicken to the gods—the old gods—within and without the church. The holidays were on the same dates and in the same form. The Indians by custom and habit gathered from miles around, and prayed and danced and worshipped and sang to the gods of the *place* in a new temple.

This saving of the old relationship to the unseen universe played so great a rôle in the lives of the Indians that it helps to explain the hold of the Church upon the people of Mexico. The Church not only saved the Indian from extermination by giving him an equality with the white man, but it saved his sense of place in the universe by giving him an instrumentality to perpetuate his beliefs; to practice his religion. The Church now housed two kinds of gods, the old and the new; observed two practices, the old and the new. The new practices had meaning only because they were so near the old, observed in the same places, on the same days, with the same dresses, the same dances, the same songs, the saints even looking like the old gods and just as personal. It saved the Indian's sense of the meaning of life, and as much as anything else, preserved him from complete moral degradation, from spiritual annihilation.

One must see the Church and the priest as two rather distinct institutions. The priesthood in many places was transitory; the church was permanent. The people were the Church; they were one with the saint of the little community who watched and guarded it. The priest was only a servant of the saint, and was paid as one. There are villages in the mountains of Oaxaca where a priest is allowed to enter a church only with the consent of the elders of the community, and by their invitation. The Church is of the people, and the saint is their very soul.

Friar and priest, Franciscan and Dominican monk, bishop and prior, replaced in the imagination of the Indian the authority of the older priest. The Church had consciously or unconsciously participated in the transfer of the old religion into the new; the new became a part of the old. The Indian, in turn, accepted the new priest as authoritative, as he had the old, and permitted himself to be corrected and punished by the new spiritual power, as he had been by the old. The Indian built the churches under the guidance of the priest and the monk, as he had built the temples, the pyramids, the castles, under the leadership of the old religion and its priests, as a labor of love, of veneration, of force, of duress, of faith, and of fear. These emotions are not distinguishable in the mind and heart of man; fear and veneration, punishment and reward, go together. The Indians who built the churches worked without pay, without food, and at the cost of sweat and blood, of pain and sorrow. So had the earlier temples been built. But they were built also by love and faith and hope, adorned by the affectionate reverence for the saint who was the protector and the guide—the God who mitigated and understood, punished and rewarded. It is only the cynical, the crass, the ignorant, who fail to understand the simple emotions of a simple people trying to find a foothold in this world of ours, trying to find it by transferring to some visible form, something that they can touch and feel, sing and pray to, bring their sorrows and their hopes to, something that can mellow the tribulations that afflict them in a stubborn and unyielding world. The churches were built by love; the churches were built by force. Both were there at the same time. The separation between good and evil is so narrow, the transmutation of one into the other is so subtle, that in the live-a-day world the distinctions may not be made, and if made, are frequently afterthoughts, re-readings of past experiences in terms of present needs.

The Church had witnessed the tragic fate of the Indians in Cuba, in Puerto Rico, in the Antilles. Abuse of the Indians in the islands had very nearly destroyed them. The same result was threatened in Mexico. From the Church's point of view, the Conquest was for the sake of conversion, for the

A LABOR MEETING IN FRONT OF A FACTORY
CLOSED BY A STRIKE

sake of saving the millions of souls from damnation, and their destruction would have been the greatest of sins, the damnation of these millions of souls. To save them gave the Conquest a moral purpose, and save them it would, at any cost. The objectives of the Church coincided with those of the Crown—the discovered lands and the people on them belonged to the King. They were held by the conquerors in feudal tenure as a sort of trust for the Crown. The defense of the Indian against the cupidity of the conqueror was a defense of the long-run interests of the Crown against the immediate aims of exploitation by the *conquistadores*.

Just as the Church had preserved the Indian's self-respect by saving his faith in his own gods, and by giving him the additional Christian gods and saints, so the economic and social organization after the Conquest saved the traditional *mores* of the Indians among themselves. Rights, privileges, and prerogatives of the Indian lords and masters were in a measure respected in relation to their own subordinates. The native social organization was made to serve the ends of the conqueror.

It thus came about that the leader of the Aztecs who had most stubbornly fought the Conquest, Cuauhtemoc, became a vassal of Cortez, and, as vassal, placed at Cortez's disposal the rights and prerogatives that he enjoyed over his own people. The *repartimientos* inaugurated by Cortez as "the only way to hold the country" consisted of setting up a system of tribute for the conquerors to be collected and delivered by the native chiefs. By this method, the exactions of the Spaniards were satisfied while much of the original sense of right between the natives and their own leaders was retained. Cruel and fearful as it was, that system played no small rôle, in combination with the influence of the Church, in preserving the Indians from extermination. It may have been the basic reason for the survival of so many thousand Indian communities even to this day. It saved them their way of life,

41

even though it hardened and narrowed it. It preserved their sense of justice, even though it increased severity. The individual was saved by his group because the group was saved.

Older Indian fealty to their gods, the great awe which the older deities had inspired, the habit of setting aside land to be worked communally for the maintenance of priests and the embellishment of the faith facilitated the acquisition of power and influence by the Catholic Church among the Indian population. The easy transition that the Indians made from their own stone idols to the saints within the Church and the continuance of many practices which were part of their older faith made their identification of the new and old faiths serve both the Church and the Indians.

Such influence with the Indians and the government gave the Church a preponderant place in colonial Mexico. It did not take long for the Church to acquire great wealth and great power. Its churches, temples, monasteries, colleges, and hospitals were to be found in all great centers of population. The office of priest came to possess an influence, dignity, personal standing, and well-being that made it the most respected profession in Mexico. Few civil and military officers could look forward to such an assured income, to such a place of usefulness, to such public and private honor as could the members of the Church or any of its dependencies. After the first years of conflict were over, after the early sacrifices and martyrdoms, the priests of Mexico, apart from the few who were delegated to *misiones* among the savage tribes of the north, and the Church which they served, lived in a world seemingly as secure, as wealthy, and as powerful as the Catholic Church had known, even in the best days of medieval Europe. Here among a primitive people that they protected and defended, taught the new arts, civilized and used for the benefit of the Church, as well as for the benefit of the Indians themselves, both the Church and the orders that were parts of the Church contributed to the development of an institution and a way of life that had, in its day, the elements of grandeur, power, dignity, and usefulness. But the Church was destined to succumb to influences of which its success made it unmindful. Its work seemed to have been well and easily done; too easily, in fact, to be permanent—too formal in its ends to be practical, to be inbred in the details.

CHAPTER 5

CONFLICT OF CHURCH AND STATE

THE Church and the State were both universal. The Indian village was particular. The strife between Church and State in Mexico is part of a general conflict between the village and the nation; between the conqueror and the conquered; between the Spaniard and the Indian; between the foreigner and the native; between the rich and the poor; the European and the Mexican; between a culture that looked to ideals from abroad, and a culture that was steeped in ideals that were indigenous.

That conflict has raged within the Church and without, between the Church and the State, and within the State itself. There has never been any homogeneity either in one or the other. There have always been many churches and many states in Mexico, as many, almost, as villages. The rule of centralized power, even in its most prosperous days, whether of Church or State, has been nominal, superficial. That has always been true; it is true today. Therein lies the meaning of the conflict. On one side, there was a theory of a Church, a theory of a State, a theory of an economy, a theory of a body politic, a foreign, a Spanish innovation in all these matters. On the other side there was always something else, something native, unyielding, something that would bend but not break, bend and rebound with greater violence, with bitterness. The conflict has now lasted four hundred years, and still continues. The strife has been one of plural cultures against an attempted universal formula. The literary folk, the governmental folk, the soldiers, the priests, the statesmen, the theorists, have been the believers in and the practitioners of a common faith, a common government, a common empire. Emperor, king, president, country, nation, have fooled themselves and others by making much sound and fury, by talk, by writing, by preaching. But at the bottom of it all was a particularism, a series of particularisms, that would not yield. The villages consented through duress, and gave the appearance of being what the preachers, teachers, soldiers and politicians pretended them to be; but the impression was self-generated by those who propagated its doctrine, and the evidence was superficial. The little Mexican villages, the thousands of little villages, never belonged to the Church; never belonged to the Empire; never belonged to the State; never belonged to Europe; never belonged to Mexico City. The village supported these institutions, tolerated them, worked for them, suffered for them, even at times seemed to love them; but that was make-believe; that was because of duress, because of acceptance of the inevitable; always there was a slow gnawing at the roots of the new and foreign institutions. It is of such a texture that the conflict between the Church and the State is made. It is a conflict of the village particularism against the Church imperialism. The specific struggle between Church and State, of which so much is made, is only an incident of lesser importance. The centralized Church in Mexico was defeated when it was most successful, because it seemed so successful.

The hasty conversion of millions of natives, claimed, for instance, by the early Franciscans, proved to have been only a superficial, even though an impressive, ceremony. The Indians, attached to their old faiths, habituated to the old practices, accepted the ceremonial baptism, in a language they did not understand, and with a purpose they could not comprehend, as something strange and charged with mystic meaning, but quite beyond their ken. The Church may have taken the ready submission of the Indians as evidence of their conversion to Catholicism; to the Indians it was perhaps a means of winning grace and favor from the new gods that had come with the new masters of the country. The conver-

45

sion was soon over. The habituation to Christian doctrine and practice had not even commenced. Catholic theology, the system of Catholic doctrine, was beyond the intellectual ken of the Mexican Indian, and rapid conversion by baptism of great multitudes did nothing to increase their insight or enhance their understanding. This contrast between rapid baptism, on the one hand, and gradual accommodation to practice and appreciation, on the other, made the hold of the organized Church nominal on the mass of the people, and tended to confine it to larger cities where the Spanish and *mestizo* elements predominated.

In spite of its power, the Church had its difficulties, even during the colonial period. The important conflicts during the colonial period were between the regular and the secular clergy, between the religious orders and the Church. These struggles began in the early days of the second Archbishop of Mexico, and continued until the very last days of the Spanish régime. The friars had the support of the people, and frequently of the local governments; the Crown sided with the Church. The king repeatedly instructed the colonial administration not to permit members of the religious orders to enter Mexico without a license, and even ordered the destruction of convents built without permission. These struggles are illustrated by the strife between the Bishop of Puebla, Don Juan de Palafox, and the Society of Jesus. It led to the preaching of sermons against the order by the Church, and against the Church by the order, expulsions, excommunications, judgments, counter-judgments, exile: all the earmarks of civil conflict, all to no purpose.

It was during the war of independence (1810–1821) that the serious difficulties of the Church really commenced. Until then there had been, with minor exceptions, peace within the Church. The Church had grown in power and influence, in prestige and wealth. The independence movement for the first time seriously affected the moral position of the Church and contributed to that changed attitude of mind which made the later attacks upon it feasible. In the war against Spain, the champions of rebellion often found support among the lower clergy. In fact, two of the greatest leaders of the movement—Hidalgo and Morelos—were humble priests. They were denounced, condemned, and excommunicated by the Church, and turned over to the secular power (that is, to the Spanish army), to be shot as traitors to Spain. It takes no great effort of the imagination to see that the leaders of the Church incurred not merely criticism, but hatred, from the sponsors of Mexican independence. The nascent nationalism of which the independence movement was an outcome learned to identify the Church with foreign control, a belief strengthened in the last hundred years of Mexican history.

Internal division was peculiarly unfortunate for the Church at the very moment when the new ideas of the French Revolution filtered in as part of the independence movement. The organized Church, by espousing the cause of the Spanish Crown, found it more difficult to defend those special rights and prerogatives it wished to continue—especially when the more liberal elements in Mexico achieved power. By becoming partisans of the losing side, and by excommunicating and morally supporting the killing of the leaders of the revolution against Spain, who were drawn from the ranks of the Church itself, the Church made its position morally untenable before those very elements which it later had to conciliate. That it failed to make a satisfactory adjustment was largely due to its failure to observe neutrality in the early days of the conflict. Neutrality might have saved it from the charge of opposing national independence, and from the charge of allegiance to foreign imperialism which, during the last hundred years, has so frequently been hurled against it.

Moral divison within the Church, and conflict of opinion with the leaders of the early independence movement were particularly unfortunate for the Church, because, as soon as

47

the revolution against Spain was over, the question of the relations between Church and State became acute. Clearly enough, such an issue would have arisen anyway. But the feeling of fear and hostility which the Church had roused in its opposition to independence, found this issue, when it did arise, charged with asperity and bitterness.

The conflict between Church and State was fought out about two issues: the *patronato* and the *fueros*. The Spanish Crown had secured from the Pope title to the lands of the new world. But this deed (and it is to this original grant that the claims of the Spanish Crown to the new world are always referred as a primary source) did not prevent the Spanish king from exacting from Popes Alexander IV, in May 1493, and Julius II, in July 1508, Bulls that practically placed the Church under the dominion of the Crown. In fact it has been said that "the Crown had almost exclusive power in the establishment and organization of the Mexican Church." These rights, going under the general name of *patronato*, delegated very extensive prerogatives to the Crown.

The Church was denied full use of the tithe of ten per cent, or *diezmo*. It had to receive special permission to build its temples, churches, hospitals, monasteries. No priest or friar could enter the country without consent from the State. The Crown named the bishops of the Church before they were confirmed by the Pope. The lay government laid out the territorial limits of bishoprics, of dioceses. A *presentación* (gift) was required for all clerical offices from bishop to sacristan. The State retained the right to punish the servants of the Church and to interfere with the punishments inflicted by the Church. No edict of the Pope could be published or executed without permission of the Crown, which claimed the right to resolve ecclesiastical conflicts. Such were the major original claims of the lay government in its relations to the Church.

With the coming of independence, the question immediately arose whether the old rights of the Crown had passed to the new State. The State took the position, as a matter of course, that it had inherited all of the powers of the Crown in Mexico: military, civil, and ecclesiastical. The Church, however, insisted that the prerogatives over ecclesiastical affairs, which before had been exercised by the Crown, had now disappeared. The prerogatives of the Crown were, in the eyes of the Church, personal to the king. Independence had, by destroying the power, nullified the prerogatives of the Crown; they did not pass to the Mexican republic.

Conflict between Church and State was now inevitable. Under the rule of *patronato*, the Church was subordinate to the Crown. The difference that arose never really caused the rights of the king to be challenged. When the Society of Jesus was accused of attempting to assume or to presume upon the powers of the State, it was ruthlessly expelled. No serious challenge of the right of the king to expel the order developed. The government may have been criticized for the ruthlessness and arbitrariness with which the order was torn from a soil that it had helped to conquer, baptize, and enrich; but the right of the Crown was apparently accepted by all concerned. After independence, the Church denied that the Mexican government inherited the powers which it had recognized as belonging to the Crown.

The Church repudiated any master. This repudiation of the claims of the State made the Church a competitor of the State in matters of political policy, for it insisted on making those decisions which previously had been made by the Crown. The conflict between the two institutions became a conflict for survival. The Church could not accept the prerogatives of petty tyrants, without responsibility, risen to power overnight by means of *cuartelazos*, and likely to be driven from office again by another *cuartelazo* the next day. For its very existence, the Church needed a powerful government that would give it security and peace. No such government could be established without its aid, yet any attempt on its part to shape political policy was met by the challenge of the liberals who feared domination of the State by the Church. The Church's very claim to freedom became its undoing; the conflict became one of principle, and the Church lost in the end.

As part of the struggle over the patronato, must be counted the additional dispute over *fueros* (privileges). The Church declared itself the only religion within the State, claimed exclusive control over education, freedom from taxation for its properties, and immunity from civil authority. One Mexican bishop expressed this attitude by saying that "from the time that these things are directly or indirectly consecrated to the service of the faith, they leave the human domain, enter into the category of things called of divine right and become by their very nature excluded from civil jurisdiction." Further, the position of the Church was that "ecclesiastical immunity was not derived from the civil law and consequently could not be abrogated by it." With such a theory, in the face of a State that had been shaped under the impact of a struggle against absolute monarchy and foreign dominion, and in control of people who had been influenced by ideas emanating from the French Revolution, the position of the Church was difficult indeed.

More difficult was the fact of a powerful Church and a weak State. The might of the Church was not staggering to the imagination when compared to a great imperial power that reigned from the distance of three thousand miles, but it loomed large when contrasted with a government that could not hold its own against a few bellicose and poorly drilled soldiers in command of an unruly sergeant. The State was weak, too weak for comfort, when compared with the Church. The Church, in attempting to retain the powers of the Crown for itself, contributed to the intensification of nationalism, and nationalism, expressed as sovereignty under the influence of the French Revolution, made the conflict inevitable. From one point of view, the whole history of Mexico, from independence to the Diáz régime, is a conflict between two ideas: the idea embodied in the Church, and the idea of the individualism, democracy, profit-making, business investment, and free thinking of the middle-class revolution, which in Mexico was represented not by a business middle class, but by a political middle class that wished to acquire the wealth and the power of the Church, and had only the political ideals of the French Revolution with which to do it.

Instability of political institutions, lack of political faith or honesty in public officers, persistent subversion of all principles of government, unending change of policy and program, perpetual shifting of political personalities, and absence of party government gave the Church a position of strength that seemed invincible. Here was an institution that maintained its unity, that held on to its organized institutions, that practiced the old faith, that followed the same principles. Here was something to tie to; here was a rock among the billows, seemingly impregnable, eternal. The conflict between Church and State in Mexico assumed large proportions because the State was a volatile, changing, unstable institution, and the Church, by contrast, seemed stable and continuous. Those who believed in the Church had something definite, something real and personal to lean on, a doctrine, an organization, a recognizable basis of order and stability. If they sought to use the Church as a means to dominate the government, it was in part, at least, because they sought to achieve stability for the government by giving it the support of the Church, and, if necessary, the control of the Church as a stabilizing force. The fact that there were other influences—the fear of loss of power, the sharp conflict of ideas, the basic differences in attitude toward the place of the Church within the social organism—merely made the fol-

lowers of the Church more certain of their position. If the government had been strong and stable, if the political leaders after independence had had sincerity, persistence in policy, simple faith and honesty, or constant belief in some principle of government, then the conflict might have existed, but it would have taken a different form, such as conflicts have assumed in other countries where the state is strong.

To make matters worse the Church was rich and the State was poor. The Church was rich in lands, buildings, and income. The government was poor; it was always in arrears; it was never able to meet its obligations. The demands upon the government from a thousand and one aspiring politicians, and many times that number of satellites, and an innumerable host of soldiers, corporals, sergeants, lieutenants, captains, majors, colonels, and generals, each threatening and frequently starting a revolution, were such that any discernable wealth became subject to demands, claims, and exactions that increased with each administration and with each yielding, which only whetted the appetite of the government.

During the three centuries of peace and protection under the Spanish Crown, the Church had prospered. The churches, the convents, the temples, multiplied; the priests and friars increased; the possessions of the Church accumulated rapidly and constantly. The wealth of the Church was so great in comparison with the riches of any one person, or even of the government, as to become with the years a depository of credit, both for private enterprises and for the government. The Church acted as banker of the colony. As long as there was little commerce, as long as there was a small middle class, as long as wealth was in large estates, and as long as the *mestizo* element (which had no land) and the *criollo* element (which inherited the land from its fathers) were content, one because its appetite had not been stimulated, and the other because it still had enough, the Church had little difficulty.

The ideals derived from the French Revolution, the developing credo of middle class economics, the notions of individualism, the opposition of the liberals to corporate ownership in guilds and churches, their insistence upon the circulation of wealth for the earning of profit, made the "dead hand" of the Church seem a great menace to the well-being of the people, a danger to the sovereignty of the nation. We are dealing with ideas. The notion of nationalism, of statehood, of individualism, of a Church, are all ideas. Belief in a supreme church gave way to belief in a nation that was supreme. The conflict with the Church as an idea came in Mexico about the same time as the conflict with the Emperor as an idea, and at the same time that the ideas of middle class philosophy were developing, at the same time that notions of political democracy were coming to the fore.

In addition, the indebtedness of the rural properites in Mexico to the Catholic Church became a source of great difficulty to it. Every property owner wanted to see his lands freed of mortgages, and the only means of freeing the hold of the mortgage upon the income from his property was to deprive the Church of its power to hold property or to make loans upon private lands. In fact, the economic position of the Church on one hand, and of the private property owner on the other, made the struggle an inevitable one. In the course of the conflict, the Church lost the greater portion of its wealth.

After independence, Mexican rural property had fallen in value and in producing capacity. The years of rebellion weakened the ability of rural property either to raise its rentals or to cover the interest on its capital loans, not to speak of paying off mortgages. The turbulence after the independence constant rebellions, pillage, and destruction, increased the poverty of private property owners. Bankruptcy was unavoidable. The alternative to bankruptcy was repudiation, but repudiation against the Church, the greatest creditor, was difficult, and the difficulty was solved by an attack upon the Church. Writing as early as 1836, fifteen years after independence, Mexico's most thoughtful historian (Mora) said, in speaking of the problem, that "the legislature must take the only means of escape, which consists in sacrificing the claims of communities (churches) against private property."

There have been various estimates of the wealth of the Church. No one of them is accurate. That it was very great is agreed by every student of Mexico. A conservative Mexican historian, Lucas Alemán, a good member of the Church, and the intellectual leader of the Church party in his day, estimated that at the end of the colonial period "not less than half of the real property and capital of the country belonged to the Church. Most of the remainder was controlled by the Church through mortgages. The Church was the landlord, the banker, and the trustee of the period."

Under these circumstances, forced loans by unfriendly governments against the Church are understandable; but these loans were exacted by every government and for every kind of reason, good and bad, honest and dishonest. Even Iturbide, the military leader of the Church party, imposed a forced levy upon the Church in Puebla, Mexico, Guadalajara, and Vera Cruz to the extent of 600,000 pesos, immediately after independence, and even before he became emperor.

Clearly enough, a powerful Church, sure of its own position, attacked by vacillating and unstable governments, could not remain indifferent to the kind of political rule that dominated the country. The forced loans, natural to governments hostile to the Church and in straits because of their inability to meet the demands of their ever-growing needs, played their rôle in forcing the Church into hostility. The only way the interests of the Church could be protected was through favorable governments, and favorable governments could be secured only through the influence of the Church; yet every move in self-defense forced it into politics and increased the insistence of the charge that the Church was participating in politics and trying to control the government. The Church was forced into political activity, as a matter of self-defense, and every political move it made hastened its ultimate ruin, because it roused new sources of opposition, and gave new reasons for attack, criticism, and fear.

After independence a sort of peace might perhaps have been established if the Church had agreed to pass on to the State the powers previously exercised by the Crown, if the Pope had recognized Mexican independence, if a species of Concordat had been signed defining the relative rights of each of the institutions. But the refusal of the Church to accede to the demands of the State in the matter of the *patronato*, the insistence of the Church upon maintaining all of its old *fueros* (privileges), the refusal to recognize the independence of Mexico, the refusal to come to some agreement with the government through a Concordat, weakened the government, increased its instability, and, in the end, strengthened those attitudes, practices, and passions that destroyed the power of the Church itself.

The economic bias that had its origin in the French Revolution and in the industrial philosophy that had taken shape in Western Europe complicated this issue between the Church and the State. The philosophy of individualism and capitalism, the opposition to guilds, the denomination of property that did not circulate by the opprobrium of "the dead hand," gave the opponents of the Church a powerful weapon. The curious fact was, of course, that no economic middle class worthy of the name existed in Mexico. The revolution, however, had produced a political middle class, and had given power to lawyers and scribes. The struggle between State and Church in Mexico was a conflict between the lawyers and the priests, and the lawyers won. A changed attitude toward property, the belief that it must belong to an individual rather than to a church, a guild, a brotherhood, a state, or a community, the assumption that there is some special virtue in such possession which property loses if it is held and used by other than individuals, became a mighty instrument in the hands of those fighting the Church. The ready assumption that progress, civilization, liberty, were all bound up with a destruction of the economic possessions of the Church that these properties ought to come to "circulate," that their circulation would increase the wealth of the country, was useful as an instrument, but turned out in the end to be a poor excuse for what happened. We are again in the realm of ideas, of the way individuals and groups look at the world about them.

The "dead hand" of the Church assumed a moral significance which was contrary to the new ideas of economics and politics, of freedom, especially freedom of commerce. The properties of the Church, in harmony with these new ideas, ought to be put into private hands, into circulation. They ought to become part of the market, of purchase and sale. Such a process would, it was argued, increase the national wealth—especially the wealth of the land speculators. In Mexican practice, however, it made little difference whether the property was in private hands or not. In fact, most of the landed estates in private hands were not for sale. They were held under a rule of primogeniture and were, practically speaking, as "dead" as the lands of the Church; that, however, was not the point. Nor did the absence of a middle class that would buy and sell make any difference. Here was an opportunity for the liberal politicians to enrich themselves at the expense of the Church, and to destroy its power: that was important. That was what happened in the end. The issues were, after all, matters of principle, matters of faith, new ways of viewing the world. The new ideas and the old could not subsist together. French nationalism and a feudal Church could not live in peace at the same place and time.

A complicating factor came from the way in which the Church developed as an institution. Instead of being spread out among the thousands of smaller communities in the rural districts, the clergy tended, for reasons that are explicable enough, to crowd into the larger cities. The influence of the Church was felt most in the cities, and a large proportion of the income of the Church was spent upon the churches in the urban centers. The church organization and religious life in the rural communities remained largely distinct. The priest, as a representative of the Church, remained a stranger within the rural community, a visitor upon the occasions of special *fiesta*, so that outside of the larger cities he was not a regular participant in the lives of the common people. It meant that marriages, baptisms, burials, Sunday services, and even mass were either rarely performed according to the rule of the Church, or, if regularly performed, officiated over by members of the community, who in the tradition of the older religion exercised the functions of the Church as they understood them, a mixture of Catholic and pagan practices. The rural villages were thus independent of the Catholic priesthood, and were not aware of the meaning of the conflict which the priesthood carried on with the government. This lack of understanding contributed to the weakness of the Church in its struggle with the State. The inadequate distribution of the Catholic clergy in the rural communities existed even before the expropriation of the Church lands by the laws of the Reform, and was noted by earlier historians.

What was true then became more pronounced after the destruction of the monastic orders, and is more obvious at present. We have, therefore, a Church that claims national representation on the grounds that it ministers to the religious needs of the country at large, which in fact it has never succeeded in doing. It has done so less and less each year since the period of independence, and is, for both political and economic reasons, unable to achieve a nation-wide distribution of the priesthood at present.

The Church had and has, however, intimate personal relations with the people of the cities. This limited contact gave the Church its peculiar bond with the landowning classes of Mexico, and has made it seem hostile to the mass of the people in the social upheaval of the last twenty years, weakening the Church in its struggle with the State.

Just as the Church's greatest support came from the middle and upper classes in the cities, so its greatest enemies were developed there. It was in the cities that the ideas of the French Revolution, the growth of Masonry, the immigration, after independence, of middle class foreigners who were French or under French influence, and the development of nationalism, were mainly in evidence. It was in the cities also that the conflicting parties, who fought over spoils of office, saw in the Church a doubtful friend, if not an enemy. The Church was looked upon as a good instrument for prestige in a conflict, and a source of wealth in case of need. The new middle class immigrants who could find no lands except as they took them away from the Church played up the opposition that has grown more intense with the years. They helped to make the *mano muerta* (dead hand) of Church property seem contrary to science and natural law.

But it is to be remembered that all of these conflicts, struggles, and ambitions were of the upper and middle classes, and restricted to the cities of Mexico. The mass of the common people remained outside these struggles, and, on the whole, when drawn in, came as soldiers who fought for ideas they did not understand. The Church, by confining its direct ministrations so largely to the people of the cities, by confining its personal contacts so largely to them, by being so largely immersed in their struggles, found itself weakened when conflicts within these classes arose. This close relationship tended to make the Church itself an instrument of conflict or a reason for dispute. The Church could not lean back upon the mass of the people. The mass had a religious existence, nominally Catholic, but largely outside the direct ministrations of the organized Church, and were unconscious of the elements of the conflict.

It was perhaps natural for the Church to be so largely confined to the larger communities. It was there that Spanish was spoken, that Spaniards largely dominated even after the revolution against Spain, whereas in the country the opposite was true: primitive, varied languages and cultures existed. It is not implied that there were not hundreds of priests that lived in little villages, who spent long and hard lives on mule back going from town to town ministering to the common people. It is merely insisted that for the size of the country, for the many thousands of communities (over sixty thousand), for the large proportion of the population that lived in the country districts, an unequal distribution of priests characterized the Church in Mexico all through its history. Out of this poor organization came a natural and inevitable allegiance on the part of the priests to the interests of the upper class in Mexico, which led in times of conflict to serious weakness within the Church. When the Church lost some of its supporters in the large cities, it could not lean back upon the rural population, for among them religious life and church organization were two very distinct phenomena. Their religious life was real, vital, immediate and powerful. It was organized locally and in terms of local *mores;* whereas the Church organization, with the priest as the agent, was rather distant, rather foreign, rather infrequent. Here is to be found much of the weakness of the Church as a religious organization, and also much of the failure of the Church to maintain itself within the country at full strength when the rural sections came to supplant the city and the middle and upper class elements in Mexico, in the shaping of public policy. If the Church had continued, through the centuries, to fight the Indians' battles, if it had been associated with them in all of its history in Mexico, the story would have been different.

CHAPTER 6

THE DEFEAT OF THE CHURCH

THE Mexican Indian is parochial. His universe is exceedingly limited; the mountains that circumscribe
his horizon define his intellectual and spiritual world.
The gods he worships are the local gods. The saint is the saint
of the village, and not infrequently conflicting claims of rival
saints have led to long conflicts between villages. The gods
are local; the saints are gods, physical gods who contain
within themselves a miraculous power. The notion of an organized church, of a universal Catholic Church, is beyond the
experience of the isolated primitive communities. The priest,
if he does not reside in the community, is an honored visitor
who performs useful services, but who really does not participate in the essential religious life of the village. That religious
life goes on without him just as well as with him. The majority of Mexican villages are outside the Church organization
although they are what they conceive to be Catholic. This
contrast between the village and the clerical universe shaped
the difference between the primitive people and the educated
class in the larger communities that sees the Church in its
universal relationships. The conflict with the State has been,
in part, a struggle of the Catholics of the middle and upper
classes against the government. It did not involve the smaller
communities, which were neither interested nor concerned.
The Church operated in their little villages as it had always
done under a local community organization. The absence of
the priest was not noted. He had never come more than once
or twice a year anyway and this time his mule was ill.

It must be clear by now that the stage in Mexico was so
set that peace between the Church as an institution, with
its claims, powers, prerogatives, and privileges, inherited

61

from the colonial period, could not fit into the scheme of political institutions and ideas that became prominent after independence. The attack upon the Church in 1833, and the more serious attack in 1857, were the natural and inevitable outcomes of two different ideas and ideals that have found it impossible to live side by side, each with its full claims. The powers of the Church were old, venerable, and great. The Church represented an ideal society and claimed for itself the prerogatives that had accrued to it over a period of three hundred years. As an institution it could not fit into the political set-up that followed the independence. Not only were many of the ideas that ruled these governments incongruous and iniquitous, in the eyes of the Church, but the governments were weak human instruments, volatile, unreliable, and frequently motivated by a personal cupidity, which made the Church a good source for private gain. The governments, on the other hand, stood for what they believed to be true liberty, freedom, democracy, nationalism, individualism, commerce, industry, constitutionalism, and private gain from the exercise of the profession of business.

The Church, with its great corporate wealth, was an impediment in the development of a middle class. And the development of a middle class, the power of a middle class, the third estate of the French Revolution, was, in its day, in the eyes of its protagonists, a very sacred idea indeed. The Church's desire to continue its special *fueros*, in particular the powers that it held over its members in all cases of civil and criminal jurisdiction, was an infringement of the sovereign power; its insistence upon control of education was an interference with the right of a free citizen to his conscience; its insistence upon exclusion of all other faiths was a further claim to a monopoly of belief that was contrary to freedom of thought (a freedom that had an ideal value but little bearing in practice within the Mexican scene). The issues were clear, and to all this is to be added the fact that the weakening of the power of the *criollos* and the rising power of the *mestizos* as politicians and intellectuals, gave to the *mestizos* an ambition to emulate their previous masters by becoming land owners through acquiring the properties of the Church. Personal interest and moral idealism found a common basis in the attack upon the Church. The ends of freedom, liberty, and justice, as well as the enrichment of the new class which had come upon the scene of power and influence in Mexico, were served by the spoliation of the Church.

The struggle was on. The Church, in defense of its ideals, used such powers as its prestige, wealth, and influence made possible. The middle class, that is, the political middle class which had risen to replace the Crown and its satellites, did likewise. The 1857 constitution led to a bloody and murderous three years' war. Regardless of the side represented, Church or State, liberalism or conservatism, the armies, whether inspired by the Holy Cross or by the banners of freedom and democracy, were equally cruel, equally ruthless, and equally unmindful of even the ordinary decencies which warfare by common consent imposes upon opponents. The Church, defeated, looked abroad and gathered itself for a new struggle under the banner of Emperor Maximillian. That venture failed, and with it vanished the last hope of the Church to retain its prerogatives. Unfortunately for the Church, the memory of that foreign invasion strengthened the feeling among the leaders of the liberal groups that the Church was not only feudal in its attitude toward Mexican social and economic institutions, but also antinational, "unpatriotic," and willing to barter away Mexican nationalism, Mexican democracy, Mexican freedom, to save its own *fueros*.

The later history of the Church in Mexico derives to so large an extent from this belief, orginally generated during the war of independence, and later strengthened during the French invasion, that one could almost draw this discussion to a close here, and call it all of the explanation needed to clarify the conflict which has since continued.

The Díaz regime which followed soon after brought peace to Mexico, and with that peace a quieting of the passions that had raged for so long a time. The Díaz government was a compromise between the contending groups on the basis of peace and prosperity, of an apparent offering to each group an opportunity to satisfy its own heart's desire. In time the Church found itself with some of its wealth, power, and prestige restored to it. But unfortunately for the Church, it became committed to the system that characterized the Díaz régime. We have indicated in a later chapter the essential policy of the Díaz régime. It may be described here by saying that it attempted to give Mexico peace by a rapid and forced industrialization in the course of which the communal holdings of the Indians were to be destroyed, and the foreigner was to be favored as against the Mexican. Although it is true that there are evidences that the Church was uncomfortable under this aegis, and that during the years 1900–1910 the Church in various congresses voiced the grievance of the common people, yet it was a very weak voice and without effect upon the meager public opinion that existed in the country.

The Church seemed tied to the Díaz policy, and when the Revolution came the Church again found itself on the wrong side. It opposed revolution. It opposed the policies of the Revolution, and when it had an opportunity, attempted to secure for itself something of the freedom of action that it had enjoyed in the older days. In the effort, it found its natural companions in those elements in the republic that were opposing the social program of the Revolution. These elements were the large landowners, frequently Spaniards, and the large investors, almost exclusively foreigners. In other words, the Church again laid itself open to the charge of siding with the foreigner against the Mexican, of being "unpatriotic," of seeking to destroy Mexican nationality. During the revolution the Church had not even as in the independence some of its clergy who took the popular side. If the Church had had a few martyrs to the cause of "Zapatismo" or "Agrarismo," if some of the members of the clergy had followed the Indian and the peon in their battles for land and for freedom from the peonage of the large estate, if, as in the earlier days of independence, the Church could have had an Hidalgo or a Morelos in the cause of social change, as it had in the cause of political change, then the recent history of the Church might have been different. But it proved to be the opposite. The Church found itself on the unpopular side of the battle in Mexico, and has suffered the consequence of defeat. Its activities as an instituion came under the increasing opposition of the older liberals and nationalists, as well as of the new revolutionists, who now have added proof that the Church as an institution is aligned with those elements in Mexico that stand against the development of social justice and nationalism. Whatever the answer of the Church, clearly enough it has gone unheeded and will be so for a long time to come.

In the last hundred years the Catholic Church in Mexico has been reduced to a hierarchical skeleton. It has lost its lands; it has lost its power; it has been largely destroyed as an organization. But this change has had little effect upon the essential faith of the common people. The people are no less Catholic today than they were a hundred years ago. In fact, the change has chiefly affected the educated classes in the cities, where the weakening of the Church and the cutting down of the number of priests has made itself felt. Out in the thousands of little villages, where most of the people live, the Church goes on as it has since the conversion—without a priest. The life of the community was organized around the church, and the church was built around Saint John, or Saint Thomas, or Saint Caralampio, or some other saint.

Around him the old religion was entwined. He had replaced the older gods in full or in part. In some places the older traditions still persisted. To the new saint the same credence and obeisance was made that had been made before the older gods. *What Mexico has had all through the centuries is a local religion—the religion of the village*, with an occasional greater saint in the neighborhood for special veneration. Upon this local faith, the Catholic Church, with the help of the Spanish State, built up a national superstructure that connected with the Church universal. But apart from the cities this connection was unsuspected by the mass of the smaller communities. They knew nothing about it, and know little, if anything, about it now. The idea of centralized hierarchy, a Pope, a City of Rome, a theology, a universalized idea which was carried by a universalized institution, of these the mass of common folk have remained innocent. What has happened is that the superstructure of the Church has been well nigh destroyed. But it really never existed in the minds of the people in the villages and in the mountains among the Indians. Whether the Church is re-established or whether the priest is allowed to come again once every six months, the local religion of the village will go on as it has in the past. The superstructure inherited from the Conquest has here, as in the matter of race, economics, and politics, largely disintegrated. What has been left to the little village is a cross, a church, a saint. The cross is new; the church replaces the older shrine; and the saint takes the place of the older deity.

The village has returned to its older practice, its older way of life, in the matter of belief—a way that it had really never left, but which the universal institutions of Church and State had assumed and reckoned, and counted as part of themselves. The little village has returned to its particularism. In the process of attrition, the stubborn, native, and unyielding traits have proved stronger and possessed of greater endurance than the foreign, the universal. In a sense, the old has won against the new. The self-contained Indian community has reasserted itself, and the universal Church, one of the great institutions brought by the Spaniards, has been largely destroyed, liquidated.

CHAPTER 7

SPANISH DOMINION

MEXICAN politics began with the war of independence
against Spain. For three hundred years, Mexico's
destinies had responded to the colonial policies of
the Spanish Empire and to the economic and political aspirations of the Spanish Crown. Spain shaped the politics of
Mexico as it shaped the politics of its vast empire. Although
local needs and personal cupidity of the representatives of
the Crown frequently frustrated its laws and decrees, it is
still true that Mexican politics were Spanish colonial policy.

An interesting feature of this colonial policy was its almost
unaltered character. Within a hundred years after the Conquest, if not before, Mexico's internal structure was set to
a form and hardened; after that, it persisted as a type. It
stood still for nearly three centuries even though much
change took place in the world abroad. Such change failed
to affect the Mexican scene. This scene was characterized
on the political side by a centralized government and a centralized Church, manned by specially delegated Spaniards
who exercised their power largely for their own and the
Crown's benefit.

Spain's colonial policy was characterized by the subordina-
tion of the interests of the colony to those of the mother
country, the use of Mexican funds, not merely for the Crown,
but for the partial support of Cuba, Puerto Rico, Venezuela,
Colombia, and the Philippines as well, by a sharp prohibition
of types of industry, a narrow confining of the channels
through which commerce might flow, an emphasis upon the
development of mining, an attempt to keep Mexico from all
intellectual intercourse with the rest of the world, the limitation of immigration, the frowning upon too much travel, by

68

an attempt to maintain Mexico closed to the world and confined to the services of the Spanish Crown and the Spanish administrators in Mexico.

Spain's outstanding achievement is that it gave Mexico a unified political administration. In this, Spain succeeded where the Aztecs had failed. The conquerors found the country torn between a host of warring groups, and gradually welded into a common administration the territory from Guatemala to California, from Yucatan to Texas, New Mexico, and Arizona. All of the little Indian republics, Tlaxcala, Cholula, the Tarascans, the Zapotecs, the Mayas, the Quichés, the Mijes, and the rest, even the northern tribes that had fought, resisted, and fled into the mountains, were gradually brought under a general administrative plan. The orders of the viceroy were obeyed east and west, north and south, obeyed and received with respect.

With this unification came internal peace of a kind that Mexico enjoyed neither before the conquest nor since independence. True enough, the peace was comparative. Banditry was prevalent; small Indian uprisings occurred; conflicts among the Spaniards themselves were not unknown, nor was conspiracy against the Spanish Crown entirely absent. But in spite of that, Mexico had what amounted to peace.

Two elements in this peace may explain its duration. First, it rested upon a caste system: colonial society had four distinct social classes. At the bottom of this caste system was the Indian. There were gradations even among the Indians: there was the slave taken in rebellion, branded and carried to the mines, the plantation peon, the villager who paid tribute, the Indian who retained his freedom by escaping to the mountains. There were also Indians who were allowed to enter city trades, and some who secured minor positions in the Church. But in spite of these variations, the Indian was at the bottom of the scale, the beast of burden.

Just a little above the Indian was the *mestizo*. He gradually grew in numbers, importance, and influence. Nearer to the Indian than to the white man, closer to his mother than to his father, denied most lucrative employments, barred from better social contacts, the *mestizo* became a class apart. He lived more frequently in the cities; he worked at the semi-skilled occupations; he was later to be found in the mines and on the plantations, where mixture with his white master was more persistent. He was in closer contact with the white man; he was more influenced by the white man's habits and standards; he acquired a taste for the white man's food; he copied the white man's clothing; because of his father he looked more like a white man than the pure Indian did, and slowly learned to feel more like him.

Above the *mestizo* was the *criollo*, white, of Spanish parentage, born in Mexico. He inherited the wealth, lands, and prerogatives of the conqueror. He was a stranger in the country of his birth, with no political power; this was in the hands of the Spaniard born in Spain, who ruled Mexico in the name of the King, and for their own benefit, for three centuries.

All the groups in the country opposed the foreign-born Spaniard who governed the colony. Against him, when the time came, was developed the first manifestation of national sentiment. But the unity against the Spaniard did not bring the *criollo* closer to the other classes. The only thing he had in common with the Indian and the *mestizo* was his hatred of the Spaniard. The *criollo* had for the Indian even less sympathy than the Spaniard had. The *criollo* was in constant conflict with the Indian, especially over land. In fact, the Spanish Crown, in seeking to mitigate the position of the Indian, through administrative measures, caused the chagrin of the *criollo*. Between the *mestizo* and the Indian there was no great division in the first years of the colony. A common position of inferiority kept them together. This unity, however, broke down after independence, and has since been a factor in the political history of Mexico.

The division of the Indians into separate races, and the population into castes, during the three centuries of colonial government was one of the causes for continued peace.

Another reason was that the Spanish Crown, after the Conquest, made no serious effort to destroy, at one fell swoop, the social organization it found in Mexico. After the Indian's capitulation, he was allowed to retain a semblance of his community, his religion, his way of life. In 1555 Charles the Fifth ordered that "the laws and good customs which the Indians had had for their government and politics before and continued after they became Christians, and those who retained their laws and customs but had not as yet accepted 'our sacred religion' should be protected and guarded in the exercise of their own government and politics." Thus the Spanish Crown attempted to preserve the Indians from too sudden a break with the past and prevent the obliteration of all that was meaningful to them as human beings and members of organized society. The campaign to destroy their religion was superficial, and native ownership of land and its communal utilization were continued to a surprising degree. Indian villages were left as they were and protected in their holdings, even if their holdings were reduced. The tribute exacted was a continuation of a practice prevalent before the Conquest, and was collected, as before, by the native Indian chiefs.

During the three centuries after the conquest there was much change, but it came about slowly, in bits, in different places at different times. The years of slow attrition worked against the Indians, and the uprisings that occurred testify to their restlessness. As a whole the rule of the conqueror rested upon as little interference with the internal unity of the different groups as was consistent with the interest of both the State and the land owners. The masters had changed, and the system changed slowly with them.

Exclusion of the native population from the government

was, in the long run, to prove fatal to Spain; was to be one of the causes for the overthrow of Spanish power. In the end only those tied to Spain by birth had a real concern for the maintenance of the Spanish connection.

Concentration of all power in the hands of the Spaniard meant that with the passing of Spain experienced government disappeared. With it also passed most of the prestige of both government and Church. Obedience as a principle and submission as a habit were destroyed by the rebellion. The lack of administrative experience, the absence of a strong government, the ignorance and recklessness of some of the governors, the ruthless disregard of life and property, the pillage and destruction of most of the large cities, the confused party alignments during the independence movement, all made political stability impossible. The destruction of centralized power and the emergence of sovereign states without administrative unity or historical justification led to military and political anarchy. No one seemed able to obey orders; no one seemed capable of commanding obedience. All power was temporary, momentary, all authority derived only from direct force, and the necessary force was dispersed in many groups and individuals. There was nothing that bound the country together. All active elements were driving in different directions.

The revolution militarized Mexico. The military forces of Spain had been small, with the army officered and recruited from Spanish sources, and with some local militia made up of the wealthier elements in the community. As a result of the eleven years of warfare, a new military element grew up. Hordes of Indians, who for three hundred years had remained subdued, discovered that they could sack, rob, and burn with comparative impunity. Adventurers discovered that if they could make a living in no other way, they could do so by force of arms. Centralized power lost both its prestige and its capacity for controlling the country. The cruelty of both sides, the killing of prisoners, the burning and looting of cities (which was widely practiced by both sides) stimulated an appetite for loot. The end of revolution saw Mexico filled with armed bands which, when the excuse provided by the struggle against Spain disappeared, discovered other excuses that served the same purpose. The chaos which was to fill Mexico for nearly seventy years found its origin in the struggle for national freedom, and in the interval from the end of the colonial administration to the beginning of the Díaz régime all government may be said to have disappeared in Mexico.

CHAPTER 8

GOVERNMENT BY VIOLENCE

AFTER more than ten years of bitter civil strife, Mexico's independence was achieved by treason. D. Agustín de Iturbide, who between the years of 1812 and 1820 had ravaged, killed, and burned in the cause of the Spanish Crown, joined the Mexican side, was embraced by one of the leaders of the independence movement, and became the instrument of national freedom. With Iturbide, to augment the rebel forces, came the army that had fought under him. This fact of a personal leader taking his personal army from one side to the other and making common cause with his former enemies helped to lay the foundation of the military chaos that has troubled Mexico ever since.

The war of independence, which lasted from 1810 to 1821, had the effect of an earthquake. It destroyed the governing classes of Mexico, drove the Spaniard from the country, and removed from office experienced administration. It left the country filled with ambitions stirred to life by the blind fury that had raged so long a time. It destroyed the capital, property, prestige, and power of the only class in the country that had exercised powers of government. Guerrero estimates that there have been at least four thousand military battles in Mexico. He also estimates that in the war of independence more than 600,000 lives were lost. Not a church tower of all the 12,000 temples but was robbed of some of its bells to be melted into cannon. Pillage, murder, robbery, violence, and rape were the constant rule of the years of war for independence, regardless of which side lost or won, regardless of who was the leader: priest or general, Indian or Spaniard. It had become a war of castes, with the Spaniard as the chief victim, but with all of society victimized. The cities of San

Miguel, Celaya, Guanajuato, Valladolid, Zitácuaro, and others, were destroyed, burned, and pillaged. It was a war without quarter, and everything that came within range of the conflicting groups was destroyed: *haciendas*, palaces, towns, and villages.

In the face of such a record one must always recall with profound gratitude and admiration the humanity of Don Nicolás Bravo, who released three hundred Spanish prisoners who had fallen into his hands, after having just learned that the Spaniards had shot his own father. By contrast such examples merely darken the picture.

Manifestations of violence were rooted in the social and political structure. The Indians and *mestizos* who had been slaves for three hundred years, bound and tied, abused and used, compensated themselves in a day for centuries of injustice when they came to be soldiers against the Spaniard. Justice, if justice be the infliction of one wrong for another, and if revenge be an element in justice, balanced the scales at one time, and the sudden swing was frightful in the pain that it produced. The evil of this practice lasted beyond the conflict with Spain; it became a habit. The bitterness of the struggle for independence laid the foundations for a morale that made violence a necessary element in politics and political technique.

Iturbide became the first emperor of Mexico by violence. His followers, in military uniform, invaded the constitutional congress and bullied it into making him emperor. He then dissolved by fraud and force the body that had yielded him legal sanction. That after all is a good epitome of the political history of Mexico. Iturbide who was merely a poor officer in a small army with none of the prerogatives of a great leader, a great statesman, or a great demagogue, was audacious enough to invade an unarmed assembly engaged in attempting to form a new government for a people who had never governed themselves. By that one act, Iturbide initiated the political technique of Mexico: the way to power is by violence. Perhaps no treason to Mexico has had more direful consequence. It was the beginning of a history that has been smeared with blood and filled with treachery and revolution, for no aim but power, no cause but political status.

Mexico became independent upon the eighteenth day of May, 1821. Within three months there was the first *pronunciamiento* (military declaration) against the new government. Felipe Garaz, in Tamaulipas, refused to obey its orders. This rebellion was barely suffocated when Santa Ana declared himself the "Protector" in Tampico. No sooner was he reduced to submission that there was a new *pronunciamiento* in Jalapa, and General Echávarri who was sent by the government to suppress the new rising, rose in rebellion in his turn. Rebellion, revolution, uprising, disobedience, repudiations, threats, plans, programs, marches, counter-marches, attacks, and retreats became the order of the day. Treason to the superior became the norm, almost a respectable mode of conduct, the easiest and the safest means to promotion, power, glory, pillage, riches, gold lace, bluster, further treason, and, finally, death and dissolution. Every soldier might become a general, and every soldier on the way committed treachery as often as was convenient and profitable; every general ultimately died as a result of such treason. The commander lost his power of command; the followers knew naught of obedience, nor the equals of confidence. No one was sure of anything except that he could trust no one, that disobedience was the safest and most remunerative rule before violent death overtook one. There were, therefore, no rulers who were obeyed, no ruled who did not rebel, no citizen who would not wriggle out of any commitment, either fiscal or moral. Government was dissolved by the disappearance of respect, loyalty, confidence, and faith.

When Iturbide was forced to abdicate, the states of Guanajuato, Morelos, San Luis Potosí, Zacatecas, and

Oaxaca formed a league against the federal congress, while Texas, Coahuila, Nuevo León, and Tamaulipas formed a "junta" in defense of the congress.

In 1823, two years after independence, Guatemala proclaimed its independence. In Texas, a priest by the name of Tres Palacios rose against the congress and enlisted the frontier Indians in his cause. Guadalajara proclaimed itself independent. Querétaro issued a revolutionary plan. Yucatan declared a revolution in favor of *centralismo* and established its own government. In Sonora, another priest declared a revolution against the "Plan of Vera Cruz." The Congress of Oaxaca declared its independence from Mexico, and Colima separated itself from Jalisco.

Dissolution of organized government was in full swing; administration became less and less central and more and more local. Politics became more intense as they became more localized, and political passion rose higher and higher as the changes of government became increasingly rapid, bloody, and violent. Parties splintered into bits, each bit having a central personality, and each conspiring against all of the rest.

Such governmental disruption made the distinctions between *políticos* and *bandidos* a nominal one, and the congress issued the same law against political conspirators and road bandits. Pillage, highway robbery, assaults, and attacks upon towns and cities, with any pretext or no pretext, became a mode of expected and accepted behavior. A common bandit, Aspericueta, assaulted the town of San Miguel and pillaged it in broad daylight. Another robber attacked the city of San Luis. Whether these attacks were political, semipolitical, or pure banditry was hard to discern, and, so far as the public was concerned, not distinguishable at all. Pillage and robbery were the same whatever the slogan under which they were committed. Gabriel Yermo rose in Cuautla, Vicente Gómez organized a *liga santa* in Puebla; Reguera fortified himself in Cerro Colorado and attacked the roads that lead to Tehuacán; a sergeant rose in rebellion in Querétaro; Hernández in Cuernavaca; General Calderón in Mexico; Rosenberg and Gardoa started a rebellion in Tepic; in Oaxaca, Lamadrid organized a band that called itself by the simple and honest name of "The Assassins."

Dissolution of Mexico seemed inevitable. The loss of Texas was but one item in the general turmoil. Governors carried on wars against governors, such as the attack on Coahuila by Nueve León, with the idea of annexation. Yucatan declared its independence in 1841, and if it had not been for the war of the castes, the Indian uprising, which forced the state of Yucatan to beg for outside aid, its independence would have been consummated. In fact, Yucatan asked the United States government to intervene in favor of the whites in the state, and offered itself in annexation as a reward.

What was happening between the states was happening within the states. The *jefes políticos* were becoming independent of the state governors and the *caciques* of the *jefes políticos*. The army which the central government might have depended upon to protect it and to maintain order broke up (for the same reasons which led to disintegration of centralized administration), into bands and parties that had neither principle, discipline, responsibility, order, nor organization. The army ceased to be an instrument of peace for the central government, and became the main cause of internal disorder and disharmony. The scene was laid for sixty years of chaos.

The violence learned during the struggle for independence was repeated and perpetuated until it became the rule in political conflict. From the beginning, the killing of prisoners on the ground that they were trying to escape became a habit. This practice, known as *ley fuga*, (developed by President Bustamante in the early days of the Republic), has since been used by everyone aspiring to power in Mexico, by everyone exercising it, by every petty military officer, every policeman with an eye to orginality. It has been a rule of politics, of war, of rebellion Prisoners almost always want to escape. Bustamante had prisoners who "tried to escape" while being transported on mule back with their feet and hands tied, after they had surrendered on the promise that their lives would be spared. That could not and did not prevent their being shot as it has not prevented many other prisoners from being shot under similar circumstances. Bustamante, too, is credited with the invention in 1824 (three years after independence was achieved) of the "Court Martial" for general and wholesale use. To such heights of cruelty and savagery did his conduct reach that an opposing general, Barragán, issued a ' Peaceful Manifesto" asking that if the war must continue it should be as among civilized peoples. What Bustamante achieved in cruelty was a minor matter compared to the excesses of a later ruler of Mexico, Santa Ana, who was of a caliber to compare with the bloody tyrants of the remote past.

During the years of dissolution after independence, the army was not only the safest but also the most lucrative career. It was the one profession for which no one needed any special training, and in which all could, with sufficient audacity, achieve equal heights. The lucrativeness of army life made all other employments both dangerous and of little monetary value. The army was the chief gainer from the general dissolution. The weaker the organized community became, the stronger was the army; the weaker the centralized army became, the stronger were the smaller units within the army. The dissolution arose from the ineptitude of the new governing class, the immense distances, the bad roads that made these distances seem even further than they were, the self-appointed character of all authority, the destruction of wealth that followed in the wake of independence, and the continued pillaging and robbery, the almost universal illiteracy, the breakdown of all social and economic ties, and the continued sowing of hatred and discontent among the different classes. All these influences contributed to make the military career the safest and most profitable of all the professions. It was a profession in which honor, glory, riches, and power were to be had for the asking, and quickly, provided one could ask with arms in one's hands and brazen disregard in one's bearing.

In fact, government service, especially that of soldier, became almost the only dependable means of livelihood. The public funds could almost always be collected by force, fraud, threats, and promise. It was the only fund outside the Church that was fairly certain of periodic reappearance. It would be essential only to defend access to the public treasury. The federal army of those days has been described in the following words: "For every two men that carried a gun there were two commanders that ordered them about, one official who commanded the commanders, one musician who played the tune and one retired officer who criticized the operations and collected his gratuity."

In 1845, Benito Juárez, while governor of the State of Oaxaca, said in an official document: "The commanding generals enjoy an absolute independence of the authorities of the states, and in the absence of a public spirit, and the ignorance of the masses, have at their disposal the physical forces with which they have regulated the destinies of the nation." The fear and hatred of the army was such that it was always difficult, even in the face of foreign invasions, to secure the necessary military contingents. In the City of Mexico, an attempt to take a census in 1836 revealed 104,000 inhabitants, with only 15,000 males. So great was the repugnance against possible military draft that there was a general attempt to escape being counted. Of the males shown to be in the city, the majority were young boys or old men. From this census arose the saying that "in the City of Mexico every man is entitled to seven women."

The meaning of military rule in Mexico was early illustrated in Mexican history. Within the first fourteen years after independence practically every prominent general who had participated in the independence movement had been killed or exiled, or was in hiding with a ransom on his head. One need but mention the outstanding figures of those days— Iturbide, Guerrero, Bravo, Negrete, Echávarri, Morán, Barragán, Andrade, Bustamante, Quintanar, Pedraza, Facio, and others—and we see that all of these were either murdered, shot by a military squad, exiled, or escaped in fear of their lives. With such a beginning it is clear that it was not easy to bridle so restless a military clique, and those who might have done the bridling—the common people, the peasants—had neither power nor interest in the bloody affrays that were staged every few months among those who called themselves the masters of the public and fought to secure power and spoils from the government. Rule by the military meant rule by the strongest military officer, and there were always men who believed themselves both stronger and better fitted to govern than those actually in power. That was natural, inevitable. Military officers with an army at their backs usually have not only a good grievance but also a strong conviction of their superior merit as well. In Mexico, time has generally proved them right for a period, until a stronger and more virtuous officer appeared on the scene, as he usually did within a few months.

A good civil reason was always available for a military attack against the government. It might be said, of course, that whatever the excuse was it was sufficient, and therefore good in the eyes of the military cliques who supported it. Since in the army the means to income is through promotion, and as the mass of subordinates is always greater than the superior officers, then in a country where a lieutenant may achieve a captaincy, a captain become a major, a major rise to the position of a colonel, and a colonel become a general by the mere device of supporting a new revolution against an old one, it has always been easy to find military support for a new governmental venture. Military, as well as civil, power passed to the new group, and in the management of public funds forced loans, as well as forced takings, were possible. All this has been done, as becomes military men, in the name of a good cause, and with a clear conscience. It is not suggested that these military men were neither honest nor good. It is merely pointed out that when an army finds means to achieve its own particular ends as an army, without regard to the broader ends of the community within which it exists, that army's definitions of honor, honesty, and public service are likely to depart somewhat from the customary civil definitions of those terms. We are dealing with a sort of moral relativity. As the distinguishing feature of the army is that it is armed, it is inclined to achieve a preponderance in determining what is right and what is wrong that makes civil definitions rather ineffective.

One reason why the army has been the source of so much difficulty, is that it, like the Church, was a society apart. In the military organization of the Mexican Republic, the army was completely beyond civil control. It continued the old Spanish tradition in which the army was subject only to military law. Just as under the canon law a priest could be judged only by the Church, so, under the Spanish and later the Mexican rule, a soldier could be judged only by military law. Under the conditions which prevailed in Mexico the solider was immune for most crimes, especially if the offender was an officer even of the lowest rank. In spite of the fact that the Constitution of 1857 abolished these military privileges, the tradition of military immunity largely persists. Mexico has thus from the very beginning been saddled with a special military class supported from the common treasury, in effect the greatest drain upon the treasury, but without the ordinary channels of public control and public responsibility, ready to join any movement that would advance the cause

GENERAL FRANCISCO VILLA

of its own members, regardless of the needs of the country. Being subject only to its own law it gave account to no one. It collected what money it could from the budget through rebellion, forced loans, pillage and theft, and continued to plague Mexico from the earliest days of independence to very recent times.

A rebellion was a serious matter for the government but not for the army. The army merely found in a rebellion a means of increasing its income, promoting its members, and securing funds not easily available before. The rebelling group took possession of such towns as it could, equipped itself with the goods that were available, took over the public funds and collected what it could by forced loans, and avoided battle. The longer it avoided battle the greater was the likelihood of success. The government forces would either desert, or the government would go bankrupt, whereupon the loyal forces would themselves join the rebellion. For the government defeat was fatal, but for the rebellion, not at all. The rebels, if beaten, could gather their scattered forces, operate in small groups in the mountain fastnesses, live on the country and await a new opportunity. The government was usually defeated in the end. There were nine successful rebellions in the first fifteen years of Mexican independence.

The government was almost always at a disadvantage. It did not dare trust its loyal troops. It had to support, equip, feed and please them, else they might any day become enemies. The army, of course, cost the government money all the time, but when a rebellion was brewing it was found necessary to refurnish, reequip, and rearm the loyal troops. The funds that had been set aside for that purpose usually found other outlets, so that a rebellion proved a drain upon the government, a burden upon the populace, but, by the same token, a boon to both the loyal and the rebelling groups in the army. The loyal group received more than double its legal allotments. It had already received the budgetary allowance set aside for the army; now that there was danger in the air it received a further grant of money from the mortgaging of the future income of the government. The defeat of the rebel army was not a matter of vital import to the military supporting the government. They could always join the rebels and they frequently did so, after they had received from the government all that the government had to offer. Revolution, from the army point of view, was a sort of private business with few dangers, much honor, and promotion at public expense. It is only in terms such as these that the Mexican army of the early independence period can be described: an instrument of evil and pillage, without public purpose or public interest and without honor in the ordinary civil sense.

Between 1821 and 1845 the army destroyed the federal government of Mexico ten times, not counting the innumerable *pronunciamientos, levantamientos,* and rebellions that did not succeed, and not counting the innumerable local uprising against governors. The purpose each time was either the placing of a new president in office or the forcible removal of the one in power. The object of the military, however, was always the same: remuneration for the success of the new leader. During the conflict the prospective government was lavish in promises. With power achieved, the government found itself incapable of satisfying the greed of its military supporters. As Francisco Bulness says:

All wanted to be cavalry colonels, or at least infantry colonels. All wanted to be heads of military expeditions against real or imaginary bandit groups, against peaceful or savage Indians, with unlimited expense accounts. All wanted to have the income from ports or fiscal offices, all wanted gold, either private or public, all wanted concessions, *haciendas,* houses, titles, to establish gambling houses, all wanted their exemptions to cover past, present and future crimes. All wanted everything and the president, instead of being the leader of a government and governor of an army, be-

84

came the servant and slave of an army of an unstable group of bandits.

In the years between 1821 and 1845, the military budget exceeded the total income of the government fourteen times. That is, more than half the time the government income was less than the assigned military budget of the country, which did not include other means of emolument not specified in budgetary accounting. The purchase price of the presidency exceeded the total income of the nation for the years 1832 to 1850, with the exception of the two years 1835 and 1836. In the twenty-three years from 1823 to 1845 the total income of the nation was $291,236,796. In these years the army had assigned to it $326,506,715. Such was the situation in a country that had no roads, no ports, no railroads, and no peace.

When Comonfort came to the presidency in 1855, Mexico was in a state of turmoil even worse than usual. Justo Sierra says, "There wasn't a day without a *pronunciamiento*, without sedition, without its rebelion, in some part of the republic." It seemed as if the country were in eruption like a volcano. The political situation "hid a crater."

Constant turmoil made economic development impossible. Apart from the destruction and pillage that were consequences of the repeated uprisings, each new armed force that called itself a government could, and did, change the laws. Every *jefe político*, commander, governor, *cacique*, president, or whatever he and his armed force called him, made laws, raised and levied taxes, increased the *alcabala*, punished, fined, confiscated—that is, he extracted all that he could as fast as he could, with as little regard for the future as was possible. Economic stability was impossible, enterprise impossible. Nothing remained that was safe, but land. Cattle were killed, buildings burned, and crops cut, foraged, or destroyed.

We may summarize by saying that the military chiefs who repudiated the civil governments, the governors who repudiated the central authority, the *jefes politicos* who repudiated the governors, the *caciques* who, hidden behind their mountain barriers, ruled, abused, and governed without regard to the world at large, the military uprisings that turned their defeated elements into bandits who, in turn, lived upon each other, or the government, or the peaceful residents of city or country, all these groups succeeded in making life a hazard, property a nominal possession, and honor something to be upheld with a gun.

CHAPTER 9

VIOLENCE AND THE IDEAL IN POLITICS

A POLITICAL theory, if it is to be useful, must reflect a society within which the idea it formulates is operative as a way of political conduct. From that point of view the theory of a feudal system, of a centralized government and Church, a powerful aristocracy, an ordered peace based upon serfdom and semi-slavery, with a modicum of charity and kindliness, was descriptive of the state of affairs as they existed in Mexico before independence and after it for a long time, even as they exist today in certain spots. The ideas of the French Revolution which were imbibed by a few liberal middle-class people, who were discontented with the Spanish régime because it excluded them from power, were not representative of Mexico. There was no base of equality in Mexico. There could be no democracy; there could be no freedom. In an agricultural country, democracy, equality, freedom, can only be based on small-scale land ownership, town meetings, popular militia, common language and culture: equality in fact. That could have been achieved in Mexico only by a destruction of the large estates, the division of the lands to peons and villages, and the deprivation of the army and Church of special privileges. Political democracy in Mexico waited for a complete and profound social revolution; but such was farthest from the ideas of the leaders and directors of the movement for independence. The *criollos* wanted the spoils of government and not much more. The ideas of democracy helped undermine the prestige of the Crown and provide moral justification for the rebels, but were to find no application in the new government.

During the struggle for independence and after, a new order of ideas invaded and permeated the small educated classes. These new ideas were adopted in theory, but the old practices continued. The ideas of democracy, liberty, fraternity, and equality received lip service, but the Indian remained a serf; the landowner remained an *hacendado*. The power of the sword was still the dominant power. It was as though a new light had entered a dark cavern, but most of those in the cavern were too blind to see it and too lame to profit by it. Mexico was glued to its past and could not break loose. The new ideas were foreign to the social and political system. The old institutions and the new ideas came into conflict. It became a conflict between an ideal society and a real one, between a theory and a fact.

For a century the conflict in Mexico had been between an ideal and a fact. The fact was anarchy, and the ideal, peace. The fact was servitude, and the ideal, freedom. The fact was petty military authority, and the ideal, political democracy. The constitution of 1857, like its various predecessors, was a formula that could not be applied, a political doctrine that had no roots in the soil. It was foreign, unreal, immaterial. The constitution, adopting the French model, declared men to be naturally free and politically equal. The *peon* was tied to the soil, although he was the mass of the nation. The *leva* (forced military service), was in force. There was no freedom of the press, or of opinion, or of worship. In theory, death for political crimes was abolished; in practice, it continued. The whole history of Mexico was torn by this conflict between theory and fact, theory foreign to fact. The ideals of the independence movement were outside both the experience of the colonial and the ancient *mores* of the Indian. The constitution of the 1857 remained inapplicable.

Independence from Spain left the major political issues still to be settled. And the history of the last hundred and twenty years is in part a history of the attempt to settle them. The conflicts have been violent, deep, and persistent, because no formula acceptable to any one group has been applicable to the whole situation. Mexico had been a colony for three hundred years. It continued all of the colonial institutions after independence, except that of allegiance to a foreign crown. The theories that justified the rebellion proved unworkable as instruments of government. The basic question, "What kind of government shall Mexico have?" remained unanswered. "Shall it be a monarchy, an aristocracy a republic, a democracy?" "Shall it be a centralized or federated government?" Each of these questions was answered in the affirmative more than once, some many times. Again, "Shall Mexico maintain the old institutions of Church and army, as during the colonial period?" To this question too, many answers were attempted; and it was not till 1857 that it received even a partial answer.

Here was a government, modeling itself upon democratic institutions, attempting to operate with a form of popular suffrage, but with a base of divergent uncommunicating race groups, with general illiteracy, with a system of serfdom that embraced the greater part of the population, with a poor income from the mines (which had been seriously impeded in their operations by the turbulence of the war of independence, and which had never recovered), with much of the land in the country exempt from taxation because it was in the hands of religious orders, with much of the remaining land in the hands of large estates (whose owners successfully prevented the taxation of their property), with an army that lived by public disorder, with commerce limited to luxuries for the upper classes and with ideas of liberty, equality, fraternity in conflict with ideas of order, religion, Church, faith, God, and King.

Independence, as we have seen, destroyed the central government and dispersed its powers. Government became local, personal, and direct. Districts that could hide themselves behind mountain barriers defied central authority and established independent governments. There were entire regions that had governments of their own and obeyed only their local chiefs. Alvarez dominated in the mountains of Guerrero; Mejía and Olvera ruled in Querétaro; Lozada, in Nayarit; Juan Méndez, ruled in the Sierra of Puebla as late as 1876. Regalado governed the region of Tlahualilo; Cravioto ruled in the mountains of Huauchinango in Tamaulipas. These are but samples to illustrate the chaos that overtook Mexico. They do not include such purely Indian groups as the Yaquis, who never accepted governmental control, and whose autonomy was respected by the local and federal governments. This administrative localism invaded all parts of Mexico, even the Federal District. The Indians in Xochimilco gave Juarez a military contingent during the French invasion under the assumption that they were aiding a friendly nation.

This military and political dispersion was further increased by each *hacienda* that became, during this time, a political, military, and economic unit within its own borders. The plantation not only exercised all the powers of a civil government, imprisoning and castigating those who lived within its confines, but armed and militarized its *encasillados*, either for defense or aggression, against its neighbors or to take part in some larger political movement. This breakup of general authority strengthened localism, not merely in the country districts, in mountainous regions, and on plantations it even existed in the larger cities, where the *barrios* came to be dominated by a sort of petty feudalism, petty tyranny, and petty *cacique*.

Political units of the type that we have just described do not easily lend themselves to written constitutions. The gap between the ruler and the ruled cannot be bridged by a legal document. Such government is altogether too personal, too military, too autocratic to be subject to legal restrictions, and its powers and activities overrun legal channels. This was true of Mexico not only in localities, in counties, in states, but in the federal government. The will of the ruler was for practical purposes the law of the land. Those who were discontented with the government might, and did, rise up in rebellion and overthrow the undesirable president, but the political structure and form went on. The leader of the new revolution, regardless of the pretext, regardless of promises made, regardless even of desire to do differently, might find himself doing the same as the others, or nearly the same. The leader of the revolution became the president if he was successful, was shot or exiled if unsuccessful. The rest went on as before. Opposition groups were effective in overthrowing a government they did not like; they were ineffective in keeping within constitutional bounds a government they had brought to power.

Revolutions on political grounds from 1810 to 1910 in Mexico have therefore been negative. They have destroyed, torn down, driven president after president from office; they have not succeeded in forming a new institutional base, because there has been no local democratic units for governmental structure. This makes it possible for a student of Mexican political institutions to say, when speaking of the Constitution of 1857, "The Constitution of 1857 was never followed in the organization of the public powers, because if it had been complied with the stability of the government would have been impossible . . . and the constitution was subordinated to the primary needs of existence."

The written constitution has served as a source of revolutionary agitation and turmoil. The failure of a government to comply with the constitution was a good reason for a new rebellion; the impossibility of governing within constitutional limits notwithstanding. Constitutionalism was, therefore, and still is, a source of conflict. Consider the difficulties over *sufragio efectivo no reeleccion* (effective suffrage and no re-election). The fact is simple enough: a country with such internal disharmony and petty localism cannot operate under a political document that assumes as a basis that all are equal before the law. The facts belie the theory upon which the document is based. The *peon* did not have the same powers of enforcing his will as the *hacendado*, the middle class, as the military class. The law was equal for all; but the application was according to caste, power, social prestige. The political constitution presupposed a community of individuals; which in fact it was not. Mexico is a country of indigenous, or semi-indigenous village groups, divided according to family and clan distinctions. Within the political clan all was possible; outside of it, nothing, except what was winked at or considered unimportant.

The nonexistence of party organization, the lack of any sense of the rights of minorities, the complete absence of democratic habits and practices, made democracy a farce from the beginning. He who had the power won the government, and as soon as he was in power he despoiled, persecuted, and robbed his opponents and contenders for public office. As the group or individual in power was in fact legislator, judge, and executive at the same time, his opponents had no recourse but rebellion. Government was thus a very personal matter among groups of individuals, without serious regard to party politics or party ideals, but with very serious attachment to some individual attempt to make the world safe for themselves and their friends, and, in the process, as uncomfortable and unsafe as possible for their political and personal enemies. Persecution of opponents was certain, regardless of who came to power. It was one of the few political certainties in Mexico. The other certainty was the *cuartelazo*, the military uprising against the party in office. Politics, therefore, for over sixty years—from the days of Iturbide, who initiated the program of acquiring power by treason, to the days when Díaz took over the reins of government— came to be oppression by the clique in power, to be met in turn by a *cuartelazo*. That was as certain to be the course of

92

events as the rising of the sun. The only uncertainty was the length of time that any particular group could keep itself in office; even for this time and experience made it possible to calculate an average. For the federal government, during the sixty years from Iturbide to Díaz, this average was less than a year.

Revolutions were perhaps an educational movement in Mexico, a costly one, it is true, but a substitute for the lack of any general education. Their consequences were bad in most ways. They led to economic ruin and political instability, but who would say that they did not contribute to the spreading of knowledge among the masses, to the mixture of the races, and to a leveling off of the cultural content among the different elements in the population and among the different races? It may also be true that they helped to spread the Spanish language among the people, since Spanish was the only common speech among the wandering groups as they traveled from one part of the country to another. It is a rare wind that blows no good. Even the rebellions may have been useful for the development in Mexico of that nationalism, of that spontaneity, which has made the recent revolution and its social program possible.

The break-up of organized society as a consequence of persistent turmoil made for an increasing dependence upon personalism, upon family ties. The family and its friends became a political unit for defense and aggression. It has remained to this date a basic factor in all Mexican politics. The *compadrazgo* (the *compadre*, godfather, relationship) in Mexico is a matter of great importance in the social cohesion of the family. It still has something of the nature of the older feudal ties between the lord and his subordinates which led to a sort of mutual protection and fealty against the rest of the world. It has remained a source of protection of the weak left abandoned in the world because of the loss of relatives through death. The *compradre* takes over the protection of

93

the *comadre* and her children. The acquired family is thus larger than the natural family, and is still a basic factor in politics. One's friends, family, and *compadres* share the fortunes of the head of the group, enter office with him, go out in revolution with him, share their bread and risk their lives for each other. It is perhaps the only tie of solidarity in the upper Mexican groups, and especially among the *mestizos*. The Indian has his village fealty, the rich *criollo* his wealth and power, but the *mestizo* has this enlarged family as his source of strength and power. As the *compadre* is almost always a person of superior position, the relationship of adoption enhances the personal status of the adopted, provides protection against injustice, aid in case of need, and prestige all of the time. In the cities, where life and property are safer, the element of *compadre* is of minor importance, but in the country, with its isolation, it is still significant.

Because of the purely personal character of Mexican politics, the leader has always surrounded himself with his family, his intimate friends, his body servants. It may be a democracy on paper, but even the members of congress must be *gente de absoluta confianza* (people of absolute confidence). This is not criticism. This is description. It has always been true in Mexico, is true today, and will continue to be true until such time as party government becomes a fact in the political organization of Mexico. Until such time it is inevitable that the leader of the government should seek to surround himself with those whom he can trust and to whom he may entrust his life. Every politician of importance in Mexico is always in danger of paying with his life for his public career. That, too, is simple fact. The history of Mexico from the days of independence to the present is replete with stories of murder and assassination and summary military death. That toll is inevitable under the circumstances. Personalism tends therefore to become actual nepotism. Under the Díaz regime the president's son carried out large public works at public expense, was chief of staff, and was his father's private secretary at different times. The president's nephew was once chief of all the police of the republic, at another time a deputy, and at another time governor of Oaxaca. It has been said that "We have seen in all of the congresses of the union all the relatives of General Díaz, all the relatives of his political aides, his sons-in-law, his brothers-in-law, his cousins, his doctor, his dentist, his buffoon, his panegyrist, in short, all of his personal friends and companions have lived perpetually in the congress of our 'constitutional government.'" The whole scheme of political relationships is built up on that principle. The man in office is surrounded by friends. Each, according to his needs and abilities, receives such benefits as are at the disposal of the leader and within his powers. In return the recipient of the favor expects to render such services as are peculiarly at his disposal and within his powers. Nothing that can be given is denied, and no sacrifice that can be demanded is refused. When the friend enters office all of the friends about him move into power. When he is out of office they, too, are out, but the group continues as a group until the next opportunity arrives.

Speaking of General Díaz, Andrés Molina Enríquez says:

In effect, all of the ministers and all of the governors have always been tied to General Díaz by personal friendship. The *jefes políticos* have in a similar fashion been tied to the governors. In their turn, the *presidentes municipales* have been tied to the *jefes políticos*, and to these the *vecinos* of the local villages.

This is significant as a political method because it takes the place of party, of party principle, and of national patriotism. In a country where social and racial divisions are as great as we have indicated, patriotism is difficult to define. No common unity is possible, even in the face of foreign invasion. That has certainly been clear in recent years, when definite groups would have welcomed American intervention if, in the process, they could have destroyed the policy of the Revolution.

Up to the present period, and in a sense even at present, peace in Mexico, when it has existed, has been a peace achieved by the submission of, or loyalty of, or friendship of these minor rulers in their special spheres. Peace has been brought about by permitting the small *cacique* full powers within his special province; his loyalty has been purchased permitting him to protect his friends, his family, and his *padrinos*. Democracy in the sense of individual initiative and operation has simply not existed, even in the large cities. In the smaller towns, villages, *haciendas*, *pueblos*, it has never existed. It could not exist. The principle of government was a principle of loyalty to the little chief; the little chief, in turn, rendered loyalty to the still greater chief in the capital of the state or in the City of Mexico. *The small group has always followed its local leader against anyone, even against the great leader.* Herein is the root of the political problems in Mexico. It is in identifying the interests of the leadership of the local community with the interests of the leadership of the larger community that peace may be had.

This reduction of government to a private concern made private participation in public funds a natural and inevitable part of government. No office holder knew how long he would be in office. It might be a day, a week, or a month, but almost never a year. With a new revolution, and one was always brewing, would come not only the loss of the office but likely also proscription, exile, and, in case of poor luck, death. One had achieved office by revolution, by the infliction of injury, by the exercise of passions and fanaticism. One expected to be driven from office the same way. Political passion was at its highest, at boiling heat all the time. A change in office meant for the officeholder, the political party or government of the moment, all the consequences of a great triumph—or a great tragedy.

What was true of the individual officeholder, the need for making use of the opportunity quickly and without much scruple, of getting what could be had from the public treasury, was also true of the government in office. It could not take time to examine, to verify, to supervise, to charge and condemn. It needed money; it needed it quickly. A new revolution was around the corner. It needed money for the army, for supplies, for creditors. It took what it could get from its own party officeholders who, as tax collectors, shared with the government what they received. The government received, as a favor one might say, what the government officials paid over after deducting their salaries and the cost of acquiring office—which to them meant free effort for party ends, risk of life and goods, damage done by others when they occupied office, and insurance against future loss because of participation in the office of government. That is, after all, a considerable bill to collect, and yet a legitimate one from the standpoint of the temporary officeholder who risked his life in aiding his party to office, who stayed in office at the risk both of his life and his goods, and who was almost certain to be driven from office by violence, death or exile. It is in such an atmosphere of political government that the tradition of Mexican party organization and administrative morale was formed. It is true that under Díaz there was a lull in this process, at least in its most violent forms, for a period of thirty-four years; but it might be said that it only became more systematic, and therefore less obvious.

That Mexican politics revolves about the Mexican treasury is perhaps the most significant fact about its organization, and, as things stand, inevitable for a long time to come. Outside of the government there are no sources of income in Mexico that are secure, definite, self-perpetuating, and available. All wealth in Mexico, at least all wealth in private hands, is precarious, limited, constantly subject to danger from public attack, or theft through robbery or rebellion, and this has been so for a hundred and twenty years, especially among the Mexicans; foreigners have greater security both in their possessions and in their persons.

Political activity must, therefore, be financed by governmental funds. Governmental income must finance the party in power. There is no other source. It is this simple economic fact that makes the party in power so strong; it has secure access to the only available finance. The party in power does not wish to relinquish office, because of all its adherents would automatically be deprived of the only definite source of income available in the form of jobs, commissions, franchises, and prerogatives. It is this that makes revolution so frequently the only means of removing a party in power. Until other sources of income can be developed through industry or agriculture, so that the mass of younger people who are coming up can find an adequate means to a livelihood outside the government and the spoils of politics, political partisanship, conflict, and revolution are bound to occur with greater or lesser frequency.

Díaz pacified Mexico by compromising with the local leaders and converting them into instruments of the government. In the world of such little loyalties all outsiders were natural enemies, and all transitory people subject to tribute and robbery. Banditry was natural in a country broken by inaccessible mountains, and reft into a thousand little political loyalties, with no recourse to the outside, and with no contacts with the outside world except when foreigners came for purposes of exploitation. The only means of tying these local chieftains to the central seat of power was to transform the bandit into a policeman at public expense. It was this principle which Díaz used so effectively in pacifying Mexico. *Pan o palos* (Bread or sticks). If they will coöperate, feed them from the public treasury; if not, exterminate them. Peace was therefore achieved by making the bandit the symbol of authority, and by so doing, tying his loyalties to some central principle. His official tyranny and oppression became less disastrous than the persistent and irregular banditry in which each one who had lost his fortune or wished to make one took up banditry as a profession.

Peace in Mexico was, therefore, achieved by giving formal sanction to little tyrants; justice and police power were exercised by them. Slowly, as the central power became stronger, accounts and accountability were introduced; inspection was enforced; trial and judgment were exacted. As power accumulated, the central governing body became more and more arbitrary and severe, and the little tyrants lost much of their initiative. They had helped build the central power by loyalty and support, and later were reduced to impotence and obedience at the threat of extermination. When Mexico achieved peace it was by means of tyranny on a large scale. When it had rebellions, it was because of tyranny in many places on a small scale. There was a transfer from local banditry to national tyranny, from petty oppression and violence to universal peace by oppression everywhere.

This system of pacification has many illustrations. D. Manuel Doblado, as governor of Guanajuato, was the first to introduce the system of converting the bandits into police. In the days of Díaz, the army was largely recruited from criminals sent by the states. The *rurales* (rural police) that made Mexico "the safest country in the world" were composed of highway robbers or *salteadores*. The brigade that protected the roads from Santa Fe to Toluca was made up of such a group.

Under the Díaz régime, power was gradually concentrated in the federal government and specifically in the president, until every governmental activity emanated from the president. The election of the president, maintained in form, ceased to be effective in practice. The powers of the legislature disappeared, not only in the national Legislature, but also in the state legislatures. What was true of the elective officials was similarly true of the judicial officers. They were appointed with an eye to a common policy, and this policy was enforced by direct intervention of the executive, both in local and in federal matters. It is important to observe that the constitutional forms were maintained. The legal channels were still in existence, but administrative procedure had supplanted political and elective machinery. The will of the nation was the will of the president and of his subordinates. All this was made possible under Díaz because he had succeeded in satisfying or suppressing those elements that had hitherto made trouble. The conflict among the political groups was ironed out. The conflict with the Church, which had existed since its inception in Mexico, was now at a minimum, and the Church was allowed to recover a part of its old prestige and power. The incoming industrialism opened sources of income and promise of wealth to many classes in the community. The internal difficulties—the great internal disharmony, the excessive poverty and misery of the masses—were overlooked. Individual recalcitrants were suppressed without mercy and without favor. There was but one ruler, one power, a dictator who had managed to unite in his own hands all of the agencies of government for a period of nearly thirty-five years. He did all this without seriously changing the character of the relationship between the classes. In fact, the position of the poor had become worse because of his continuance and extension of the policy of destruction of village holdings, his taking away village lands and turning them over to individuals.

Theoretically, Mexico under Díaz was not only a democracy, but a democracy of the advanced type. It guaranteed to the individual all of the rights for which any liberal could ask. In fact, it was an oligarchy that accepted the dictatorship of an extraordinary man for the maintenance of those privileges, prerogatives, place, and power that it desired. The laws either were not applied, or were applied with an eye to the person involved. The rich, the powerful, the well-connected, the foreigner, the circle around General Díaz, did as they pleased, obeyed such laws as suited them, enforced such laws as served them to greater riches or more power. Where the law interfered, it was disregarded, violated, forgotten. It was a personal government with the consent of, and for the benefit of a small group of foreign and native holders of claims of family, politics, power, and foreign influence.

The rest of the population was largely outside the law: the will of the ruler being the law. The mass had no rights that must be respected, no influence that made itself felt. They had no representatives before the court, no judges to listen to their pleas. Resistance was met by force, by the *ley fuga*, by forced levy into the army, by forced migration from place to place, by forced labor in the *henequén* plantations in Yucatan, or in the fields of the Valle Nacional. The will of the dictator was supreme. Worse, the will of each little dictator, from the governors of the states to the *caciques* of the districts and the sergeant of a few *rurales*, was as good as the will of the big one, because the poor and the meek and the downtrodden and the exploited had no voice that could cry for help. Mexico was at peace at the price of tyranny, humiliation, oppression, and foreign approval.

But Díaz failed. The peace that he gave Mexico proved transitory. It proved transitory partly because it was too well done. In the thirty-five years the local *cacique* had been so tied to the central government as to cease to be a source of loyalty. He had been converted from a local leader to a local tyrant, from a local friend to an enemy. When the Díaz government was destroyed it required a new revolution to develop a new local leadership with local support. The pendulum swung back again from tyranny to chaos. The process of finding a happy medium is still going on, and is still in the way of organization.

This combination of economic, cultural, and racial conflict, this history of conquest, exploitation, and cruelty, of political chicanery and dishonesty, has left a deep sense of distrust within the mass of Mexicans, especially among the *mestizos*. The Indians do not trust the white man or the *mestizo*, and with good reason. They have had four hundred years of cheating, broken promises, robbery, and theft from their white conquerors and their white neighbors—a history of perverse dealings that even at this date has not come to an end. In spite of the Revolution, there are many places in Mexico where the Indian is exploited by the neighboring *mestizo*, white man, or foreigner. But the Indians trust one another within their own communities. Internally there is faith and discipline and loyalty. Where the race and language have survived, where the older traditions have been preserved, there the Indian retains his internal unity and his faith.

This is not true of the *mestizo*. The mixture of bloods has brought with it a cultural by-product that has carried into the small community the bitterness and distrust that have arisen out of the centuries of exploitation and political chicanery. *Son desconfiados* (they are suspicious) is an almost universal description of the small rural community, especially if the community is of mixed blood. They have been betrayed so often, promises have been broken so many times, that no other result was possible. Disbelief has become natural; it is their most effective, and, perhaps, their only, means of defense. The fruits of experience indicate that any promise made will probably not be kept, that any leader will betray, that any undertaking will remain uncompleted. Under these conditions a social revolution is difficult.

Spiritually, the regeneration must be deeper than can be expected from mere physical violence and physical conquest. The battle may have been won against the government, but the battle for internal unity and internal faith must still be won. It will be a long time before the simple faith of honest men can be developed so that a promise, an undertaking, or a program will be more than a gesture which everyone assumes, with good historical justification, to be no more than an excuse for further self-emolument, for further pilfering, further evil, and further extortion. I recall a little scene in one of the villages near Actopán, where tanks were being constructed by the local educational agent for the curing of skins, and a coöperative undertaking was being established. The leader of the community was an energetic little man who limped and had to use a cane. He had recently been shot and wounded by the opposition leadership within the village over a battle for the control of the community. This man, standing with his followers, who were being asked to buy shares in the coöperative, repeated over and over again, "*es obra seria, es obra seria*" (it is a serious undertaking). Not once but a hundred times did he repeat it. It was serious. It was honest. It really was to be carried through. It was not meant to rob and cheat. It was serious. It was for your benefit. Only with great difficulty did a few of the men permit themselves to be persuaded. Experience had taught them to believe in no outsider, and even to distrust their own neighbors.

An investigator of the Department of Education in the district of Xocoyocán in the State of Tlaxcala, writes:

The most offensive and calumnious stories are being spread about me by word of mouth from one person to another. Without paying any attention to these rumors I have gone about my work of visiting and interviewing the people. I have the feeling that they are distrustful and false and say things opposite to what they think. This feeling is confirmed by the sanitary delegation and even the Governor believes that the state is shot through with hypocrisy, disunion, and lack of confidence, and resists all attempts at any coöperative undertaking.

He also told us that he finds the people exceedingly difficult to work with and he finds that his worst enemies of one day become his most loyal friends the next, and that the friends of yesterday have suddenly been converted into the bitterest of enemies, and apparently without any good reason.

It is for these reasons, among others, that politics in Mexico are still charged with the fever of armed conflict. Rebellion and murder are still elements in political technique. The last 120 years of almost constant turmoil have left an expectancy of violence in the settlement of public disputes. Violence is a traditional means, and the recent Revolution has reënforced it. Even in the days of Díaz it was the supreme instrument of political technique. No understanding of Mexican politics is possible without an appreciation of this habit, especially in certain political groups. The acceptance of death by violence is almost passive. One who has traveled in Mexico and has talked to the people will have learned this simple fact. One asks about certain people *"Ya lo mataron"* (He has already been killed). *"Lo iban a matar"* (They were going to kill him). Passions lie smoldering in the breasts of Mexicans ready to be easily stirred. Because there is no other recourse, violence is a handmaiden of justice. Political life is still lived with a gun at hand. There are villages that have been torn internally for generations as they are in our family feuds in the Kentucky hills, except that in Mexico, it was an accepted and almost universl phenomenon. The families were, and are, small political parties. The feeling of hatred between certain families, especially where conflict over land, Church, or power has come to embitter an old feud, is such that there can be for a long time to come no healing tonic. A new generation, with new ideals and a new distribution of power, is essential before peace can be had.

For the time being, murder is still a political instrument. One thinks of the past politicians in Mexico and remembers such names as Calleja, Cruz, Concha, Bustamante, Lozada, Márquez, Rojas, Miramón, Santa Ana, Cobos, Jaruata, and others. One thinks of more recent times and remembers Pancho Villa and Pablo Gonzáles, Huerta and Negrete. As long as there is no party organization, peace is impossible; and until the mass has something to defend, has interests to protect, party organization is impossible. Until such a day, murder will remain the ultimate political instrument. It may be private murder, such as an assassination (Villa and Obregón were both assassinated), or it may be military murder such as that of Carranza. Or again, it may be death in battle, by small or large armies, or it may be death by treachery, like that of Zapata, or death by a firing squad after surrender, like that of Felipe Carrillo Puerto who, with five brothers, was shot by minor military officials to save Yucatan from his liberal policies. When will Mexico change its habits? When will it be a different Mexico? That is the question.

Mexico has the promise of peace in it; but the fulfillment must be found in the thousands of little villages which either have or can acquire real stability and unity, and which need and want peace as an essential of life. Until then, as long as politicians and soldiers can at will shift public policies, change laws, betray aspirations, and make promises meaningless, the old habits will be employed for old ends, and politics will continue to be what they have been: the threat of murder, pillage, force, fraud, and treason until the end, which is death.

CHAPTER 10

POLITICAL ISSUES AT STAKE

I N THE last three chapters we have given more emphasis to the *nature* of the political conflicts than to the issues over which they were developed. The reasons for this are that the issues were incidental to the strife. Something in the profound social disequilibrium that Mexico inherited made the conflicts inevitable. That something was the attempt to transform Mexican society into a world of modern ideas—liberalism, constitutionalism, individualism, and, later, modern capitalism—without destroying its feudal structure inherited from Spain. In the conflict the issues were frequently submerged, and the narrower interests of personalities and localities came to dominate and supersede the larger issues. Properly speaking, Mexico was not a nation at the time the Spaniards departed for Spain. It was a colony with sharp internal, economic, cultural, and class divisions, in which the army and the Church and the large landowner attempted to retain the prerogatives and privileges of the days of yore, even though that system of institutions had become incompatible with the new world of ideas and practices that was developing as a result of the independence movement and other influences abroad in the world.

The first of these new struggles was the attack upon the army as a special and separate state within the State, an institution that lived within a body of *fueros* (privileges) that made it immune from civil control. The second was an attack upon the Church which, like the army, lived as a state within the State. The third was the attack upon the plantation, which also was a state within the State and almost immune from governmental control. The major political issues of Mexico since the Conquest are centered about the struggle with these three major institutions that were left as a heritage from Spain.

Another series of issues, of minor importance but cutting across all the others, concerned the kind of governmental organization, the kind of institutional set-up Mexico ought to have. That was never settled in theory until after the defeat of Maximillian, in 1865. From the time of independence, the issues of centralism versus federalism, of monarchy versus republic, of oligarchy versus dictatorship, and innumerable variations of these, were all tried out or projected. A written constitution was always prepared and always disregarded in practice. The Constitution of 1857, which finally set the kind of government, in theory, was soon in dispute, resulted in the Three Years' War, in the Maximillian adventure, and finally, under the Díaz régime, was a mere formal document good for nominal show in a world that asked for democracy.

In practice, dictatorship has been the rule regardless of the theory. It has been the rule because a society so divided within itself as Mexico has been cannot practice a democratic government which presupposes a certain similarity of ideals, interests, and a certain cultural unanimity. These Mexico did not have, but it gave lip service to democracy and carried on in the only way it could, by tyranny more or less disguised, more or less beneficent. Politically, the type of government has consistently been a false issue; no government lived by the rule which it set before the world. Constitutionalism, regardless of type, was frequently merely an additional excuse for a new revolution, on the ground that it was being disregarded, which it always was.

The three revolutions which have profoundly altered the structure of Mexican political and social life, from 1810 to 1930, were first the independence, second the *Reforma*, and third the Revolution of 1910. The first destroyed Mexican dependence upon Spain; the second attempted to destroy the colonial system derived from Spain, and was only partially successful; the third has attempted to destroy the plantation and to free Mexico from foreign tutelage. The first revolution arose out of a conviction that the time had arrived for the Mexicans to govern themselves, that the time had come when the Spanish administrator was to be superseded by the Mexican one, when the *criollo* should replace the Spaniard. The second arose out of the failure of the *criollo* to give Mexico peace and security. The war with the United States demonstrated that which needed no proof: the political ineptitude of the Mexican governing classes. Those who had inherited the power from Spain could not use it. The conflict with the United States set up in bold relief the failure of the army, of the Church, of the politicians, and of the upper classes. It was the final test of the pure whites, the *criollos*, and their defeat spelled their end. The *Reforma* attempted to bring Mexico abreast of the more modern political organizations of the world; it attempted to abolish special privileges (*fueros*) in the army and in the Church. It also attempted to destroy the feudal structure of a landholding system that was derived from the Conquest. In the last effort, the reform failed, and the task remained to be accomplished fifty years later, and is still only partially achieved.

Of the three great social upheavals in Mexico, the first brought the *criollo*, the Mexican whites, into power; the second brought the middle class and the *mestizo* into power; and the third brought the Indian peasant out of oblivion.

From another point of view we may summarize the hundred years of conflict as one between two broad ideals of society. One group wished to go back to the good old days of Spain, to the colonial system. In the light of the persistent turbulence and misery, the peace and quiet of the Spanish régime seemed good and ideal. They had had peace, order, security, prosperity. The ideal, the best of all ages, seemed to have passed away with the coming of independence. Like many reformers, these would have put their future into their past. What was needed was a king, an aristocracy, a Church secure in its foundations, a common faith, a disciplined army, and security of property (most of the large landowners were Spaniards once more). The leaders of this group had a vision of an ideal society, feudal in social economy, colonial in politics, medieval in religious organization. The difficulty with Mexico, from their point of view, was that independence had disturbed the natural social structure, and that the only way out was to restore it. That, for them was the end to be sought by all good citizens, patriots, and Christians. This group finally compromised with Díaz because with him they found peace and much of security for those institutions which had escaped from the previous rebellions.

The other group had a very different objective, a very different explanation of the ruin of Mexico. The fault was, according to them, that the work of independence had not gone far enough. Mexico had secured freedom from Spain, but had retained all of the colonial institutions of the older régime. It had retained the Church with all of its wealth, its privileges, its power. And this Church was largely manned by foreign bishops, Spaniards. The war of independence had left the army in its old form, with its *fueros* (privileges), a state within the State. The land system, the large plantation, was intact as before. What Mexico needed was a completion of the task undertaken by the war of independence. The Church, the army, the large plantation, all would have to be modified or destroyed, to be brought into conformity with the principles of modern democracy, a democracy based on French ideas of equality, liberty, and fraternity, and American ideas of federal government with a division of powers.

The first group wanted a monarchy; the second a republic. The first sought to achieve peace by reëstablishing the colonial system in full; the second wanted to achieve peace by completing the work of independence and destroying the residue of colonial institutions in Mexico which, from their point of view, made peace impossible as long as the old system continued.

Between these groups there could be no peace. The first group looked to Europe for a model, the second to the United States. The first derived aid and comfort from the European monarchies, the second from the American republic. This second group also made its peace with Díaz. The promised benefits of capitalism which the Díaz régime initiated—railroads, mines, factories, banks, foreign investments, property —all of these contained the promise of "progress," of civilization, of liberalism. The old society would now be destroyed, not by rebellion, but by the "natural law" of competition, the "survival of the fittest," by the doctrine embodied in Herbert Spencer's "Social Statics." This compromise did not affect the common people. They had played a minor rôle in the politics of Mexico, and no one expected that they would change. The end of the Díaz régime, when it came, proved that both of these groups were wrong. A new political element was to make its appearance, and a new politics was to be developed.

This new politics was to bring into Mexican political life the Indian, who had been deprived of political existence after the Conquest. It was also to be a politics centering around the destruction of the large estate, which had its origin in the Spanish Conquest. It was to be politics with an attempt further to weaken the Church which came with the Conquest, and it was to result in giving the village community again, for the first time in four hundred years, a measure of political power, power that it had lost when the Spaniards destroyed the native social and political organization. It was also to be an attempt to destroy the capitalistic policy of the Díaz régime, upon which both camps in Mexican politics had found bases for compromise. It was, in short, on political grounds, to attack the chief political by-products of the Conquest: the Church, the army, the caste system, the large estate, the centralized government, and to undermine the capitalism and liberalism of the Díaz compromise.

We may conclude this chapter by asking a question. What is Mexico's most insistent need? Peace! Internal peace, a sense of stability, of permanence, of security: that is the pressing need of Mexico. Not in all of its history has Mexico had peace. The day of dissolution is always at hand. Tomorrow may bring a new government into power, new politics, new people, a new philosophy of life. All may change within a day. That fact has been at the root of Mexican political and social existence: revolution, conquest, defeat, victory. A new revolution, a new plan, a new constitution, a new government, a new program, a new *personaje* was always in the making. That fact has corroded and influenced all of Mexican temperament, all of its personal and social existence, its very philosophy of politics. Mexico needs peace, and it has revolution. It needs quiet, and it has turbulence. It wants to work and play, to paint and sing, to live in joyous abundance, and it has poverty, violence, treason, and passion.

The reason is simple. Mexico is not a nation. It is becoming one, but the process is painful and harsh. Mexico can never have peace unless it achieves internal unity and harmony. It cannot do that unless it destroys the enormous disequilibrium that lies at its roots. The revolution may not necessarily be violent, though it probably will be. But violent or not, peace in Mexico is at present neither possible, nor, so far as internal unity is concerned, desirable if it means the continuance of a state of affairs that has made the Mexico of the last hundred years a Mexico with two revolutions a year, a new president every eight months, and a new constitution every ten years.

So ingrained is the habit of revolution as a political instrument, that even the thoughtful Mexican accepts it as inevitable. So natural, for instance, was the Revolution of 1910 considered, that Mexican scholars compared it to the inevitableness of the sea in motion, or the light of day. It seemed to them that it was the only instrument toward peace, the only way out of a social disequilibrium which apparently provided no relief except through violence, no release except through social upheaval. Writing in the early days of the Revolution of 1910, Manuel Gamio said:

We must consider the revolution as a natural event, entirely natural; we must march with it and not against it. To place obstacles in its course is like attempting to quiet the sea or blot out the light of day.

PART TWO

REVOLUTION

CHAPTER II

UPHEAVAL OF THE MASSES

THE Mexican Revolution, beginning in 1910, was a repudiation of the Díaz compromise, not by those who were a party to it, but by those who were left out of the reckoning. Both the conservatives and the liberals of the earlier conflicts had made their peace under Díaz and were content with the fruits of the bargain: the conservatives with what they were saving and reconstructing of the old, and the liberals with what they were garnering from the fruits of industrialism and "progress." This compromise was ruptured by the common people, the peasants, the Indians, the city laborers. They not only repudiated it, but more or less destroyed the basis upon which such a compromise had been possible. The Mexican Revolution has sought to bring a third class into the political arena, and in the process has at least temporarily weakened, if it has not fully undermined, the influence of the other two classes, which we have called the conservatives and the liberals, that is, those who aspired to a purely feudal and those who dreamed of a purely capitalistic state. These dreams were destroyed by the upheaval of the lower classes. The uprising itself, however, was not responsive to any plan. It was incidental. It was pragmatic.

The Mexican Revolution was anonymous. It was essentially the work of the common people. No organized party presided at its birth. No great intellectuals prescribed its program, formulated its doctrine, outlined its objectives. No great military leaders staked their reputations on its outcome, and in so far as the Mexican Revolution gave birth to political parties, these arose out of the conflict. The program of the Revolution is still being written; it has been in the process of writing since 1910. The military leaders who have achieved fame in the movement were children of the upheaval: Pancho Villa, Obregón, Zapata, Calles, Amaro, and others like them. They were all unknown, unheralded, children of peasants, of Indians, barefooted in their childhood, more or less illiterate. The Revolution made them, gave them means and support. They were the instruments of a movement; they did not make it, and have barely been able to guide it.

How different this from the French and Russian revolutions! There was not a Rousseau, a Voltaire, a Montesquieu, a Diderot in Mexico. There were no important intellectuals on the side of the Revolution. The whole educated class belonged to the dictatorship and its satellites. The gulf between the rich and the poor, between the landowner and his peons, between the office holder and the common folk, was so profound that the grievances of the common people found no voice. During the Díaz dictatorship the intellectuals had their eyes turned to Europe, especially to France, and were interested in Positivism. Those who thought of social problems at all read Spencer and talked as if the "State versus the Individual" were the new Bible, the new credo, the natural law. The theories of racial superiority, the notions of Gobineau, which are now referred to by Mexicans as "that arrogant doctrine of the superiority of the white race," were taken seriously. The movement for the destruction of the communal holdings, for the alienation of government land, for stimulus to foreign immigration, for the special favoring of foreign investors, found support and justification in the belief that Mexico must become a white man's country. This belief was preached by Mexicans newly risen to power who felt themselves so far above the common peons that they denied, in fact, the value of their own inheritance. All that was native was ridiculed, looked upon with contempt. That which was European and American, especially in the later years of the Díaz régime, seemed significant and important.

Under those conditions it was difficult, if not impossible, for the Mexican intellectuals to achieve understanding of, and sympathy for, the common people. Even today the intellectuals are playing an insignificant part in shaping the program of the Mexican Revolution. They are now children of the Revolution, in sympathy with its broader aims, but their participation has been of minor importance. This is due to the lack of contact even today between them and the common folk. The two classes still live in worlds so different that they do not understand one another. The gap between the city and the country is so great that no mutual appreciation seems possible. In every conflict the City of Mexico has been in the wrong, on the losing side. There is not a single book upon the Mexican Revolution, written by a Mexican, that is comprehensive enough to stand as an interpretation of the movement as a whole. There is not even a definitive study of the agrarian problem, produced by a Mexican intellectual, and this is the situation most insistent in its demands for solution and most productive of passion and conflict.

There are speeches, leaflets, and pamphlets by the thousand. Innumerable laws have flooded the country, laws covering every type of social problem. Salvador Alvarado, the energetic governor and soldier, whose coming to Yucatan was like a cyclone that destroyed a feudalism rooted deep in the soil, Salvador Alvarado, who abolished slavery in Yucatan, boasts of having issued more than a thousand decrees and laws. He, perhaps more than any other Mexican who took an active part in the Revolution, attempted to formulate its program. But no Mexican intellectual would admit that Alvarado was an intellectual or that he formulated the program of the Revolution.

Mexican intellectuals have contributed specialized studies of Mexican problems, some of which are of very high quality. One can mention the work of Covarrubias, of González Roa, of Gómez Morin, of Gamio, of Lombardo Toledano, but none of these is comparable to the generalized statements of the Russian scholars. There is no Lenin in Mexico. There is no doctrine, no program, no definite end, no crystallized formula which must be achieved at all costs, no pattern for the reform of all mankind, or even for all of Mexico. The whole thing has grown piecemeal, in patches, in places.

It would be misleading to leave this discussion without mentioning the influence of Andrés Molina Enríquez, who, in 1909, published what is, up to the present, the most important single study of Mexican social problems, *Los grandes problemas nacionales*. Speaking in this book of the influence of the French Revolution upon the destruction of the large feudal estates, he said,

Such a work we would like to see among us . . . and it is necessary that it be done and it will be, either by such peaceful means as we have indicated, or by a revolution which sooner or later will come. Such a work will do a great deal to save our nationalism.

This was said in 1909, a year before the Revolution began. Within eight years the author of these words played an important rôle in the writing of Article 27 of the new Constitution of 1917 which, in a large measure, is an application of his ideas to the land problem of Mexico. Later, when General Calles was Secretary of the Interior, this same author wrote an exposition of Article 27 which is the most interesting as well as the most important explanation of the changed legal position of private property in Mexico. But it would be a mistake to assume that the work influenced many people, or was widely read or widely known, or that it particularly shaped the course of the Revolution. The Revolution came, and it was fought by men who knew nothing of this volume. The ideas of the Revolution were forged in the battles for social justice. When the time came to write its victories into law, the author, who had foretold the Revolution, became an adviser and legal counsellor of the committee that was preparing Article 27.

So piecemeal has the Revolution proved to be, that no general movement affects all of the states at the same time. National laws are enforced in one state and not in another; revolutionary doctrines are proclaimed in one place and not in another. This is true in regard to the agrarian problem, in regard to the Church, and in regard to labor. While in one part of Mexico the central government may be supporting and protecting labor, in another the local governor may be persecuting, hounding, and even shooting labor leaders, all in the name of the Revolution.

The negligible participation of the intellectuals has, over long periods of time, been paralleled in the matter of the military history of the Revolution. It was not a revolution that was fought by large armies. There were, it is true, some fairly large battles during the Revolution, but over the whole period these represent only incidents in the way of military history. The real battles of the movement were fought anonymously by little bands of peasants and soldiers to vindicate their right to overthrow the government. *Small groups of Indians under anonymous leaders were the Revolution.* If the leader was successful, if he was shrewd and quick, and if luck was on his side, he won many skirmishes and escaped with his life. His little band grew after every successful battle. New elements joined it. He acquired more ammunition, more arms, more horses. If he was defeated or killed his little army melted away, its members returning to their native villages to settle down. Gradually a sort of professional army grew up. The experience of being a soldier, of seeing the world, of going armed and having a horse, of profiting by a skirmish by pillaging the clothes and arms and supplies of the defeated, became a habit. This was better than the routine of the *hacienda*, or life in the village. It was adventure, and in a good cause, too. There were speeches and bands and parades and strange places.

The habit of fighting grew upon the Indians who had

"joined up," and thus it was that the larger armies of the later revolutionary days were recruited. It was an individualistic army. Each general controlled his own men. They were his because he had gathered them in his marches, had fed and armed them. Pancho Villa, when he entered Mexico from the United States, had four friends with him. He equipped his army by theft and robbery, later by the spoils of successful skirmishes. He took the best horses from the *haciendas* and exchanged cattle for ammunition, across the border. It was in this way that an army developed. When individuals achieved certain standards of fame, prestige, and special terror, they were referred to as colonel or general. Gradually the larger groups, fighting a common enemy, would coalesce under the most successful of the leaders operating in the same region and become a formidable army. Pancho Villa had forty thousand men at one time. Obregón is said to have brought eighteen thousand mounted cavalry when he entered Mexico City. He started out in Sonora with a few hundred men and without any experience as a soldier. He lost no battles, and at every one he increased his army. When Carranza began his war against Huerta he had seven hundred and fifty men, and he was the governor of a large and rich state, not an unknown peasant who rose in rebellion. These seven hundred and fifty were divided into three columns of two hundred and fifty each, which were ordered to march south, one group by the west, one by the east, and one through the middle of the country.

Armies provisioned themselves along the way with whatever fortune provided, and armed themselves at the expense of their enemies as they marched along. Zapata boasted that he never bought a gun. When divisions of the army grew large enough to be important, there were generals. Every time a realignment was made in the revolutionary groups, it was a question where this or that general would line up. His mobile, unorganized group shifted its allegiance as the

GENERAL EMILIANO ZAPATA

particular leader desired. It was not a national army; the revolutionary armies belonged to the individual leaders that had created them. Strong personalities welded powerful fighting elements out of these groups. They also had to face, at any time, the prospect of treason and rebellion. It took years for the army to overcome its voluntary tradition. The soldiers owed allegiance only to the man whom they followed. He owed allegiance only to himself and to such idea of the Revolution as he had in his own mind, and to such a leader as he wished to follow for as long as he thought it convenient to do so.

Things are different now, but the change is very recent and may not prove permanent. The work of General Joaquín Amaro and of General Calles has transformed the irresponsible army to a disciplined machine, but even so, Escobar rebelled as recently as 1929 and took half the army with him, and later Arnulfo Gómez and Serrano turned on the government. The older tradition of a personal army is dying, may even be dead, but it would be presumptuous to assume that the Mexican government can now count on its military as a unit in all internal emergencies.

It is important to understand all of this if one is to appreciate the anonymous character of the movement. Without intellectual leadership, without military organization, the Mexican people have made their Revolution, and, in the process, have defined the concrete, specific objectives which they wished to achieve, many of which have been achieved in localities. It has not been a national revolution in the sense that all of the country participated in the same movement and at the same time. It has been local, regional, sometimes almost by counties. The Valley of Oaxaca, for example, is *agrarista*; the mountain areas in the same state are opposed to the Valley and indifferent to its needs. The Isthmus of Tehuantepec, in the same state, remained for years untouched by the currents of the social upheaval, and only now is discovering that such a movement has taken place. It is attempting to reap some of the benefits of the Revolution after it has passed into history as an accomplished fact in the Valley of Oaxaca. This is fairly typical of the whole history of the movement.

It is characteristic of the Mexican Revolution that the cities have been reactionary and the country radical. The root of the difference in the rôle of intellectual and peon lies deep in Mexico's social organism. It has been and still is a country with two cultures, the urban and the rural, and so great is the gap between them that they have marched, and still march, in different directions.

In the history of the movement the dominance of Mexico City has played a leading rôle in the repeated betrayals which the Revolution has suffered. The City has approximately a million people, about one sixteenth of the total population of the Republic. Far smaller are some of the other cities: Guadalajara, Puebla, and San Luis Potosí. All of the other large cities in the country combined do not equal the population of the City of Mexico. The rest of the population is scattered in some seventy thousand little villages, many of them with less than a hundred inhabitants. Their average population is about three hundred. Only three per cent of the rural communities have between three and four thousand inhabitants.

The sharp contrast in size is further heightened by the contrast in character. The City is modern; the country is primitive. The City is of today; the country is of thousands of years ago. The City has radios, automobiles, electric lights, music, opera, fine buildings, and paved streets. It speaks Spanish, French, English, and German. The country has nothing; no lights, no roads, no elaborate buildings—nothing; frequently knows not even Spanish. One must see this contrast if one would weigh the influence of the City in the shaping of the life of the country. This contrast is sharpened by the fact that Mexico City is made up largely of bureaucrats. It is not an industrial city; it is a city of government officials, government clerks, foreign diplomats, representatives of foreign concerns, and their house and body servants. Labor is largely servant and service labor: chauffeurs, merchandising clerks, beauty-parlor attendants, night-club keepers, pulque venders, uniformed door lackeys, and soldiers. There are a few factory workers, street-car motormen and conductors. It consists of officials and lackeys, with an intermediate group of intellectuals. It is beautiful and aristocratic, with fine museums and open air schools, but it is not an industrial community.

To this city flock all aspiring politicians, scoundrels fleeing from local indignation, those intriguing for goods and power, those who feel injured in their interests or desirous of injuring others, those seeking favors, those trying to get something that does not belong to them, or to get back something that has been taken from them. All find their way to Mexico City, to the antechambers of the ministers, to the halls and palaces where influential people gather. There are to be found the representatives of every business in the country, foreign and native, honorable and dishonorable. They are all trying to find the way to some special advantage, some favor and some right. Such a city is the natural enemy of the country, particularly of such a rural country as Mexico—illiterate, primitive, toil-ridden, stolid, suspicious and resentful of outside interference. The City of Mexico has been and is at present the great enemy of the Mexican Revolution. It has been only within the last few years that public opinion within university circles and the school system has been converted to the Revolution, and even here the conversion may still not be complete. The newspapers, *El universal*, *El excelsior*, and the others that have come and gone since the Revolution, have been outspoken, bitter, and relentless enemies of the Revolution and of the rural country.

It is natural that such a city should not understand the country of Mexico. It belongs to another world. Soto y Gama once said,

I watch which way Mexico City thinks and then I think just the opposite, for that is the way the common folks in the rural districts think. Then I know that I am right.

Zarco, one of the great figures of 1857 constitutional fame, said of Mexico City, even then,

It cannot be denied that Mexico City has many illustrious people, but it is evident that here public interests are neglected, that here all becomes corrupt, that here, thanks to luxury, intrigue, and bad habits, even the most honorable people become tainted.

The influence of Mexico City, as well as of the other large urban centers, frequently made the betrayal of the Revolution inadvertent, unconscious, and inevitable. It was part of the conflict between the city and the country, part of the conflict between the sophisticated political and urban attitude toward life and the elemental and primitive rural existence.

Every time the city succeeded in absorbing, culturally and socially, a leader of the people who had been sent to it, that individual became a traitor to the original ideas and aspirations for which he had fought and which had made him a leader. Anyone who has seen a picture of a Mexican general as he was when he took up arms in defense of his village, and a picture of the same man after he had come to power, will understand what happened. In the earlier days he was dressed in cotton shirt and trousers, *huaraches* (sandals) and a sombrero, the distinctive features being brilliant eyes that illuminated a rather emaciated face and lean body, the rifle and the belt of cartridges being the only sign of modernism. The later picture shows modern clothes, brown shoes, a felt hat, a heavy gold chain, a certain portliness, a greater sense of ease and comfort. He has succumbed to the city. The process is a simple one which few have escaped.

The conflict between the city and the country in Mexico is so profound, so deep, that no compromise seems possible. The city has always won in its struggle against the individual by attrition, by wearing down. The repeated rebellions during the last twenty years have been, from one point of view, the sending up of new leaders to take the places of the old ones for a time, until they too have been overcome by the good dinners, the automobiles, the flattery of friends, the adoration of leeches and parasites, the ambition of family, the ease, comfort, and good will of the city.

It might perhaps be worth while to attempt to describe the process by which this happens, the process to which so many of the best of the leaders of Mexico's social movement have succumbed, and which has caused so many repeated uprisings. When revolution begins in a locality, some young *mestizo* or Indian—energetic, fearless, and bold, animated with a zeal for the common cause, possessed of a strong personality, a sincerely honest human being, but simple and nearly illiterate, moved by the sorrows and injustices of his little village, filled with a desire to avenge himself upon its immediate oppressor, and to vindicate for his community those rights of which it considers itself deprived—develops into a successful leader. He proves a good soldier, a good officer. He is quick; he is relentless; he scruples at no sacrifice; he risks his own life and that of his friends, and if he wins he rapidly acquires reputation, followers, and increasing power. But all of this time he is a peon; he dresses as he has always dressed; he eats what he has always eaten; he reads no newspapers (he may not even be able to read); he makes few, if any, speeches; he sleeps on the ground as he has always slept; he is surrounded by people who speak his language and believe as he does; his aim is simply the conquest of power for the division of the large *latifundia* surrounding his village. If fortune favors him, and if his movement happens to coincide with a larger movement in other parts of the country, he soon finds himself marching at the head of a large column on his way to the capital of the state or of the country. With the opposition defeated and the government overthrown, a new government must be formed. The great leader of the movement must have men he can trust and must reward those who have been useful and important in the achievement of military victory. This young soldier, who two years ago was a barefooted peon, may suddenly find himself in control of a government department, of a ministry, of the governorship of a state, or of some important civil or political office.

His experience has widened enormously, but unless he possesses the genius of an Obregón or the very great intuitive strength and integrity of a Calles, he soon succumbs to the new place of power. He is poorly trained; he knows no more of the complexities of the social and economic organization than he did before. He must depend upon scribes, lawyers, and politicians for advice. He finds himself seated in a revolving chair at a mahogany desk in a large room lavishly furnished, with many worthies frowning down upon him from the walls, with thick carpets on the floors and uniformed obsequious attendants to carry out every wish. He becomes *Señor Ministro;* visitors bow and scrape in front of him and run to open his door. He begins to be showered with presents; flattering things are said to him; he adapts himself to the new environment as best he can; he changes his clothes, his manners, his food; he acquires a large house, begins to entertain. His wife and family acquire social position; the newspapers praise him; a new world of friends and companions appears on the scene. They seem good fellows at heart, only they speak a different language. They are interested in different problems; they do not place as much emphasis or the same emphasis upon the grievances that he fought to correct and that brought him to power. It is a good world, but a world with different ideals. There are theatres, movies, and music. He has to become a patron of the arts. Books are dedicated to him. He becomes a dispenser of favors. He is flattered and praised. Gradually, he loses interest in his older aims; they seem further off, less important. The people about him agree with him on every subject except the one he fought for, the one his village bled for.

He wakes up one morning and discovers that he thinks differently. He has not changed his mind; his mind has been changed for him. He begins to be more careful, more conservative, less ardent in his old beliefs, less accessible to his former companions in the country. The more he becomes like others in the city, the more favor he wins; and the more favor he wins, the more he becomes like the people who favor him. He has been swallowed up by the city. Portes Gil, who has kept his older zeal in a degree that few have achieved, said while he was still president of Mexico:

The Revolution has had individuals that have enriched themselves while in power; it has had to lament those who were frightened by the truth; it has had to mark on its dark pages some of its members who through vandalism and arbitrariness have become rich, some of them fabulously rich. But it has not been side-tracked by these events. On the contrary, the fact that the Revolution has been able to swallow so many of its children merely proves its greatness as a reconstruction movement.

The city swallowed them. But, as he says, the mass goes on. A new revolution breaks out. The older leaders are denounced as traitors. New battles follow the old pattern and end the old way. For a little while the new leaders remain loyal to the path marked by the village, and then gradually they, too, succumb to the city. It isn't treason; it is submersion, spiritual submersion in a strange environment.

There is another phase that helps explain the pragmatic and tentative character of Mexico's social movement. It is essentially an agrarian movement. The other aspects of the Revolution have been incidental by-products and trimmings.

The motivating drive has come from the inhabitants of little scattered villages, small population groups, with simple ideas and simple attitudes toward the world, who wanted land, their own land, as they saw the matter. The older *mores* of communal ownership, of village unity, of common control and direction reasserted themselves. The upheaval was profound and deep and bitter, but voiceless. The Indians, the peons, were neither scholars, nor philosophers, nor politicians. They could write no laws; they could not interpret them after they were written. The popular movement, seeking blindly to undo the plantation system, to destroy it, had no intellectual leadership that came out of its own experience. It had to seek its advisers, lawyers, speech-makers, politicians, and statesmen from other elements in the community. These, even when honest, even when sincere, derived from a different experience. They had read foreign books, books by economists, publicists, books by syndicalists, socialists, anarchists. They had read American books, French books, German books, and English books. With notions derived from foreign experience they attempted to explain and fit what was going on in Mexico into intellectual terms that came from totally different sources.

With the best of intentions, the intellectual spokesmen frequently misjudged the direction. They were trying to pattern Mexico as if it was going through some socialist revolution, or as if a syndicalist state were being built. It was neither one nor the other. The elemental cry was land— land and water. Land, water, and later, schools. But especially the cry was for freedom, the right of the village to carry on as it was attuned to carry on, in response to the older community organization. The scribes, the lawyers, the politicians, the learned ones in foreign law have succeeded at various times in encumbering the movement with a degree of legalism and foreign doctrine that would have side-tracked the whole process if they had persisted.

It is in this connection, too, that the concern of the intellectuals in what they call the national interests is against the village interests. The little communities know nothing of the nation. When I told them that I lived at a distance of a ninety-day mule-back trip, the Chamula Indians shook their heads and said it couldn't be because I should fall off. The villages have received little from the nation; they have no very direct connection with it. The city folk, with their urban intellectualism, have attempted to subordinate the interests of the rural community to the interests of what they call the nation. In their view the nation is the city plus the country. The city dominates; the country is an incident. Every effort of the Indians, the peons, the villagers, has had to meet this barrier—natural, if you will, but foreign to the agrarian movement. The result has been repeated misunderstanding, bitterness, treason, and betrayal—conscious or unconscious —of the needs of the rural community which made the Revolution over and over again. The agrarian revolution has had to break through the impediment of an intellectual guidance that was foreign to it, and foreign to the basic interest and drive of the rural population. The intellectual element has consistently served to restrain, to modulate, whereas the true desire of the rural districts has been to be thorough, to uproot the old scheme of things.

I recall a meeting in a large community in the state of Tlaxacala. Some three hundred peons, from twelve villages, had gathered for a meeting to which had come representatives of the National Agrarian Commission. They met in a large adobe building, as the town had denied them the only adequate meeting place that was to be had. Old boxes and tin cans had been collected to serve as seats. The people were poor, barefoot, with their clothing torn and patched. An elderly man, with a sparse, straggling beard, unrolled a paper and read painfully in a quiet voice,

We are tired of being betrayed. It is time that the laws be enforced.

It is time that we be given our lands. The Revolution is over now. We are accused of being bandits. We are not bandits. We only want our lands, and we want a school, too. If our leaders continue betraying us we will be forced again to try to take our lands back with arms in our hands.

While the crowd in the room cheered and shouted, the other leaders embraced the old man. This picture has had its replica a thousand times in the last twenty years, and similar incidents will occur in the future until the social movement finds some level of equilibrium.

The pragmatic nature of the Revolution derives, therefore, from the lack of intellectual leadership; from the great gap between the city and the country; from the cultural divergence between the urban and the rural districts; from the sharp geographical differences in the various areas; from the inept intellectual servants of the Revolution, reared and educated in an environment which makes it impossible for them to forego notions derived from foreign political and social literature, who have attempted to apply these notions to village needs; and from the attempt to identify the interests of the nation with the interests of the city, and to subordinate the needs of the rural districts to the needs of the city.

CHAPTER 12

ROOTS OF THE CONFLICT

WHY did the Mexican Social Revolution begin in 1910? That is an interesting and speculative question to which there is no satisfactory answer. The apparent causes that would explain the social upheaval had existed for a long time, and might have justified an outbreak at an earlier date just as logically as at a later one. Looking backward over the Mexican scene we must find a combination of circumstances that, taken together, make the social upheaval of 1910 seem reasonable, in accord with the facts as we know them. But it must always be clear that historical explanations are the weaving together of threads with a view to giving them meaning and logical focus. They are connected and explained by the observer as a series of antecedents; they derive meaning from being placed in juxtaposition and given a seeming direction, which they may have had, even if the individual items were unrelated in purpose or unconscious of a common direction.

In appearance, 1910 was the best of the years of the Díaz régime. It was the year which commemorated the centennial of the beginning of Mexican independence, and a great celebration was staged to impress the world with the prosperity, progress, and greatness of the country, and the greatness of the chief under whom Mexico had found peace for the first time since independence. A large host of foreign diplomats gathered in the City of Mexico to celebrate the event. The governments of the world vied with one another in showering honors on the eighty-year old dictator. He was weighed down by the gold medals, crosses, orders, and ribbons bestowed on him. The City of Mexico was filled with festivity, with soldiers in gala uniforms, with parades and bands, banquets and speeches, with distinguished scholars and diplomats from the world abroad. The credit of the government was high; its budget was balanced; industrial activities were going forward at a rapid rate; peace reigned. Mexico was famed as the "safest country in the world." Mexico City was being beautified. New buildings were going up; an expensive opera house and a new legislative palace with a dome modelled on American types, were being built of iron to typify the new achievements of Mexico: industrialism and democracy. In fact, the visitor, the stranger, the city dweller, the governmental employee, and the foreign investor had every reason to believe that the future of Mexico was secure. At last, a hundred years after the initiation of independence, Mexico had fully entered the family of nations, with high honors and much promise. Its future seemed brilliant, its progress assured, its peace permanent. Yet the sound of the jubilee had barely passed away when all of this structure toppled like a house of cards; its best promises were as the dust, and its greatest figure an exile in Europe, a disappointed and morose old man.

What had happened? Many things, too many to weave into a common picture. In the thirty-four years of his government the dictator had aged; his hand had weakened; he had lost his grip upon the smouldering passions that he had once stilled by the alternate use of iron and gold. He was past eighty years of age, and all the members of his cabinet were advanced in years. Not one was under sixty. It had become an old man's government. That in itself aroused opposition from the younger generation of good family who had been kept out of office and public affairs for so long a time.

In the days of rebellion and revolution the leaders in government had been young. The men who had created the Díaz régime were young people, but they had held on and grown old in power. The country was at peace. Wealth had increased, and with it sophistication. The children of the

"THE MOORS AND THE CHRISTIANS"
A religious dance

rich were being sent in increasing numbers to schools in Europe and the United States. They had learned something of democracy, popular suffrage, regular elections, freedom of the press and of speech, party organization, and popular participation in politics. When they returned to Mexico, they naturally wished to exercise their youthful ambitions and aspirations and remodel Mexico to their hearts' desires; but every avenue was closed. They could not speak, write, or publish; they could not organize; they could do nothing but admire and worship at the feet of the greatest of all men, Díaz. The young men of wealth and standing could not enter business: that was mostly in foreign hands. They could not enter politics: there was none. They could not hold offices: these were preëmpted by the older generation. In the state governments, as well as in the federal government, the leading officials were aged men, governors who had been elected and reëlected over a period of thirty years. Such men owned the states with the consent of Díaz, and permitted no younger men to enter.

That is an important and an interesting factor in the change which has come over Mexico. It was a change from old age to youth. The Revolution was conceived by young men; it was fought by young men; it has been controlled and guided by young men. It was, in a sense, a new generation displacing an older one. If the Díaz government had permitted itself to absorb the energies and ideas of the younger generation of the wealthy, the educated, the liberal groups who had benefited by the peace and the increased wealth to get their educations in Europe and the United States, then the course of Mexican history might have been different.

For over thirty years Mexico had gone without political activity. Party organization was non-existent. The powers of the local *caciques* had ceased to depend upon local support, and had come to be derived from the central dictatorship.

All public offices had come to obey a single principle: the will of the dictator. Mexico was less democratic, less capable of being democratic, at the end of the period than at the beginning. Peace had been maintained by suppression, by favor. Individual judgment and influence had disappeared, except as they reflected or coincided with the will and the direction of the central influence. Under those circumstances it was like a bomb exploded in the night for the old dictator to declare, in 1908, in an interview with Creelman, that Mexico was then ripe for democracy, and that he would welcome the development of political parties. People have argued about the motives of this declaration. Some have seen in it the astute old dictator using bait to bring his enemies out of hiding, and thus more easily to destroy them. Others have argued that it was the sincere desire of an old man who, with the good of his country at heart, wished to pass to his grave with the feeling that he had left behind him a permanent and peaceful political institution.

Regardless of the motive, the effect was the same. The statement stirred the political passions that had been smouldering for over thirty years, and brought once more to the front the irreconcilable forces that had torn Mexico for so long a time. The end of the Díaz régime was to be the end of the compromise, for, in reality, the older forces were not fused even by the peace of thirty years. The conservatives had regained much lost ground; the liberals had achieved much in industry and industrialism, but the ideal society of either group was still far away, and with the disappearance of the cementing compromise, there was danger that the old battle would begin anew, with additional causes that came from the changed position of Mexico: a greater *latifunda* system than Díaz had inherited, a much greater capitalism than was in existence when he came into power, and at the same time, a new current of ideas about social justice derived from abroad, foreign ideals of labor and social policies.

The danger of conflict was clear; the older habits, even after thirty years of disuse, were not completely atrophied. This danger was made still worse because the Díaz statement that Mexico was ready for democracy was not true. It was less ready than when Díaz had taken office. The thirty years had served to undermine and destroy even such habits of local power, prestige, and influence as the chaos of the older day made possible and necessary. The prospect of shifting from tyranny to democracy in a country such as Mexico, where the mass of the people was illiterate, where peonage was still in effect, where labor was completely and fully suppressed, where freedom was unknown and political initiative non-existent, where the large landowner ruled like a monarch, where the industrialist was a foreigner protected against the Mexicans, where disregard for law was more natural than obedience to it, where the racial and caste differentiations were as sharp as they had ever been in the past hundred years, where the Indian communities had a smouldering hatred of the landowner and his governmental satellites because of the damage they had done to the communal holdings, and where the government offices were filled with relatives of all the *científicos* who made up the coterie around Díaz—to speak of a shift to democracy in such a situation was as irrelevant as the earlier shift from colonial government in the same direction had been. It was just as impossible to operate a democratic government with universal suffrage and regular elections in the Mexico of 1910 as it had been in the Mexico of 1810. The shift was not possible, because Mexico had remained fundamentally feudal in social structure, and was now saddled with a foreign capitalism which used the feudal base for its own greater ends.

Into this situation was injected conflict among the foreign interests that had been invited to exploit Mexico's resources. This friction was chiefly between American and English oil companies. In his latter days, Díaz apparently favored the

English against the American investors, on the grounds that it was politically safer to do so. At any rate, the early Madero movement against Díaz found favor in certain American quarters, and was, perhaps, financed in part from American sources. Be that as it may, competition of foreigners for special favor and privilege did not contribute to the stability of a government dependent upon the life of one human being. In their greed to monopolize Mexican resources for their own exploitation, conflicting foreign interests roused among the Mexicans opposition to all foreigners.

More important, however, was the development of a body of independent labor in Mexico, especially on the railroads. The railroad builders in Mexico, to supply themselves with labor, had to go about the country and buy off the debts of workers tied to the *haciendas*, free them from plantation control, and then hire them to construct the road bed and lay the tracks. It was thus that the railroads were built, rail mechanics developed. A labor force, mobile and free, grew up. In the end, this freedom of movement on the part of labor effected that change in mental attitude without which a social revolution in Mexico would have been very difficult. Here for the first time a free, mobile industrial group of substantial size was created, which moved from place to place, lost its older traditions, and became an increasingly powerful factor in molding a new attitude of the common people toward life. This heritage from foreign, especially American, industrialism, has received inadequate attention from even the best students of Mexican problems.

With easier transportation came increased migration to the United States—a temporary migration—of Mexican laborers. On his return to his native land, the Mexican immigrant brought ideas that were, in essence, revolutionary in the Mexican environment. It is no accident that so many of the earlier leaders of the Revolution had had longer or shorter sojourns in the United States. Nor is it an accident that the earlier revolutionary movement had its most effective and most vigorous support in the northern states, where American influence was most conspicuous, and where access to the American border both for supplies and escape was most convenient. It was in the states of Coahuila, Chihuahua, and Sonora that the earlier Revolution had its most effective stage and most irrepressible character. Of the conspicuous leaders of the Revolution, Madero, Carranza, Pancho Villa, Obregón, and Calles all came from states that border on the United States.

What is true of the Revolution in general is especially true of the labor movement. The C.R.O.M. (*Confederación Regional Obrera Mexicana*), the most conspicuous and successful of Mexican labor movements, drew many of its best leaders from men who had worked in American industries and had been members of American trade unions. Ricardo Treviño, one of the outstanding Mexican labor leaders, spent seven years in the United States, and was a member of the I.W.W. He is but an example, a type.

Another phase of American influence in the developing Mexican Revolution was the rôle played by the American Federation of Labor, especially the personal influence of Samuel Gompers upon the development of the Mexican trade union movement and upon the careers of some of the Mexican labor leaders. American influence, largely because of increased migration to the United States and contact with the ideas and practices across the border, played no small part in making the ideas born of the new experience incompatible with feudal Mexico.

The United States played a further part as a haven of escape for many of the leaders of the early revolutionary movement, and also as a base of operations. Madero and his group had propagandist headquarters in the United States. The Magón brothers were later persecuted and imprisoned in the United States; but even imprisonment served their ends. In Mexico they would have been summarily shot by the Díaz government. Pancho Villa escaped and lived in the United States more than once. Felipe Carrillo Puerto while in exile worked as a longshoreman in New Orleans.

These are mere indications of the many and various threads that made for so profound a change in the Mexico of Díaz, and that have slowly developed not merely a new kind of Mexico but a new type of Mexican.

Such influences, though significant, were perhaps but incidental. More important were changes in the internal social politics of Mexico. Of these, the systematic and widespread attack upon the Indian village and its communal holdings was of greatest consequence. This undertaking was not a new one. The *conquistadores* had initiated it nearly four centuries earlier. They, too, attempted to destroy the Indian villages, and succeeded in robbing them of their best lands, especially in the valleys. Only the Spanish Crown and the Church had stood as barriers against the too rapid destruction of these communities. The struggle between the plantation and the village persisted during the entire period of colonial administration. After independence the position of the village became more precarious. The plantations were now relieved of control by the Spanish Crown; they were more dominant in the government, and they succeeded more easily and more frequently against the unprotected Indians. Confiscation of Church lands, and the growth of a new class of large landowners merely increased the pressure upon the village.

Under the Díaz régime, this attack became a national policy. Utilizing the *Leyes de Reforma* which, in the previous attack upon the Church, had prohibited corporate holdings, the Díaz régime found a legal justification for its attempt to destroy the communal holdings. Against the illiterate and unsophisticated Indians it was easy to prove lack of title to the land they occupied. If title had to be conceded, it was converted into private property; the Indian was given a

piece of paper for land which he had held from time immemorial, and then induced to exchange this paper for a drink.
He was too innocent of the meaning of the procedure to
understand that tomorrow he would find himself a stranger
upon the land where he had been born, which he had tilled,
and in which his parents and grandparents had been buried
for generations. This policy, which had gone on slowly in isolated places, from the time of the conquest, was now converted into a national program, and pushed rapidly by adventurers and land seekers with the connivance, as well as
the active support, of the national government.

The law of June 25, 1856, *Ley de Desamortización*, as it was
known, had led to a break-down of the communal land holdings of the Indians who, perforce, came within the law by
being communal land-holding groups. The attempt to carry
the law into execution among the Indians had resulted in a
series of uprisings. The villagers in Michoácan, Querétaro,
Vera Cruz, and Puebla rose in rebellion and forced the government to modify the law. These and other difficulties gave
rise to a change in the law in October of the same year, a
change which made compulsory the division of the lands
within the communal villages themselves.

The program here undertaken by the federal government
had been discussed soon after independence with a different
result. If we turn to a report laid before the constitutional
convention of the state of Mexico by one of its committees
as early as 1824, we find the following:

The committee thinks . . . that while it would be of much utility
and convenience to the public to reduce . . . to private ownership
the lands which are at present held in common by the villages, it
fears that lacking the necessary agricultural implements with
which to cultivate the lands individually distributed . . . they will
abandon them to their own and the village's disadvantage, or they
will be left without lands, thus increasing their poverty, and will
be obliged to make constant demands that new lands be given
them, in opposition to the interests of the surrounding landowners.

This will give rise to conflicts both ruinous and prejudicial.

This was the judgment of the State Legislature of Mexico, which at that time included a large part of south central Mexico: Hidalgo, Tlaxcala, Morelos, and Guerrero. The laws of 1856 took just the opposite view. It is to the consequences of this legislation and its application during the years 1856 to 1910 that much of the cause for the Social Revolution must be laid. The destruction of common land ownership really resulted not merely in serious interference with the internal unity of the village community, with its internal discipline and traditions, but in effect reduced the standard of well-being of the villagers. The common ownership of land provided wood for fire, for the making of charcoal, for building materials for the little huts, for the burning of pottery. It provided pasture for animals both large and small, and space for the wandering and browsing both of chickens and turkeys. It eliminated the possibility of sale and disposal of the child's inheritance by an extravagant or ignorant parent. It eliminated the cost of transfer after death or by sale. Possession and use of the land was easy and natural. If one had tools and some capital, he tilled. If misfortune deprived him of these he earned his income by making charcoal or pottery, or finding other uses for the natural resources within the village boundaries.

The division of the lands automatically reduced each individual to the limits of his own little parcel, made for the development of social and economic classes within the villages, for facility of sale or transfer to the easier enhancement of the surrounding estates, and for their greater pressure against individual owners. Instead of having to confront a community jealous and on watch for its lands the *hacienda* now had an individual who was a prey to all sorts of influences that could not be exercised against a community. The centuries of communal tradition and communal usufruct made the individual Indian an easy prey.

Andrés Molina Enríquez testifies in the following passage from his own experience of nine years in the services of the state of Mexico:

Many times . . . the *mestizos* initiated the procedure for the break up of communal land holdings of Indian villages, have bought up the lands, have influenced the distribution of the individual titles, and immediately collected them, paying the costs in the names of the recipients. Many of the Indians were not owners of their lands for even one day. And an investigation of the purchase price would show that some pieces of land were purchased for a few pieces of bread, a few cuartillos of maize or a few jars of pulque or other alcoholic drink. Once the Indians passed over the titles to their individual pieces of land they had no source of firewood or wood for house posts or walls, no charcoal which they could sell, no sticks upon which to make their *tortillas,* no dead wood to burn their pottery, nothing with which to feed their animals, nor any place to pasture them, no place to hunt or fish, nor the use of any fruit trees.

The Indians found themselves deprived of everything, and could only become peons of the land that they had owned the day before, or become bandits, or wander off into the city and become beggars. But even where titles were issued without any fraud they led to increasing poverty. The little tracts of land were so numerous that exactitude was impossible and inheritance and further division both costly and impracticable. They were too small to support a family.

Two little villages (Tixmadeje and Dongu) in the state of Mexico that antedated the Conquest, were deprived of their lands and torn from their moorings. The Spaniards had left them in peace where they found them, with much of their land intact. They were deeply rooted. For four hundred years, under Spain and under the Republic, these two little villages had lived in comparative peace, defending their lands against the encroachments of the large estates, against the marauding military bands that wandered up and down the land and destroyed and despoiled. Then came the law of

Terrenos Baldíos. Tillers of land without adequate titles were squatters, and all of the hundreds of years of occupation and tillage, of local shrines and deeply graven memories, of sacred graves of ancestors, all of the drama of toil, love, and sorrow which these villages had played out on the same plot of land was for naught. The lands were taken from them. A powerful neighboring *hacendado* had had an eye on their lands for a long time, and this was his opportunity. The law of *Terrenos Baldíos* was a good excuse. So it went from village to village, from *rancho* to *rancho* all over the country. The plantations and the foreign land companies were in the saddle sowing the seeds they were ultimately to reap in violence and revolution, but that was not yet. Mexico was at peace and all was well with the world.

This attack on the village holdings coincided with the alienation of federal government lands to private hands. The theory assumed that for the sake of progress the large areas in public lands should be turned over to individuals for development, colonization, and exploitation. It was also believed that private owners held under inadequate titles, lands belonging to the nation. Contracts were entered into with private companies, *compañías deslindadoras* for the purpose of discovering and surveying these lands belonging to the government. Without detailing these contracts here, it is sufficient to note that they led to a rapid transfer to a few favorites of vast areas of government lands. In the process a great deal of abuse developed. Contracts or concessions would be given to some favorite to survey and discover the national land in given parts of the country. The concessionaire would dispose of his right to a foreign company, usually to an American company which became entitled to one-third of all the lands surveyed, and had the right to buy as much as it desired of all the rest at a very low price. No sooner was the contract signed than a systematic attack began against the existing occupants of the land. Given the difficulty of proving adequate titles, it seemed easier to buy from (that is, to bribe) the new company a title to the lands than to establish in court the legitimacy of possession. The difficulty of proving title also led to destruction of the villages and the little properties that had no titles or had lost them. In the short space of twenty-five years about sixty million acres of public lands were granted to a few land-owners. In addition they absorbed hundreds of villages and small properties.

The Díaz government in attacking the age-old communal holdings, placed great burdens upon the small holders whose titles were inadequate, and extended an uneconomic system of land holding from the central valleys of the republic to the entire country. The result of this policy was to raise up regal lords with plantations greater than some of our states, and to saddle Mexico with an additional feudal burden beside the one it had inherited from Spain. In Chihuahua, the Terrazas family and the Creel family (related by marriage) had nearly 15,000,000 acres of land. In lower California, Luis Huller and Company had over a million hectares, and the California Mexico Land Company nearly 2,500,000 hectares. These are but examples that can be multiplied from almost every part of the country and from nearly every state. As a general statement, we may say that less than one per cent of the rural families of Mexico owned about eighty-five per cent of all the rural land. Fewer than 2,700 families had more than half of the property of the Republic, and 114 families owned approximately one fourth. That was not in 1910 but in 1923, when the Revolution had already succeeded in reducing and limiting to some extent the areas in private hands. The Díaz policy spread friction in the rural districts over an ever widening circle, so that when the time came it was possible to stir a revolution that found support in widely separated parts of the country on a definite and specific issue—land.

The policy of irritation coincided with increasing cost of

living and a stationary wage. The traditional agricultural wage in Mexico up to the time of the Revolution was *dos reales* (25 centavos) per day. In some places it was *tres reales* (37½ centavos). It is a curious and interesting fact that this wage had not changed in almost a hundred years. Humboldt reported it as a standard wage in the early days of the nineteenth century; this was the wage Miguel Lerdo de Tejeda reported in 1838, Pimentel, in 1861, and what later evidence we have gives a similar wage. As a matter of record, I can testify that this wage is to be found even today in isolated spots in Mexico, in the mountainous regions of Guerrero, in certain spots in Chiapas, and even in Hidalgo. Traditional relationships change slowly, and despite the general rise in wages, the old wage lingers.

This standard wage was largely a payment in kind or in token coin to be converted into goods at the plantation store. During the years since independence, and especially since the coming of the Díaz régime with its incipient industrialism, there has been a steady increase in prices. The prices for corn, wheat, and beans, which were falling in the rest of the world, were rising in Mexico after 1874. That was because of the high tariff, which, for Mexico, reversed the price trend of the world. What was true of the prices of basic foods was true also of other commodities.

Tariffs were not merely external, but also internal. The *alcabala*, a species of tax between the borders of the states, and even between different counties, made prices still higher. As in the case of wages, tradition, habit, and custom here outweigh law. The *alcabala* was prohibited by the Constitution of 1857; it was officially abolished in 1874; yet traces of it are still to be found. Any one reading Mexican newspapers will run across an item of complaint on that score every few months. In my travels in Mexico I found this tax still operative in some outlying counties in Chiapas. We have thus an industrial system developing inside high tariff walls, with a lowered standard of living caused by the increasing cost of necessities of life and a stationary wage. On the matter of price and tariff and wage, we may quote from D. A. Wells to the effect that:

A population of ten million, poor almost beyond conception, have therefore to pay from two to three hundred per cent. more for the staple material of their simple clothing than needs be, in order that some other ten or twelve thousand of their fellow citizens, men and women, may have the privilege of working exhaustively from fourteen to fifteen hours a day in a factory for the small pittance of from thirty-five to seventy cents to defray the cost of their own subsistence.

A good deal of discussion developed about low wages, and we find them defended on grounds of economic law. The following quotation from Pimentel is illustrative:

Some people believe that the wage in Mexico is so small as not to be adequate for the subsistence of the laborer. We reply then that it is an axiom of the science of economics that the wages never fall below what is necessary to maintain the working class because they would perish and, as in Mexico, the workers subsist with what they are paid it may be inferred that they do not need more for their subsistence.

We may now summarize the influences that made for social upheaval as the Díaz régime drew to an end. Díaz had succeeded in pacifying Mexico by converting local tyranny into a general dictatorship, by converting the *cacique* into a policeman, a representative of the national government. He had reduced the local *cacique*, with local loyalties, into an enemy of the locality. He succeeded, too, in making peace between the conservative and liberal elements in the Republic by promising to the first security, and to the second, progress; by giving the first an opportunity to reconstruct out of the ruins what could be saved of the old feudal order, and by giving the second the promise that industrialization, undoing the feudal structure of the country, would give them the opportunity to become prosperous. He prevailed upon them with the belief that a rapid development of mining, transportation, and foreign investment were good things in themselves. This credo fostered contempt for the Indian in higher circles, and provided the clique surrounding Díaz with moral justification for a systematic attack upon Indian villages, on the grounds that such a policy was best for Mexico. This policy extended feudal land holding to areas that had hitherto not been characterized by such a system. The *latifundia* now became universal instead of local, as it had been. The power of the landowner increased. The foreigner was allowed to acquire, both financially and morally, a position of prestige and prerogative that made "Mexico the mother of foreigners and the stepmother of Mexicans." In the process, all political liberalism, all political democracy, all political opinion was suppressed. While this was going on, prices were rising while wages remained stationary. Any attempt to improve the standard of living of the mass of the people was violently suppressed.

It was under these circumstances that the Revolution broke out. The air was filled with grievances, political and economic, moral and social. All that was needed was a spark to set the ready tinder aflame. That spark was supplied by the demand of the younger generation for opportunity to take part in politics. The demands of Madero and his group were for political opportunity to participate in the government, to stop the perpetual reëlection of the dictator. It was not meant to undo the work of Díaz, which was generally accepted as good by the Madero group. It was to change the leadership, the governing group. That was the spark that set the country aflame; the fire is still burning, still smouldering. The results have been very different indeed from those dreamt of by the leaders responsible for initiating a violent movement against the aged dictator.

CHAPTER 13

FURY AND PASSION

I T IS best to think of the Mexican Revolution as a movement made up of a series of waves having more or less independent beginnings and independent objectives. At times these movements fused together for a while, and then separated again. Some of the rebellions were initiated for one purpose and then, for political reasons, assumed a direction not inherent in them in the beginning. So rapid and varied have been the cross currents that have come to the surface in the Revolution that it is most difficult to discover any given direction in the movement as a whole. It would be possible to write a history of the Revolution in terms of outstanding political personalities and their satellites. But a true history of this type would reveal that the personalities themselves have, with few exceptions, been buffeted from pillar to post by the currents of the upheaval. Examples of this are to be found in such careers as those of Vasconcelos and de la Huerta. Both of these men have played important rôles in the revolutionary movement, and yet have been tied neither to principle or policy. The rôle of Vasconcelos is tragic both for himself and for Mexico, while that of de la Huerta is an example of treason to the Revolution, of misunderstanding of the common people, and of limited objectives that have crept in to make personal advantage predominate over the underlying urge of the uprising. Treason is an unkind word. Folly, ambition, pride, self-aggrandizement, or perhaps, just lack of understanding are better words. Another example of a similar type is Pancho Villa, like a hurricane that destroys all it touches. One could write a chronological story by taking the outstanding personalities, Madero, de la Huerta, Pancho Villa, Zapata, Carranza, Obregón, Calles,

Morones, and grouping about them the lesser individuals. But that would be giving the movement a degree of coherence and unity which it never had, which it has not even at present. Anyone who knows any considerable number of the important figures at present active in Mexican political life understands well enough that there is no direction, that the pressure must, generally speaking, come from below.

A true history of the Revolution would detail the little obscure movements as they developed and gathered force and importance in localities, fought their battles and disappeared, to come to the surface again another place. Here and there a significant figure was produced, who, for a while, typified the movement, but if projected upon the larger scene lost himself and his sense of direction. One can almost say that the Mexican Revolution has gone ahead, but that leadership has gone backward, that the people have moved to greater freedom and greater power, but that the leaders have frequently moved to disillusionment, personal interest, and self-aggrandizement. There have been a few striking exceptions, but they merely illuminate the dark picture.

At the beginning, the Mexican Revolution was little more than a minor political riot. Madero had set November 20, 1910 as the day on which the people were to rise against Díaz. But the groups that did rise, some before and some after that date, did not amount to a baker's dozen. On the 19th of November, Pascual Orozco, with twenty-five followers, declared himself in rebellion against the government in the village of San Isidro, in Chihuahua. On the 20th of November a few workers in Rio Blanco, in Vera Cruz, declared a rebellion, but ran at the first skirmish with the *Rurales*. Cándido Aguilar and Roseno Garnica rose in rebellion in Paso del Macho, in Vera Cruz. In Tlaxcala an anti-reëlectionist club did the same. A few other small groups declared themselves in rebellion on that day. On the 21st, a small group of the 11th cavalry regiment deserted. It was not until a week later that the first skirmish between the government forces and a rebel group took place, in El Fresno, near Chihuahua. There were five hundred troops and four hundred rebels, and the rebels lost. That was the beginning of a revolution thath as lasted for twenty years. It gained momentum by being unopposed. The Díaz government had lost internal strength. Had it been sure of itself it might have crushed the rebellion, even if it could not have prevented social reform.

Ideologically, the Madero rebellion was European and American rather than Mexican. It concentrated upon the old notion of political freedom and equality—the ideal written into the Constitution of 1857, which had, as we have noted, remained inapplicable. In its attempt to achieve effective suffrage and no-reëlection, the movement represented no basic need or immediate possibility. The social structure and the tradition of government were such that to postulate a revolution on such issues was to reveal merely that the leaders were saturated with European models of thought and American education. There has never been any effective suffrage, in our sense of the word, in Mexico, and there can be none until there is much greater cultural equality and social cohesion among the varying elements of the country.

The Madero revolution was utopian—lyrical it has been called—and its success was essentially quixotic. The Díaz government fell like a house of cards. It was replaced by a government that adhered to a foreign theory. The theory did not work, and could not have worked, even if the best of presidents had taken the place that was by chance given into the inept hands of Madero. Mexico was accustomed to centralized and directed government. Experience had made that the natural government that it still is. The success of Madero had to end in tragedy. The old group found Madero unsatisfactory because he talked a language they did not understand, and tried to use a machinery that would not work. The peasants, the peons, the common people, in so far as they were at all stirred by the Revolution, found Madero equally unsatisfactory. The talk of suffrage meant nothing to them. They were ignorant of it. They had never participated in government, and had no notion of the way of it. What they wanted was land, the abolition of serfdom, the abolition of the *tienda de raya*. The people wanted land, water, and schools: simple and elemental demands that had no bearing upon the political ideals of the Madero group. When the lyrical government succeeded it found itself between two foes—Zapata and Huerta, the agrarian and the reactionary. Both were equally opposed to it.

The military elements succeeded first in destroying the Madero government. General Mujica, who played a very important rôle in the development of the social movement of 1917–1920, said to me, in speaking of the fall of the Madero government,

If Huerta had not destroyed the Madero government we, the revolutionists, would have had to do so. We, who were really concerned with the social movement, found the Madero government less satisfactory each day, and it was better for the Revolution that the destruction of Madero came from a reactionary rather than a revolutionary source.

The Madero uprising had the great merit of setting inadvertently afoot the agitation that made further revolutionary developments possible. The ideals of the 1910 revolution of Madero and the social policy embodied in the Constitution of 1917 are two very different things indeed; one grew out of the other only by the accident of a time relationship.

The difficulty with the Madero rebellion was its failure to recognize that Mexico had remained a conquered nation, even if the conquerors had ceased to be armed Spanish invaders and had become rich *latifundistas*. Mexico, in 1910, had all the characteristics of a colony, and the colonists were of a different race, language, culture, and social attitude. It is the most superficial of views to assume that Mexico is like

DEER DANCE OF THE YAQUI INDIANS

some of the other nations for which a political document based on universal suffrage is a feasible source of government. Mexico has never been ready for political democracy. It is not ready for such a democracy at present. It may be ready for social reconstruction, greater division of wealth and power, especially of land, but it is not ready for our type of political democracy. Social change depends here upon direct force and centralization of power, and it has been only in so far as the power of the government has been in the hands of those who have represented the common people that such changes have occurred.

Failure to recognize that the accepted constitutional forms were inadequate for social change explains in part the persistent revolutions in Mexico since 1910. Frank revolutionary government was impossible because of the lip service that had to be paid to the constitutional norms that dictated legal method. The attempt to preserve constitutional form imposed compromise governments; the need dictated an immediate and direct application of the force that had come to power for the purpose of achieving equilibrium. That was not done. The results have been repeated revolutions.

The ease with which the revolutionary elements overthrew the Díaz régime proved unfortunate. If the government had fallen after a prolonged conflict, the struggle would have defined the situation within the country, forced a clear division between revolutionary and reactionary elements, brought some common ideology to bear upon the revolutionary groups, and disciplined both the civilian and military elements of the Revolution. As it was the revolutionary groups came to power before they had found time to coalesce either in body or in spirit, before they became, truly speaking, a party. The Díaz government fell; that is, the president and his cabinet resigned, but the clique with which Díaz ruled remained intact. The old clique controlled the army. It controlled the national and state legislatures. It controlled the governors; even the new governors named by the Revolution but slightly reflected a revolutionary viewpoint. In the executive departments nothing changed except the heads. The results should have been foreseen. The federal army and the revolutionary elements were in frequent conflict. The new soldiers looked with fear and hostility on the older troops. These in turn considered the raw recruits with contempt. The revolutionary forces resisted the attempt to disband them; they did not trust the older army groups—rightly enough, as time was to prove. In Puebla, for instance, the new recruits and the older army fought a bloody battle, with great slaughter for the revolutionary elements, after peace had been declared and the Díaz government had fallen.

The most refractory elements were the state legislatures and the federal Congress. The state legislative bodies, elected under the old régime, and the new governors, appointed by the Revolution, carried on open warfare. In Jalisco and Sinaloa the governors dissolved the state legislatures by force—a remedy illegal and violent. The federal congress made public accusation against a provisional president against whom it found cause for complaint although he was notoriously anti-revolutionary. This may be gathered from his giving honorary decorations to General Porfirio Díaz, the deposed tyrant to Colonel Reynaldo Diaz, and to other members of the federal army. This was being done by an executive come to power through the defeat of the federal army and while attempts were being made to disband the revolutionary group that had raised him to power. Seeds of conflict were being sown.

Although the Madero revolution had won, it found itself in a minority position within the federal government, as well as within the state and local governments. The majority of the cabinet members of the provisional president, de la Barra, belonged to the old conservative group; the majority of governors were conservatives; the majority in both the national and the state legislatures were frankly partisan to the old scheme of things; the local *ayuntamientos* were conservative; the influential press was conservative; the Supreme Court was conservative. Everywhere the ruling influences, including the army, belonged to the old political régime. The revolutionary group was represented in the government by a minority, as revolutionary groups have been approximately ever since. The army has rebelled against the Revolution many times; Congress has rebelled against the Revolution many times; members of the cabinet have betrayed the Revolution many times; governors have almost consistently been conservative. Even in the days of Calles, the majority of the governing personnel was conservative, if not reactionary, especially state governors and certain elements in the cabinet. If the Revolution has succeeded even partially, it has been because, in each crisis, the minority in government could and did find support in the mass, expecially among the *campesinos* who wanted land.

Felix Palavacini, who has been both a participant in, and an observer of, the Mexican Revolution, divided it into four phases: the lyrical, the waring, the social, and the constructive. Madero and his associates seemed to dream of an easy transition, of change that would not be painful: a sort of gentle and easy shift from tyranny to democracy accompanied everywhere by happy approval and joyous consent. The vision of a bloody upheaval that would last for many years, that would produce hordes of armed men wandering over the land, large armies battling for power, profound social and political changes that would endanger the very existence of the nation, was not within their ken. This explains the easy faith of Madero, his readiness to continue in office members of the old régime, his forgiveness of men like Felix Díaz, who rose in rebellion against him, and his willingness to share a revolutionary government with those who had made the old tyranny a hated instrument. This dream of peaceful transition came to a sudden end with the murder of Madero by Huerta. He was incarcerated by the man whom he had chosen to defend him, and shot on the street while being transferred to prison, on the good old excuse of attempted escape.

The warring period of the Revolution began when Carranza repudiated the bloody murder and its political implications, refused to accept a new tyranny risen by murder in place of the old, and raised the cry of *constitucionalismo* (constitutional government). The battles of Carranza with Huerta, the rise of Villa, of Obregón, of Pablo González, the driving of Huerta from Mexico City, the successful entry of Carranza's forces into Mexico, the later war with Villa—all of these are parts of the "warring period," a period that lasted from 1913 through 1916.

During Carranza's struggle against Huerta, and especially in the conflict that followed with Villa, Carranza was forced to appeal to the common people for support. The program formulated during the conflict was in itself an instrument of war. It was to be a long time before the program would become effective. But it did summarize what has since been in process of elaboration and definition. In Vera Cruz the revolutionary group headed by Carranza issued some laws that have had great influence since. The first agrarian law that of January 6, 1915, was issued while Carranza was still in Vera Cruz. The *tienda de raya*, or company store, was abolished, and factories and plantations were required to establish schools on the premises for the children of laborers. These were the first steps in a legislative program that has since grown to wide proportions, with considerable degree of enforcement. These ideas of social reform, developed during the conflict, were later embodied in the Constitution of 1917.

There had been no plan to call for a new constitution. Carranza had merely set out to overthrow the dictatorship of Huerta, and to reëstablish constitutional government. The single project, as embodied in the Plan of Guadalupe, in 1913, was to call for a new election after the overthrow of Huerta, and to continue the government under the old Constitution of 1857. Carranza was no social revolutionist. He was a large landowner. He had sat for long years as senator under Díaz, and had been governor of the state of Coahuila. He had been well schooled in the older doctrine. He was already a man over fifty when the struggle with Huerta gave him the opportunity to assume national leadership. His revolutionary program came into being while he was struggling against defeat.

The labor movement as part of the Social Revolution in Mexico antedated the Madero uprising by three years. It began with the cry of the workers in Río Blanco, Puebla, "Down with Porfirio Díaz. Long live the workers' revolution!" The answer was a bloody massacre, but the original battle had been fought, and the first social impulse had been set traveling through the country. While Díaz was still in power in the City of Mexico, a few rebellious spirits published a little paper called *Regeneración*. Among these were a few who later acquired power and prestige, and played important parts in the development of the Revolution, such as Antonio I. Villareal, who was destined to become Secretary of Agriculture for a short period, and the two brothers, Enrique and R. Flores Magón, who remained to the end perhaps the most consistent propagandists of "lyrical" radicalism in Mexico. One of them died later in Leavenworth prison, as an American federal prisoner. When his body was returned to Mexico, the Mexican congress took a recess to honor his labor in the Revolution. Antonio Díaz Soto y Gama was also among them. He became the greatest orator of the Revolution, joined Zapata after Huerta murdered Madero, wrote the intellectual programs of Zapata, and is supposed to have taught him how to read by the light of the campfire. He was for many years the most consistent voice of the Mexican *agraristas*. Now in retirement, he has become a mystic, disillusioned, but still a respected name among the revolutionary groups, a name mentioned in sorrow, but with respect. These men carried on propaganda for labor and agrarian justice under conditions which were difficult and dangerous.

The victory of Madero against Díaz intensified the socialist propaganda of the few radicals. Socialist lectures were held in the tailor shop of Luis Menéndez in a back street, San Felipe Neri. Among the lecturers were to be found Rafael Pérez Taylor and Rosendo Salazar. These, and others, were strengthened by the arrival of the Spanish anarchist, Juan Francisco Moncaleano, who held open air meetings in front of factories. He was promptly expelled by Madero. It was at this time that the *Casa del Obrero Mundial*, which was to play so important a part in the development of Mexican labor as well as in the development of the Revolution, and which is still in existence as part of the C.R.O.M., was organized. It was a sort of propaganda center that brought together most of the younger leaders and propagandists in the early days of the Revolution. It was there that early fame was achieved by many of those who later played, and still play, significant parts in the social aspects of the Revolution, especially in the labor movement. The first strikes in Mexico City were engineered from there, and it was from there that the first labor union pamphlet was written, *El sindicalismo*, by Pérez Taylor.

The members of the *Casa del Obrero Mundial* were engulfed and divided by the conflict which developed between the leaders of the Revolution: Carranza on one side, Villa and Zapata on the other. Some members of the organization followed Carranza, signed a formal contract with his government, organized red battalions, and fought in the trenches against Villa. For this Carranza allowed them to organize behind the lines, and slowly to develop a prestige and leadership that has in the main continued since. Others, like Antonio Soto y Gama and Rafael Pérez Taylor, joined Zapata in the hills of Morelos, and became indentified with the agrarian movement and its fortunes. It is interesting to note that the bitterest enemies of the trade-union movement have been those who followed Zapata rather than Carranza, and that it was Soto y Gama who raised the issue of conflict between *Laborismo* and *Agrarianismo* in 1923, when the first national convention of labor and peasant groups met. The struggle for power between these groups has continued since.

The conflict between Carranza and Villa over the future progress of the Revolution seems to have had purely personal origins. The people who did not like Carranza—and there were many of them—joined Villa. The personal enmity between Obregón and General Felipe Angeles, which forced Angeles to join Villa and become his chief of staff, was another contributory factor. Carranza's notorious jealousy of his prerogatives as "First Chief" of the Revolution, and the rather careless and cavalier manner that Villa had in obeying orders that did not please him, were still other factors. Military jealousy contributed to make the final break inevitable. Carranza, as soon as he reached Mexico City, called a convention of generals to lay before them the program of the new government, which, since the defeat of Huerta, now seemed on its way to organization. In speaking before this convention, which met in October, 1914, Carranza said, "The supreme end of the constitutionalist movement was the calling of elections to reëstablish constitutional government," which had been destroyed by Huerta. He suggested that the provisional government should initiate certain reforms.

First on the program was free municipal government. This Carranza described as the "basis for the teaching of democratic practices." Next came an attempted solution of the agrarian problem. This solution was to be brought about by the division of national lands, lands that the government

would purchase from large estates, and through lands expro
priated for "public utility." The agrarian movement actually
took a very different course from the one prescribed by Carranza. The purchase of land from private owners has been
practically unknown; the division of the national lands proved
of minor significance. Expropriation was almost the sole
means of the agrarian reform. Other aspects of Carranza's
program were the expropriation by townships of lands needed
for markets and schools, weekly payments in money to workers, limitation of hours of labor and weekly wages, nullifica-
tion of contracts for concessions which were unconstitutional,
a *catastro* on rural properties, reformation of the tariff, bank-
ing reform, the establishment of a central bank, reformation
of the laws of civil marriage and divorce. Nothing came of
these projects at this time. The armies were divided among
themselves, and Pancho Villa was preparing for further war.
Villa's army was marching on the capital. He wanted the
convention where he could dominate it, so after only four
days in Mexico City, the generals betook themselves to
Aguascalientes.

No other convention, even in the turbulent history of
Mexico, gathered under such strange surroundings. The city
was filled with generals, colonels, majors, captains, lieutenants, sergeants, and privates, and they all seemed to be Vil-
listas. In the saloons, Villista generals drank and threatened.
At the convention were all of the important Villista chiefs.
Obregón and his followers represented Carranza. The convention declared itself sovereign; the generals swore on the
national standard to defend the convention and its sovereignty. The land surrounding Aguascalientes was called neu-
tral territory, and the convention proceeded. But there was
no talk except of the problems arisen from the division of
the two major military chiefs, Carranza and Villa. Villa appeared before the convention on the seventeenth of October,
1914, made an incoherent speech, and then broke down and

sobbed. He embraced Obregón, whom he had ordered shot just two weeks before.

The convention assumed importance only when the Zapatistas arrived. It was then that the first real program of the Revolution was launched before the assembled generals of the revolutionary army. Soto y Gama, the chief of the Zapatista delegation, denounced the convention unmercifully. Soto y Gama is an eloquent man, with a capacity for sarcasm and emotional concentration that has rarely been equaled, and perhaps never surpassed, in Mexico. He derided the convention and its doings, told them the national flag upon which they had just signed their pledges was only a rag. The assembly of generals was beside itself with anger. Many a pistol was drawn. The cooler heads of Eduardo Hay and Mateo Almanza finally calmed the angry assembly. During this time the unarmed Soto y Gama stood on the platform with his hands folded, a good target, but quiet and self-possessed. When quiet was restored, he continued his speech, and in fifteen minutes that same assembly poured itself out in enthusiasm and applause for Soto y Gama. Such is the power of language.

This was the first occasion on which Zapata secured a hearing for his land program; this was the first real discussion of the agrarian program of the Revolution which was to have such wide influence in the later movement. Carranza declined to accept the dictates of the convention, but with Villa as guardian, it moved on to Mexico City, and Carranza moved out. At this time Villa could have destroyed Carranza while he was fleeing in disorder, but the city was too much for Villa. It was a new world to conquer. Here were drink and women and lights and palaces. He would not move.

The convention had named Eulalio Gutiérrez president of the Republic, but Pancho Villa remained the ruler. While in Mexico City, Villa and Zapata joined forces. They and the new president were in accord for about a week. All elements were in disorder and without direction. There were too many chiefs. Even the subordinates of Gutiérrez worked to destroy the sources of the new government's power: Zapata and Villa. Although there was apparent constitutional government in Mexico City, three public men were assassinated by orders of Villa, and one day a member of the president's cabinet, Vasconcelos, and the president's private secretary went into hiding for fear of Villa. At two in the afternoon of one of the later days of December, Villa arrived at the president's house for a peaceful interview—and brought two thousand armed men with him. The interview was heated. After that the end was in sight. Gutiérrez sought to undermine Villa's power by a combination of generals. He was betrayed, and flight was the only source of escape. The government and its assistants departed hurriedly for unknown quarters on the dawn of the sixteenth of September, 1915, and Pancho Villa was again on his way to Mexico City. He stopped off in San Luis Potosí and annihilated the army of Lucio Blanco, an army of some twenty thousand men.

Soon after that, all the elements that had come out of the Aquascalientes convention opposed to Villa, surrendered to Carranza. It was not possible to work with Villa; he was going nowhere. Like a tornado, he was without purpose, without direction, a blind annihilating force. He had to be destroyed. The forces gathered about Carranza. A program was rapidly formulated to bring them together; the Revolution began to acquire a social policy. The program grew out of conflict and necessity rather than out of theory. The soldiers turned to the ideal and to the cause of the common people as their instruments of battle, and as their justification for victory. With the aid of the workers' battalions, with the aid of the agrarian groups that came to Carranza as a result of the law of January 6, 1915, Obregón defeated Villa in Celeya, and destroyed his power forever.

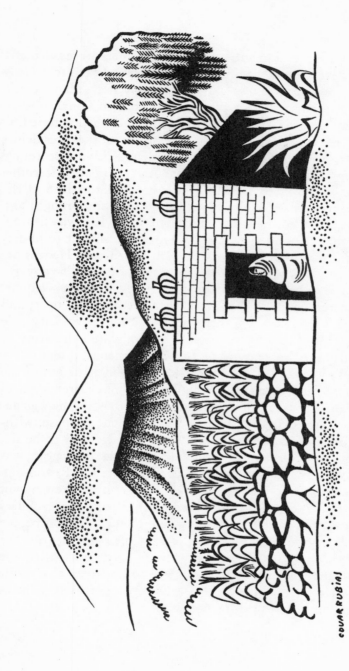

TYPICAL SCENE IN THE MESA CENTRAL

CHAPTER 14

EMERGENCE OF A REVOLUTIONARY PROGRAM

IT IS clear that the social program of the Revolution owes a great deal to the exigencies of the conflict between Carranza and Villa. It became necessary to define the objectives of the struggle, and to draw together all elements who saw in the Revolution an instrument of change. The only clear program the Revolution had was that of Zapata, and it was limited. On December 12, 1914, three months after the pronouncement of objectives that Carranza had issued in Mexico City to the meeting of generals, a much more comprehensive program was published, one destined to bring to his support many of the forces that made ultimate success possible.

In this new program, the agrarian reforms were given first place. It promised to "put in force during the struggle all of the laws necessary to satisfy the social, economic and political needs of the country; to establish a régime that will guarantee the equality of all Mexicans among themselves." The program enumerated is as follows:

Agrarian laws that will favor the establishment of small properties; the dissolution of the large estates; the return to the villages of the lands of which they have been unjustly deprived; a system of taxation that will fairly affect real property; laws that will improve the conditions of the peon, the worker, the miner, in general the proletarian classes; freedom of the municipal government; a new basis for the organization of the army; electoral reforms to make suffrage effective; reorganization of the judiciary; reform of the marriage laws; laws for the strict enforcement of the *Leyes de Reforma* (church laws); revision of the civil and penal codes; revision of the laws that govern the exploitation of the mines, oil, water, forest, and other natural resources, for the purpose of destroying the monopolies created by the previous regime and to prevent their future development; political reforms that guarantee the application of the Constitution; and in general, such laws as will assure to the inhabitants of the country the full enjoyment of their rights and equality before the law.

This statement of objective was issued, fully four years after the Revolution had begun, after the major battles had been fought, and at a time when the country was so sharply torn among warring factions that there seemed no hope of ever achieving unity again. It was the voice of a nearly defeated military group that assumed to speak for the country. It was a cry of despair. The Carranza group had been driven from the City of Mexico, and clung to a very narrow strip of coast, with the intention of escaping to sea if Pancho Villa or Zapata came nearer. It was not a proclamation by a victorious revolutionary army ready to establish a government for the purpose of bringing these reforms to pass. It was a bait for attracting adherents to the cause, a means of justifying the independent existence of an army. Had it not been for the loyalty of Alvarado in Yucatan, who supplied Carranza with large sums of money derived from the high price of *henequén* (which was at that time in great demand because of the European war), even this policy might not have saved him. But the program did bring to Carranza elements that hitherto had remained outside of his camp. It attracted the workers in Mexico City and Orizaba. It gave him the support of the *agraristas* who believed in Zapata's cause, but who, for one reason or another, did not follow Zapata in his ruthless and violent struggle against great odds. Although Carranza himself failed to realize the possibilities of his own program, nearly all of these projects have been written into law during the last fifteen years. The agrarian law, first issued on January 6, 1915, was incorporated into the Constitution of 1917, and has since been expanded consistently, until it is at present more comprehensive than at any time in the past. The labor program found embodiment in Article 123, and recently in the Federal Code. Article 130 represents the program in matters affecting the Church. So with all the other projects. A new civil and penal code has been elaborated. In fact, all of the legislative promises have been slowly fulfilled. It has taken many revolutions since Carranza's program was formulated to bring its promises into legislative enactment. On the administrative side the matter has been even more difficult. It must be emphasized again and again, that the program of the Revolution has grown piecemeal.

The reforms of Carranza, therefore, came at a time when the Mexican Revolution was torn into shreds. The breakdown of the Aguascalientes convention had left Mexico without a government, without a central power. In Mexico City, first Eulalio Gutiérrez and then Roque González Garza had tried their hands at being president, neither having power or prestige, and each fleeing from Mexico City at the threat of military occupation by Villa or Zapata. In the north, Pancho Villa was fuming and storming and marching upon Mexico City, threatening and executing all those enemies upon whom he could lay hands. In the south, Zapata, who had never officially become a party to any convention, continued his own war for lands, fighting each and every government and military power in turn, because none would concede the simple formula of lands for the people and a withdrawal of the federal troops from Morelos. In the east, Carranza, who had abandoned Mexico City with such of his followers as had not joined any one of the other military groups in the country, maintained himself on the coast. It was at this time that a social program began to be formed, that Carranza began to issue his decrees and laws which later came to be the source of much of the social legislation incorporated into the new Constitution of 1917. On February 3, 1915 Carranza promised to call a Constitutional Convention which would write into the Constitution the reforms that were being advocated during the conflict. Clearly enough, this social program was an after-thought with Carranza; it developed under pressure, in order to secure support.

The struggle, however, carried its own consequences. New ideas imposed upon the movement during the conflict, in the hour of need, became items in the central program. They represented a commitment both to the movement and to the future. It was clear that the new laws and decrees would not fit easily into the older Constitution of 1857. It was also clear that if the Revolution were defeated, the older Constitution could be made an instrument for destroying the legal and legislative achievements of the revolutionary struggle. Carranza, in discussing this matter, said,

It is certain that the enemies of the Revolution, who are the enemies of the nation, will not admit that the government shall base itself upon the reforms issued by the revolutionary army. They will surely attack these new laws as canons of a group that was not representative of national sovereignty and the national will.

The only alternative, therefore, was the calling of a Constitutional Convention that would insure the recording of the reforms enunciated by the Revolution. It was accordingly called for the 15th of September, 1916. That such a convention was called did not prevent opponents of the revolutionary program from insisting that it was illegal and unrepresentative. It has taken fifteen years to win more or less general acceptance for the present Constitution.

Justification for the calling of the Convention was made clear enough by a spokesman for Carranza:

We wish to legalize for the future what is already a fact in the present . . . that no future congress will deprive the municipalities of the autonomy that they have been granted by Carranza, that no future congress will take away from the villages the *ejidos* (communal lands) which they have already received and which they are cultivating, that no future congress will destroy the new communities that have been established by the Revolution, that no future congress will undo our labor legislation, our laws governing accidents, minimum wages, right to organize and laws governing hours of labor.

The new Constitution was to be for the purpose of placing within the fundamental laws of the country those reforms which grew out of the conflict, so that when a new congress was called to legislate for the nation it would find that "the Revolution has already been legalized."

We may recapitulate the genesis of the Constitutional Convention. It grew out of the exigencies of the moment. It had been made inevitable by the effort first to destroy Huerta, and later, on the part of Carranza, to destroy Pancho Villa. The military convention in Mexico City, called by Carranza, the Aguascalientes convention at which all of the military factions were represented, the break between Pancho Villa and Carranza, the uncompromising struggle carried on by Zapata, and the forced flight of Carranza to the coast, all combined to forge a series of needs and ideals that made the Constitutional Convention inevitable.

When it did meet, there were clearly two forces. One, the more conservative, represented Carranza, and was ready with a document for adoption by the Convention. The other indirectly represented Obregón, was headed by General Francisco J. Mújica. The Carranza group was best represented by Macias, Rojas, Palavacini, and Cravioto; the Obregón group by Mújica, Colunga, Jara, Truchelo, and Bojórquez. The radicals won the debates and carried the votes. The Carranza document was amended and profoundly changed from its original form.

Even when the Constitutional Convention was called, the Carranza government really had no social program. This can be seen in the project for a constitution submitted by Carranza to the Convention. It contains none of those articles that have since made the Mexican Constitution of 1917 a world-famous document and given it the vitality it has shown in the last fifteen years. This is true not only of the formal document submitted by Carranza, but also of the expository elucidation by those close to Carranza, who apparently wrote the original draft of the Constitution. M. Aguirre Berlanga, who played an important part in the elaboration of the original document, submitted by Carranza, devoted a pamphlet to its discussion, and in this pamphlet we find no mention of the agrarian or the labor problem. It is clear from every scrap of evidence available, either in written form or from the personal comment by those who played rôles within the Constitutional Convention, that the social program that has roused most reaction both for and against the Mexican Revolution came from sources other than Carranza.

J. de D. Bojórquez, who was one of the secretaries of the Convention, says, in speaking of Obregón,

Because of his great influence with the majority of the Convention we, the radicals, triumphed. It was his decisive influence that made it possible to write into that Constitution the saving principles contained in Articles 3, 27, 123, and 130.

The Constitutional Convention of 1917 was the most important single event in the history of the Revolution. It definitely marked off the past from the present and the future in Mexico. Whatever may be said about this Convention, and all possible things both good and bad have been said, it once and for all set a definitive legal program for the Mexican Revolution, and laid the legal foundation for all of the conflicting currents of the last fifteen years. The Convention itself was called in times of internal strife, when the different groups were still struggling for supremacy: Zapata in the south, Villa in the north, Carranza in the center. The Constitution was written by the *soldiers* of the Revolution, not by the lawyers, who were there, but were generally in the opposition. On all the crucial issues the lawyers voted against the majority of the Convention. The majority was in the hands of the soldiers—generals, colonels, majors—men who had marched and counter-marched across the Republic and had fought its battles. The ideas of the Constitutional Convention, as they developed, came from scattered sources. The soldiers wanted, as General Mújica said to me, to socialize property. But they were frightened—afraid of their own courage, of their own ideas. They found all of the learned men in the Convention opposed to them. Article 27 was a compromise.

It was one of Carranza's greatest acts that he accepted the document, so different from the one he had tried to impose upon the Convention. He accepted it as his own, promulgated it, and swore to defend and respect it and make others do the same. Apart from his failings of temper and narrowness of ideals, this submission to the Convention, a creature of his own making, would alone give Carranza an important place in the history of the Social Revolution of Mexico. He gave official sanction to the Constitution around which all of Mexico's social program has been developed.

In reflecting upon the work of the Mexican Constitutional Convention it is important to recall that it took place in 1916 when the World War had stirred the passions and the imaginations of the masses as perhaps never before. Labor parties and socialist movements everywhere seemed to be coming into increasing power and influence. Lloyd George talked of "making England fit for heroes to live in." The common people seemed to be creeping out of their hiding places and achieving power and place in the affairs of nations; states were assuming greater control over both the human and the natural resources of the country than ever before. Experimentation was going on everywhere. This background merely intensified the social conflict in Mexico, especially as the War, and the lack of recognition from countries like the United States, England, and France had cut Mexico off and isolated it, had forced it to depend on its own resources and its own spiritual energies as never before. In one way the Constitutional Convention expressed the self-discovery of Mexico, the maturing of a people in their attempt to work out their own problems and to free themselves from tutelage, to free themselves from being led by the hand by foreigners who considered themselves wiser or stronger. It was in one sense the real birth of a new people in the world, with a separate place and a separate influence all their own. For the Constitution of 1917 has had an increasing influence over all Latin America, and is at present reflected even in the pages of the new Spanish Constitution.

It must be conceded to Mexico that it produced one of the most significant and influential constitutional documents of the present century, and that it did so before the new constitution of Germany, before the Bolshevik Revolution of Russia, and before the social by-products of the Great War had found expression in legal documents. The uniqueness of the work of the Mexican Constitution lies in that it sought to discover a way to describe a formula for the solution of its own basic problems. This formula the Convention worked out in Article 27. It attempts to reduce all property in Mexico to "conditional ownership." It permits the juxtaposition of all types of ownership, from the nomadic group having nothing more than a vague sense of right to use, to that of the modern corporation with its complex titles, privileges, and prerogatives.

In another place (*Mexican Agrarian Revolution*, Macmillan, 1929, pp. 201–203) we have described the formula contained in Article 27, as follows:

Article 27, it is obvious, has created a variety of new legal forms of landholding, and in its structure lies embedded the possibility of many other types and systems of land tenure. In fact every new law, every new limitation, creates a special form of ownership of land. It seems true that the formula was developed to meet the special social and legal need of the multifarious groups of different cultural levels that make up the Mexican community. They needed a property concept that would be broad enough to include the primitive notion of ownership characteristic of a wandering Indian group, knowing temporary possession, but having no notion of legal ownership, as well as one that could cover the needs of modern corporate and private ownership. The notion of specific limitations has thus become an instrument sufficiently flexible to cover present needs, and its flexibility makes it available for the creation of future specific types of land tenure.

This formula is broader in scope than any one of our current general property concepts. It obviously retains private property, and makes its expropriation dependent upon compensation and subject to general rules of public utility. It permits communal ownership, excludes certain types of ownership from lien and mortgage liability, limits its use in certain directions, and makes it subject to requirements for use in others. It also makes certain types of property, like subsoil and water, subject to concession. The emphasis seems generally to fall upon use, upon exploitation. The formula seems generally to favor the native against the foreigner, the individual against the corporation, but it permits all of these to use and enjoy property under specific conditions.

What Mexicans have established cannot be described as socialism or nationalism or communism, nor is it private property in the accepted use of the phrase. It is more inclusive than any one of these descriptions. The limitations already developed could perhaps be duplicated in American property law that has arisen in one or another form of the exercise of the police powers. But here all of these forms co-exist on one equal basis and require no special justification or legal defense. They are all constitutional, and any other form that may be established by the legislature in the name of public interest will be equally constitutional within the concept as contained in Article 27. This attitude toward property may perhaps be described as conditional, ownership in a variety of forms existing side by side, limited in different ways, but meeting the general requirements of 'public interest.' It seems that 'given the protean right of property, all forms of exploitation are possible.'

As long as this article governs property rights, all property is subject to such changes and limitations (*modalidades*) as the legislative power may from time to time see fit to give it. Property in fee simple has ceased to exist in law, so far as Mexico is concerned, though it may and can exist in fact, providing the legislative powers concede the special conditions under which such control may be exercised. This is the most significant legal outcome of the Mexican Revolution, and has already had, and is bound to have in the future, great influence.

The other item of great import, but of lesser significance, was the writing into the Constitution of Article 123, which consists of a body of rights and prerogatives for labor. These rules and regulations, embodied within the Constitution, were certainly not new in idea. But here, for the first time, they were collected as a general body of law and given constitutional sanction. These provisions gave the Mexican workers rights and privileges which have been fought over in the industrial nations for more than a century, and which had not up to that time been conceded anywhere to the extent to which they were embodied in the Mexican Constitution. The Constitutional Convention had taken the most progressive items of labor legislation wherever it could find them, and worked them into a common and unified body of rights and prerogatives, which in law, at least, gave the Mexican workers a status which, at that time did not exist in any other country.

Articles 27 and 123 were the distinctive features of the new Constitution. In other respects it followed the model of 1857, in form as well as in ideas. The changes in the laws affecting the Church were not of great importance as compared with those embodied in the earlier Constitution. These two articles have given the document an international position, and have played a leading rôle in defining the difficulties that have marked Mexican internal and external history since that time. The Constitution and Carranza's acceptance of it marked a turning point in the history of, and set a new goal for, the Mexican Revolution. After seven years of chaos, of strife, of bitterness, of uncontrolled and undirected passions, there had come to the surface a formula which was distinctive, new, broad in scope and revolutionary in consequence, and which contained a series of implications and prerogatives that, if carried into effect, would indeed make the

Mexico of the future very different from the colony it had remained for a hundred years after colonial government passed away.

Until 1917 the struggle was to formulate a program for the destruction of the feudal structure of Mexico. Since 1917, it has been to maintain the gains written into the Constitution.

Given Mexican experience, it is evident that a written constitution may not necessarily effect the conduct of the government. The history of the 1857 Constitution makes that clear enough. No sooner was the Constitution of 1917 adopted than it was violated and disregarded in practice by Carranza, who had given it solemn sanction. From then on, the progress of the social movement has been marked by the degree of application which the legal provisions have had. We have already said enough about the Revolution to indicate that this application has been halting, piecemeal, spotty, and incidental. It is no exaggeration to say that the Constitution as a whole has had no general application. It has been enforced sporadically, in one place and then in another, by one person and then by another.

The social program of the Revolution received little application by Carranza. He reduced land distribution to a minimum, made labor organization practically impossible, and had labor leaders killed for disobeying his orders. Under Obregón and Calles the Constitution was more fully enforced. Until 1920 neither the labor nor the agrarian precepts of the new Constitution had any broad influence, but from 1920 to 1924, both these programs found some application under Obregón, especially the agrarian program, and under Calles, from 1924 to 1928, there was more general application of both the labor and agrarian provisions. Since then there has been a tendency to slow down the application of the rules embodied in the Constitution. The articles affecting the Church were not applied at all until 1926, and then only because of the emergency which the central government felt it had to meet. These facts are merely indicative that, in Mexico, the administrator has been and still is the law in a sense that no legal prerogative, command, or prohibition can be.

Enforcement of the Constitution had to meet not merely internal but external opposition. From one point of view, outside pressure against the Revolution was valuable to Mexico. It forced a degree of solidarity and nationalism that might have been difficult to achieve otherwise. From another point of view, however, it has proved a real obstacle to the development of the social program. There is no doubt that fear of American intervention has prevented even an attempt at general confiscation of the large estates. From the point of view of the Revolution that might have proved the quickest, the least painful, and the least expensive method of settling the agrarian problem. But fear of the United States strongly influenced the Convention to adopt a legal formula which seemingly protected the owners in their rights, but which merely had the effect of prolonging the bitterness and conflict, of making peace impossible, and of making property no more secure nor better remunerated. The formula of payment for the lands taken for the needs of the villages has been complied with in law, but not in fact. It has, in addition, given rise to all sorts of difficulties, among them bribery of officials, persecution, petty wars, and murders between villages and their landowners, evils which should have been obviated long since. Revolution, protracted for twenty years, is still a reality because an attempt was made to satisfy a profound social necessity and yet keep legal appearances.

Difficulty with foreigners, American and others, arose in part out of the fact that under the Díaz régime the foreigner had a position of influence and prerogative that even the Mexican did not enjoy. In the nationalism which broke upon

SOLDADERAS IN THE REVOLUTION

the scene, the attempt to reduce the outsider to a status equal to that of the Mexican before the Mexican law injured the foreigners in those vested rights which they had acquired from the older régime. The foreigner in Mexico, including the Spaniard, has had, and still has, the attitude of a stranger, a person with a feeling of superiority towards the native. There is apparent and obvious a feeling of contempt and disregard for the Mexican and his rights, so that any effort of the Mexican to organize his institutions contrary to the beliefs and interests of the resident foreigners is met with misunderstanding and opposition. The foreign colony has neither appreciated nor approved the changes that were taking place. Tied by interests and personal friendship to the older ruling class of Mexico, they shared with them an attitude of contempt towards the Mexican common people. To have these common people suddenly rise and destroy the power and influence of the upper class Mexicans was not only unacceptable to the upper class Mexicans, but even less so to the resident foreigners, whose stakes were frequently more precarious. They demanded and expected a special treatment from the Mexican government because of the power they could wield through their own governments, a power that more than once verged upon the threat of intervention or war. Foreign opposition also expressed itself in encouragement of dissident movements against the new government. The influence of two of our ambassadors, Henry Lane Wilson and James R. Sheffield, was from both the Mexican and American points of view entirely mischievous. They aggravated and fed the flames of anti-foreign feeling. They did not succeed in stopping a movement that was too profound for any government to control, but only prolonged the agony and increased the bitterness of both the internal struggle and the external conflict. Internally, foreign opposition fed the movement for rebellion. Externally, it increased the pressure for intervention. In the sum, this opposition merely had the effect of hardening and prolonging the conflict in Mexico; it has made the carrying out of a program of social reconstruction more difficult, and has made more painful the achievement of the equilibrium so essential to internal peace.

In this connection it is important to mention the work of Dwight W. Morrow, who, in contrast to previous representatives of the United States, did that which is an essential of all successful dealings; he took the Mexicans seriously, took their movement seriously, took them at their own valuation. He recognized that other people have a moral status equal to that of the American people themselves. That, essentially, is the genius of Morrow's contribution. The solution of the difficulties was of less importance. It was the changed atmosphere, the changed relationship that the new attitude provided which has given Mr. Morrow's work so important an influence on the present relations between Mexico and the United States.

CHAPTER 15

TRAGEDY AND HOPE

THE Mexican Revolution has been tragic in the extreme. Most of the great figures of the Revolution have been killed, not in battle, but by assassination, or summarily shot for treason. Others have been driven from the country and are now scattered over the world, living in bitterness and exile. Only a few of the great figures have continued to live and play important parts in the affairs of the nation. Of these few the greatest, of course, is Calles, who, as soldier and statesman, as patriot and nationalist, as leader of men and as civic teacher, has remained the outstanding single figure of the Revolution. Perhaps no one so much as he has created the Mexico of today and tomorrow. Having been a teacher, a soldier, a governor, a president he is now a guide and counsellor. He has probably never betrayed a friend and probably never forgiven an enemy. He has remained loyal and ruthless. Some of his closest friends were killed for treason by his orders. He has been one of the few who have had a conception of a Nation, a State, a people in arms and a people in peace.

Like all social upheavals, the Mexican Revolution has had its great moments when heroism and grandeur, character and strength, faith and tragedy revealed themselves. It has been prolific of great and energetic figures. It is almost an incredible host of strange figures that has crossed the stage in the last twenty years. One way of explaining the Revolution is to say that the stage was too small for its leaders. It thrust these children of the peasant and the Indian up to the light with such disregard that they had to kill each other to make a place for themselves. If there had been party organization, if there had been a tradition of party discipline, then the course of the Revolution would have been different. But the movement was individualistic in the extreme, each leader rising by his own major strength and when national policy was to be made, there was no opinion, no unison, no common judgment; the only way to an agreement was by the sword. And so they have come and gone: Madero, Carranza, Pancho Villa, Felipe Carrillo, Obregón, Angeles, Alvarado, Serrano, and a host of others—each leaving his mark, each adding his thread to the woof out of which present-day Mexico has been woven.

Although this is not the place for a description of all the striking characters that the Revolution has cast into prominence, the figure of Zapata is of such magnitude in the social movement that a few words about him are essential. It is from his efforts, more than those of anyone else, that the agrarian character of the Revolution is derived. "Zapata" as a name has been transmuted into *Zapatismo* as a movement; and *Zapatismo* and Indianism are closely identified. In fact the words *Agrarismo, Zapatismo* and *Indianismo* have almost a common significance in the annals of the Revolution. Here, therefore, is a figure that has transcended the bounds of party and group and become the symbol of the Revolution.

Of all the figures produced by the Mexican Revolution, that of Emilano Zapata is the most clear cut. He was a man of no learning, of no broad social contacts, a simple, vigorous human being who knew little of the sophisticated and faraway world on the other side of the hills, but who knew that his people had been robbed of their land, and that it was his call to return these lands to them. A story (and there are now many stories about Zapata whose name has become a source of innumerable tales, songs and traditions) is told about him, that when he was still a child he said to his weeping father, who had been robbed of his lands, "I will take them back when I grow up." He had seen the lands of his little village,

San Miguel Anenecuilco, absorbed by the *hacienda*. All attempts of the village to get its lands back were futile. A commission of the Indians visited the City of Mexico, and sat about in the halls of the Department of Agriculture and waited for days and months. No one paid any attention to them, for they were just Indians. The trouble ended in ineffective protests, and the young Zapata had to flee to the mountains. Later he was impressed into the ninth Battalion of the Federal Army for insubordination, a regular form of discipline employed by the local *jefes políticos*, an experience that later served him well. With the first dawn of the Revolution Zapata was up in arms—rather, up against the government without arms. But the *Zapatistas* gradually armed and equipped themselves by disarming the federal soldiers. Before the Madero movement came to an end he had more than three thousand armed, equipped and mounted men. It was his boast that "We have begged from the outside not one bullet, not one rifle, not one peso; we have taken it all from the enemy."

Zapata was the first to state what later became the real objective of the Revolution. As early as 1911 he is reported to have said to one of the few newspaper men who ever succeeded in reaching him, "As long as there is a single armed *campesino*, I will not permit that the *haciendas* hold on to the lands of the villages." That was fully four years before the tide and fury of the Revolution impressed the imperative need of this reform upon the leaders of Mexico. Madero had referred to Zapata as one of the bravest and most effective soldiers of the Revolution. But when Zapata asked when the lands would be returned to the villages, Madero replied that the agrarian problem was a complicated one and offered Zapata one or two *haciendas* in Vera Cruz. It was then that Zapata returned to the hills and informed the world that "Be it known to Señor Madero, and through him to the rest of the world, that we will not lay down our arms until we have recovered our lands." And the Revolution was on again.

From the time he rose in rebellion to the day he was killed, he never surrendered, never was defeated, never stopped fighting. He was illiterate and inarticulate. A few intellectuals (one was Soto y Gama) joined him, but that was not until 1913. Another was a Mexican boy educated in an American Friends' school in Philadelphia, Gildardo Magaña. They explained and interpreted. But Zapata's conduct was not easily understandable by the rest of the Mexican revolutionists. Neither Madero nor Huerta nor Carranza could sympathize with the *Zapatistas* or could understand what sort of revolutionists they were; those that could looked upon them as the worst of bandits, as the worst enemies of society. "If they are not bandits, what sort of men are they?" They must be worse.

The Revolution in the state of Morelos, and thence all through the South, was a revolution without quarter, without compromise. "Peace at any cost" was the cry of the successive governments; "land at any cost" was the reply of the rebel of the south. The war went on for nine bloody years, until Zapata was finally murdered through a conspiracy which is as incredible as it is cruel and which shows something of the temper with which the Zapata social movement was fought by the Carranza revolutionists.

In those years the only government in Morelos, and later in large parts of the states of Guerrero, Puebla, Mexico, Tlaxcala, and even the Federal District, was in the hands of Zapata and his men. He had at times an army of forty thousand. They knew the mountains the *barrancas*, and they were fighting not a war but a revolution. It was an army without a commissary; it lived on the land. It was an army without an encampment; when a battle was to be fought the soldiers gathered in response to a call, when the battle was over the soldiers went back to their villages, hid their rifles, and turned to tilling the soil. A federal column could find no soldiers to fight, only unarmed peasants who humbly worked the land. When a campaign was on, the soliders of Zapata would change every three months, some going home, others joining the army. So it went for nine years.

The federal government, whether under Madero or Huerta or Carranza, was equally bitter against Zapata, and spread ruin among his followers. It became a war of extermination. The federal army, realizing that it was fighting a whole population, began to destroy that population. Villages were systematically burned. Fruit trees and crops were uprooted, women and children were concentrated in camps; it was war without quarter. In those nine years it is estimated that one third of the population of the state of Morelos was destroyed. During those years Zapata ruled and governed this war-ridden country without difficulty; was obeyed affectionately and implicitly like an old Aztec king, was a ruler of men. During those years there was a heavy price upon his head, and yet, never in all of that time was he betrayed by his own people, never did one of his men so attempt to bring himself to power and riches. That shows something of the quality of the unity that a social movement can develop among the Mexican Indians.

Zapata was finally killed by Pablo González and Guajardo, and when he was killed terror and fear spread throughout that part of Mexico which he had dominated. A wail of despair could be heard over the streets of Cuernavaca. Four years later, I, myself, saw on one of the posts of the Borda Garden—before it became what it is now, a tourist resort—the following inscription carved with a machete in rude characters:

Rebels of the South it is better to die on your feet than to live on your knees.

It was dated April 11, 1919, the day after Zapata had been murdered.

Only when Obregón came into control of the federal government and accepted the old condition of peace that had been offered by Zapata to Madero nearly ten years before —land for the people and a withdrawal of all federal soldiers —was peace declared, possibly because Dr. Parrés, a man known to every man, woman and child in the state as the doctor who had served with the Zapata forces all through the period of the bloody rebellion, became governor of the state; and because General Genovevo de la O, a Zapatista general, became the military commander of the local troops. Zapata had won, and so had the Revolution. It was this tenacity, the persistence which would make no compromise and accept no change from the simple demand of land for the people, which made the Mexican Revolution the thing it has come to be in the history of the country. With all of its failings the Revolution has come to mean a profound spiritual and social change in the total attitude and relationship of the different classes in that country.

It is always a difficult matter to appraise a movement as complex and many-sided as the Mexican Revolution has proved to be. The forces at play are not all on the surface, the consequences which are obvious may prove to be temporary, and those which are hidden may be both profound and permanent. The scene shifts so rapidly, the emotions and passions displayed are so keen, the individuals that have come and gone are so varied, that a kaleidoscopic review would merely reveal irreconcilable elements that play with each other and with faith for a while, then take each others' lives in hate, fury, passion and ambition. The battles are not the history of the Revolution, nor are the individuals who walked across the stages with greater or lesser truculence, with much or little humility. The laws that have been written by the hundreds and thousands are not the history of the Revolution, they are merely straws pointing which way the wind was blowing; they are merely momentary judg-

GENERAL PORFIRIO DÍAZ

ments of the people involved in the struggle; they are merely
an expression of faith in the future. What then is the history
of the movement? The answer seems to be that the history of
the Revolution is recorded in a changed attitude of the people
of Mexico toward life, toward the world, toward themselves.

The chief by-product of the Revolution is, therefore, spiritual; a discovery by the Mexican people of their own dignity,
a dignity which they were not conscious of possessing before
and which was not credited to them even by the philosophers
drawn from their midst. From that point of view, the greatest prophet of the Mexican Revolution has been Diego Rivera,
who has discovered and revealed to the world the profound
dignity and strength of his people. The frescoes of Diego
Rivera represent the best dream, the deepest aspiration of
the common people of Mexico. Some day the very ideals of
the Revolution, if they should be lost in the debris of political
turmoil and personal ambition, may be rediscovered in his
paintings. It is perhaps not too much to say that as long as
his paintings are allowed to remain on the public walls so
that the common people can rediscover themselves in them,
the Mexican Revolution will remain safe, at least as an ideal
—permanent, as a dream to be achieved.

This spiritual change is best seen and most significant in
the new attitude towards the Indian. It is in this respect
that the Revolution has born its greatest fruits, its richest
gifts. Not that the Indian has everywhere escaped mistreatment, abuse and disregard, but profoundly the Indian has
been discovered by the Mexican people, discovered in the
sense of evaluation, in the sense of acceptance, in the sense
of gladness. The present-day intellectuals of Mexico, if they
are distinguished by any one thing, are distinguished by
their appreciation of the Indian as a human being, by their
willingness to identify their own future with him, by their
willingness to seek in him the strength out of which a people
may be built. It seems to them, and I think rightly so, that

the Indians are the rock upon which the future civilization and culture of Mexico has to be built. This discovery of a race denied and suppressed, abused and humiliated for four centuries is a revolution with consequences that are greater than any material gains that may be attributed to the upheaval. It is of a nature to change the very fibre of social, political and cultural existence. The most important factor in this change is that it makes for a cultural pluralism, that it sets limits to the right of the government, in the name of nationalism, civilization, or any shibboleth, to destroy the age-old culture of the races of Mexico. It makes for tolerance of social pattern, for tolerance of belief and practice, custom and way of life. It makes education mean the giving back of a common instrumentality as a means of bringing out what the various racial and cultural groups have to offer, rather than the supplanting of the various cultures with a common norm.

Coincident with this change, in fact part of it, has been the discovery of the significance of the country as against the city. No proper evaluation of Mexican history, or of Mexican politics or economics can be had without appreciation of the fact that the attitude of governments, publicists and scholars was dominated by the neglect of and indifference to the country and the over-emphasis of the city. In this matter there is still a long way to go, but more than ever before the country as a whole (especially the rural part) has crept into the consciousness of the people who manage and control, direct and shape, public policy in Mexico. The country, with its sharply different culture, with its great variety of life, with its poverty and needs, has at last become a matter of concern to the government in a way hitherto unknown. This discovery of the country means the transition from a colonial to a national state. Mexico is becoming a nation to the extent that the whole of the country is embraced in the political conscience of its governing groups.

Until now, Mexico City was related to the country as a foreign government to a colony. Mexico has discovered itself. Soto y Gama has summarized the Revolution by saying:

Our revolution has been like an earthquake, a cataclysm that has shaken all of our social classes. I have called it an earthquake. And what happens during an earthquake? The houses fall down, public order is destroyed, the churches crumble to the ground; and here I will repeat what a poor Indian said after the earthquake in Oaxaca . . . "Todos lo hemos perdido, menos la santita." [We have lost everything except the little saint.] And so with us. We have lost everything except the conquests of the revolution.

PART THREE

PEACE

CHAPTER 16

LAND PROBLEMS OF PLANTATION
AND VILLAGE

UNHERALDED and unguided, the Revolution, like a cyclone, has shaken every part of the Mexican social structure to its roots, and yet its lasting effect will be measured by the changes it works in the land system. Its other consequences, and they have been numerous and profound, are incidental. The destruction of the old ruling class, the weakening of the Church, the awakening of nationalism, the emergence of racial consciousness, the rising power of labor, the abolition of peonage, the widening base of the government—with the peasant and the city laborer added as supports for social and political power—all of these are by-products whose meaning will, in the long run, be determined by the altered social structure that a change in the land system involves. The impact of the movement upon the Mexican *hacienda* will be the measure of the Revolution.

The Mexican *hacienda* has been the most characteristic, as well as the most unyielding, of the institutions implanted by the Spanish Conquest. Regardless of the fact that the original *encomienda* was meant to be a temporary institution and that the first land grants were made with an eye to the resident Indian population rather than to the area involved, in time the *latifundia*, not infrequently equal to a small European principality, with stone fences running mile after mile as far as the eye could see, with a *casco* (big house) in the center, a sort of castle, surrounded by a high wall, with the miserable huts of hundreds of peons set about it, became, and has in many places remained, the chief feature of the landscape and the root of the political, social and economic structure of Mexico.

The plantation with its *patrón* and *peones*, with the *capataz* (foreman) between, the *capataz*—who remained a Spaniard even if the *patrón* had become a Mexican—with the *capataz* on the place, even if the *patrón* lived in Paris—riding a spirited horse, a pistol at his belt, a whip in his hand, acting as administrator, as judge, as mighty lord over a *peon* population which was tied to the soil by debts it could not pay, by the tradition of slavery, by affection for the only home it knew—this plantation resting upon force, a direct and immediate outcome of the Conquest, the most obvious and visible by-product of the Conquest, has been the dominant feature of the Mexican scene.

While the word "slavery" has a technical significance that does not apply as a description of the position of the rural population that lived and worked upon the plantations in 1910, the relationship of the laborer to the plantation owner was so nearly like slavery that it is difficult to find another word that fits the situation quite so well. The word "peonage" is an inadequate substitute. All of the plantation laborer's life was imbedded in a web of rules, regulations, prerogatives and laws with which the plantation was endowed. The peon was born on the plantation and died on it, and from his birth to his death all of his activities fell within the sphere of his master's dominion. He was born into debt because the children inherited their parents' obligations. He acquired a debt in his own right at baptism because the cost of the *fiesta* it occasioned was advanced by the *hacendado*, and money was borrowed for the priest, for the *aguardiente*. His first clothes—made from white *manta*—were purchased from the plantation store, the *tienda de raya*, against his future wage. When he was old enough to marry, money for the festivities was borrowed from the plantation owner; when children were born, the same process led to the same end—further debt. The religious holidays were celebrated with borrowed money, sickness was marked by dependence upon the *patrón* for the payment of such medication as was to be had; and when the peon died he was buried with such honor, drink, prayer and festivity as money borrowed from the same source made possible.

The wage received—a nominal wage that ranged for a hundred years between 25 and 33 1/2 centavos—was largely paid in kind from the *tienda de raya*, and it was only on the occasional days of *fiesta* that some little money was available. The plantation offered the only place where a hut could be built, the only land where a few animals could be kept, it provided whatever church existed, it dispensed the only justice the peon knew, and gave the only protection he had. The peon could not leave, because he had no place to go. There were states like Chiapas and Tabasco, and even the state of Mexico, where the peon could find a change of master only by finding a purchaser, that is, by finding some one who would take over his debt. It was in this way that the first labor for the railroads was gathered; Otherwise, the escaping peon was brought back forcibly. Rebellion or dissidence was met by the stern, personal justice of the *capataz* who, in addition to his jail, had his whipping post and his gun; and if those failed him, there was always the forced *leva*—the truculent peon could always be dragged off into the army and exiled to distant lands. The plantation governed the lives of its peons; it also dominated and circumscribed the villages on its outskirts as well as those villages which were cramped within its confines, crowded on every side to the very church door. The *hacienda* of La Gavilla for instance had 17 villages within its boundaries, not counting the peons living as *acasillados* (resident laborers).

The plantation was Mexico. It paid few taxes. It built no roads. It imported nothing from the outside, and exported next-to-nothing. It made no effort to improve the tillage, the tools, the crops or the lives of its dependents. It was not an economic institution, it was a political one. It was not a business enterprise that had been built up by purchase and capital saving, it was the fruit of the Conquest, the result of theft, robbery and murder, of age-long conflict with the neighboring villages. It was a family tradition, a family heritage passed on from century to century, unprogressive, a dead weight upon the economic life of the country. It lived on rentals, by indirect tillage, by share-cropping, by leaving the risk of planting to be borne by the peon. This institution maintained itself by armed force, by tradition, by inertia, and by a tariff keeping the price of corn, wheat and beans high against a falling market in other parts of the world.

This plantation system maintained itself for centuries. In fact, with the centuries it had increased in size, in extent, in power. It grew powerful as the village grew weak; it grew large as the village grew small. During the colonial régime the Spanish Crown and the Church both acted as a protection to the village, an ineffective one, it is true, but still a protection against the insatiable greed for more land. But in the course of the centuries the tide went against the village. With the passing of the Spanish Crown even these insignificant restraints disappeared, and the attack upon the villages became more persistent, more successful, especially after the constitution of 1857 and the laws of 1863. From that time, the village had all against it: the power of the *hacienda*, the law of the state, and, of equal importance, the point of view of those in responsible office. It was actually believed that the communal land of the villages should be destroyed. Lands belonging to them in fact, even if not in law, were given away rapidly to people of wealth—the more wealth the better, for then, the theory went, the development of the country would follow more rapidly.

During the hundred years since the independence, the other institutions implanted by Spain had either been weakened or destroyed, but not so the plantation system. The Spanish Crown and its agencies had been displaced by the independence, the Spaniard had been replaced in power by the *criollo* and later by the *mestizo*, the Spanish race itself had been largely submerged. The Church had suffered its first serious blow when the Society of Jesus was expelled in 1767 and later had been materially changed as an institution under the impact of the constitution of 1857, the Three Years' War, and the French invasion.

But at each of these steps the *hacienda* gained in power and strength. The lands of the Society of Jesus added to the power of the plantation. The disappearance of the power of the Crown and its restraining influences left unchecked the increase of the plantation, the lands of the Church enlarged it and added new principalities to old ones, and under the Díaz régime the attack upon the villages, combined with the rapid and frequently fradulent alienation of the national and even private lands of little owners who could not defend themselves, still further extended it.

So insistent, so ingrained had the plantation system proved to be that all the influence which might have been assumed to weaken went to strengthen it. The liberalism of the independence, the radicalism of the struggle against the Church, and even the individualism of the Díaz régime, all served to increase the hold of this feudal institution upon the country, an interesting illustration of the utilization by an institution of changing ideas and forces for its own ends. In this instance, the ends, conscious or unconscious, were the destruction of the free villages of Mexico, the absorption of their lands, the reduction of the Indians to peonage, the wiping out of the village commune. It was a natural tendency —the village and the plantation cannot live in peace side by side. If Mexican history teaches anything at all, it teaches that lesson. As long as possible the plantation destroyed with increasing effectiveness the communities of Indians and *mestizos* and their way of life. And now after twenty-three years of revolution the battle is still on, with the plantation defeated on the battlefield, but not destroyed.

As the Díaz régime drew to a close the plantation system was at its height. Never, in the history of Mexico, had the *hacienda* been so powerful, embraced so large a part of the area of the Republic, contained so large a proportion of the inhabited communities or so large a share of the rural population, seemingly immune to those changes which were affecting other Mexican institutions.

In 1910, the plantation system, had the greater part of the lands and the vast majority of all the populated places confined within its boundaries. In most of the states, only a fraction of the rural population had any land at all. So unevenly was the land distributed that two per cent of the country's rural properties included nearly all of the area in private hands. In fact, in 1923, even after thirteen years of revolution, as few as 2,682 owners out of a rural population of approximately eleven million, owned 50.1 per cent of all lands in private hands. Of these, 115 of the largest held nearly a fourth of all the private lands of the country, and this is an understatement, because it does not include the many instances of ownership by the same individual of properties in different states.

It should always be remembered that the plantation system was most fully developed in the states north and south of the Central Plateau within which Mexico City is located. In 1910 the plantation held 81 per cent of all the inhabited communities in Mexico. The states that had best succeeded in destroying the free Indian villages and in reducing the population to peonage were as follows: Aguascalientes had located upon plantations 65.8 per cent of all the rural population; Chiapas, 59.7; Coahuila, 57.8; Colima, 57.8; Durango, 66.0; Guanajuato, 84.3; Jalisco, 65.5; Michoacán, 60.1; Nayarit, 63.2; Nuevo León, 60.0; Querétaro, 64.0; San Luis Potosí, 81.8; Sinaloa, 73.4; Tamaulipas, 74.6; Zacatecas, 76.1. The states surrounding the valley of Mexico show a much greater preponderance of the Indian village and a much less direct control by the plantation over the Indian community. In Hidalgo only 20.7 per cent of the rural population lived on plantations, in Morelos, only 23.7, in Mexico, 16.8, in Oaxaca, 14.5, in Puebla, 20.1, in Tlaxcala, 32.,2 in Vera Cruz, 24.0, in the Federal district, 6.9. Beyond the confines of the Valley of Mexico the plantation had absorbed both the lands and the communities, while in the more mountainous regions that surround the Plateau of Mexico City the plantation had largely succeeded in absorbing the lands even if the villages escaped as thorough reduction to peonage as characterized the rest of the country. The attacks on the villages by the plantation during the Díaz régime were most insistent in the regions where the villages persisted, and these villages ultimately made the social revolution in self-defense, rather than become reduced to the same condition as the Indians in other parts of Mexico where the plantation had been more successful.

How predominant the plantation was at the end of the Díaz régime, can be seen by the proportion of communities that were confined within plantations at that time. It should always be remembered that a plantation community is a population group completely dependent upon the owner of the *hacienda*. It has no municipal government. Every time a village was reduced to a plantation group it lost its personality, its autonomy. A statement, therefore, of the number of villages and the proportion of the total that were located upon plantations in any state indicates the extent to which the plantation had absorbed not merely the land but the self-directing life of the communities, and had succeeded in destroying their *mores*. It was essentially a difference between slavery and freedom. The village that survived, even with its lands gone, was essentially free when compared to the villages that had lost both lands and village organization.

The meaning of this may best be seen in the statement that in six states more than 90 per cent of all inhabited places were located on plantations. These states were Guanjuato, Michoacán, Jalisco, Zacatecas, Nayarit and Sinaloa. In the states of Guanajuato, Jalisco and Michoacán the plantation held, respectively, 94.9, 93.3 and 92.1 per cent of all rural communities. For all practical purposes the village community had ceased to exist in those important agricultural states. In eight more states the plantation held more than 80 per cent of the rural communities. These eight states were Querétaro, San Luis Potosí, Coahuila, Aguascalientes, Baja California, Tabasco, Nuevo León and Chiapas. In other words, one half of the states of the Republic had 80 per cent of all their rural communities located inside plantations and deprived of any municipal or local initiative. Also, it may be repeated, these states were largely outside the immediate surroundings of Mexico City.

At the end of the Díaz régime, therefore, the rural population had lost all self-direction in nearly half of the states. In only seven states did the free villages outnumber the plantation villages, and all of these were in the more mountainous part of the Republic surrounding the Valley of Mexico. These states were Oaxaca, Mexico, Hidalgo, Puebla, Vera Cruz, Morelos and Guerrero. The spoilation of the remaining villages was carried on without scruple during the Díaz régime. All the powers of government seemed bent to destroy finally the last vestige of the older Indian *mores*, to destroy the village and, with it, the power of the Indian community to carry on the older way of life.

One other point should be noted in the description of rural Mexico before the Revolution. The plantation communities were generally smaller than the remaining free villages. The 56,825 plantation communities had an average population of 97, the 12,724 free villages had an average size of 541. In other words, the plantation in destroying the free village tended to reduce it in size, to scatter its population into smaller groups, to subject it to more direct control, and to make it, both economically and politically, a less independent and capable group.

We may summarize by saying that at the end of the Díaz régime there were fewer than 13,000 free villages in Mexico as against nearly 57,000 plantation communities; that the plantation community was less than one-fifth the size of the free village; that the free villages had best survived in mountainous regions surrounding Mexico City; that the plantation communities were more frequently found in the less mountainous states; that this system of reducing village to plantation had gone on for four hundred years; that under the Diaz régime it was being pushed with greater energy than ever before; and that it was against the villages in states surrounding the Valley of Mexico where the free community had best survived that the attack was most evident.

The end of the communal villages of Mexico seemed in sight as the Díaz régime was drawing to a close. Under the influence of a philosophy of capitalism, individualism, progress and development, every agency of the government seemed bent on destroying the remaining vestiges of a social and economic institution that had resisted the vicissitudes of four hundred years of conquest, oppression and revolution. At last the lands of the villages would be broken up, granted to individuals, absorbed by large estates; the communal heritage would disappear, and with it the conservatism of the rural community, the traditional pattern of life and culture would finally give way to the more modern, the more desirable system of large-scale private ownership, with large credits, efficient production, competent utilization. Mexican agriculture would cease being a way of life and would become an economic enterprise. The rural population, it was argued, would inevitably benefit by the change. Greater production would lead to greater wages; greater wages to a higher standard of living; a higher standard of living would induce foreign immigration; foreign immigration would change the racial composition of the country; a change in the racial composition of the country would, as a matter of course, bring civilization in its train, for, as was believed and preached from all high and authoritative sources, the difficulty with Mexico was the Indian. He was inferior, of poorer quality, he had not the stuff in him for progress. If he had been liquidated—and the destruction of his communal land was the first step in that direction—Mexico would have made the first step towards civilization in the true sense of the word. That the history of the Mexican plantation gave no reason to believe any of the assumptions upon which the destruction of the village was postulated made no difference. The essence of a doctrine is frequently uninfluenced by the contrary facts, and in this instance it was blind to the patent shortcomings of the Mexican *hacienda*. That the plantation was not an efficient economic unit; that it was not progressive; that it had lasted for centuries by the direct exploitation of the Indians and peons living on it; that it had shifted its share of taxation to the tariffs, to the towns, to the merchants; that it introduced no new machinery, built no roads, developed no new crops, lived by a system of rentals and subrentals; that its owners were absentee owners, occupying their time in play and pleasure in European capitals; that it had kept Mexico feudal and unprogressive, was beside the point.

The attitude of the statesman was turned to another view —a rapid capitalistic development through the destruction of the remaining vestiges of communal land, and with it, the villages, and with the villages, the Indians themselves. The theory reckoned without the Indians. When the time came the remaining villages destroyed the program of the Díaz government and repudiated the theory of racial and social inferiority upon which it rested. They rose in rebellion and saved themselves from the fate of becoming peons upon the large plantations—peons without a voice, without land, without a community, without hope—with nothing but a burden of debt from the cradle to the grave. Rather than accept that fate the villages (each one for itself), without much concert or broad general philosophy, took their stand and fought their battle and in the process shifted the structure of the Mexican nation from its original base. It should be remembered that it was in the states of Morelos, Guerrero, Oaxaca, Puebla, Hidalgo, Tlaxcala, Mexico, Veracruz, in the states where the village survived as an important population group, that the rural revolution was fought, and the agrarian program developed.

CHAPTER 17

THE AGRARIAN PROCESS

IN THE early days of the Revolution, while Madero was still officially out of power, when the old system had still all the appearances of stability, when nothing had happened except that Díaz had resigned, and when no one seriously thought of a social program, small armed groups of Indians and peons took over by force the properties of a number of large *haciendas* and plowed and planted them guarded by a gun. These Indian and *mestizo* peasants were peons become soldiers who, for the moment had solved for themselves, the agrarian problem, or perhaps initiated its forcible solution by planting, plowing, tilling and harvesting the lands that lay within their reach and to which they had no legal title.

This movement was noticeable in widely scattered areas of the country, especially in Chihuahua, Durango, Jalisco and Hidalgo. It was most active in the states of Puebla and Morelos, where later the Zapatista movement was to acquire such force. Much of this early movement was a process of vindication of injuries recently suffered under the shadow of the Díaz tyranny. Villages moved back upon the land they had so recently lost. In other instances it was more indirect— it was an extension of the right to plant and till, harvest and use the land that the village needed but to which it had no access. It is thus that the Revolution began as a movement to recover land. In the cities the intellectuals and the leaders described these acts as banditry, as it was in terms of the legal situation of that time. But the meaning of these activities was clear. The Revolution, unless it succeeded in suffocating the demand for land, would ultimately become chiefly conspicuous by satisfying this land hunger. The attempt to stop the agrarian movement was made by the early Revolution. Madero, Huerta and Carranza all tried to stem the tide and failed, because the peasants were prepared to defend their right to land to the bitter end, and did so over a period of years.

This activity on the part of individual villages in various parts of the country was the source of the Mexican agrarian revolution. In the south, Zapata, as early as 1911, and every year thereafter until he was killed in 1919, likewise reoccupied land, but on a more systematic scale. In addition, military commanders in various places, as a means of securing the coöperation of the common people in certain localities, gave them lands or sanction to retain lands which they already occupied. There was, therefore, an agrarian movement before there was an agrarian law. In fact there would probably have been no agrarian law at all if the agrarian revolution and expropriation had not already occurred. Although the Carranza decree of January 6, 1915 is generally credited with being the first agrarian law of the Revolution, there was at least one state law in addition to the proclamation of Zapata that was issued before that.

In October, 1913, Pastor Rouaix, provisional governor of the state of Durango, published what is apparently the first land law under revolutionary auspices. It is to be remembered that 1913 was a bloody year in the history of Mexico. Madero had recently been murdered, the country was torn by internal strife, and a number of military chiefs were struggling for dominance. The law, therefore, represents a political measure of the Revolution, and is so recognized by Pastor Rouaix. The introduction to this document says,

The fact that the principal cause of discontent among the people in our State which forced them to take up arms in 1910, is the absolute lack of private property; because the absence of small land holding leaves to our rural classes no other means of subsistence for the present nor hope for the future except the prospect of serving as peons on the *haciendas* of the large land owners who monopolized the soil of our State. . . . In view of the fact that the villages of the State have been reduced to misery because the lands that they had during the colonial period have been absorbed to increase the area of the large estates, especially during the last dictatorship, so that the inhabitants of the State have lost their economic, political and social independence by being reduced from independent citizens to become servants without the power of the government to interfere even by means of education because the place they are living in has become private property, therefore. . . .

It was with this preamble that the first land law in Mexico after the 1910 Revolution got under way.

The preamble is striking and emphatic. The law is limited and conservative. Such paradox seems to have been true all through the Mexican Revolution. The preambles, the speeches, the declarations, were broad and sweeping—the practical means to bring an end to the evils complained of have been halting, roundabout and hesitant. With such a declaration one assumes that the Revolutionary government would proceed to an expropriation of the land, or at least a part of the land, and its free distribution to the landless, who have been described as robbed and in misery, as servants rather than citizens. Not at all. The law merely gives each village the right to ask for land. It must agree to pay for the same in ten years, and for the cost of surveying as well. The value of the land is to be determined by a special board of assessors upon which both the villagers and the land owners are to be represented. The owner is to receive both the value and the interest, in installments, over a period of ten years. And the landowner must have left at least 5,000 hectares (12,500 acres) after the expropriation.

Conservative as this may have been, incomplete and impractical in view of the absolute poverty of the peons for whom the land was intended, it was still important as the first of the land laws. The author of this law, Pastor Rouaix, later played an important rôle in framing Article 27 of the Federal Constitution, and when Carranza became president,

GENERAL PLUTARCO ELÍAS CALLES

served as Secretary of Agriculture and became responsible in part for the halting manner in which the agrarian laws were applied.

It was not until nearly two years later, in January, 1915, that a general law was issued. This law, let us repeat, was issued by Carranza after he had been driven to Veracruz by Pancho Villa and Zapata. It was a counsel of despair.

The decree of January 6, 1915, has become the legal basis for the distribution of land. It is significant not only as a stimulus to, but also a limitation upon, the agrarian movement. Unfortunately, it made no attempt to deal with the essentially complicated agrarian problem as a whole, and has served to impede its comprehensive consideration. In general terms, the agrarian problem in Mexico had two different types of communities to deal with, the village communities partially or completely deprived of their lands to a point where their economic position had become untenable, and the communities that during the four centuries since the Conquest had been reduced to resident plantation laborers. The reform of Carranza made no attempt to deal with the plantation community and was no attack upon the plantation system. The *haciendas* and their resident laborers were outside the provisions of the law. In fact, only within the last few months the Secretary of Agriculture remarked that "the law of 1915 did not contemplate the dismemberment of the large estates."

This differentiation in the population, implicit in the decree of 1915, has since become a conscious rule but slightly modified in 1930, and has left something like half the rural population beyond the reach of the law. Even for the villages, the law of 1915 concentrated upon the restitution of land of which they had been illegally deprived, and for which they could produce proof. Here, alone, did the law operate as a matter of right. To villages without title, a very real factor among an indigenous and illiterate population that had no

Western notions of private property, land could be given only upon proof of necessity. At its very beginning the agrarian movement was thus hampered by a series of limitations that have made its application difficult, cumbersome, and subject to unending legal manipulations, chicanery, bribery and delay. Important as this decree has been in the history of the Revolution, its conservative and partial character has seriously delayed and delays at present a consummation of the agrarian aspect of the Revolution.

The National Agrarian Commission, created by the law, with a cumbersome system of committees, each of which is subject to the kind of pressure, official and unofficial, honest and dishonest, to which administrative machinery in Mexico has always been subject, further delays the execution of the program. The complicated law has made the process of land distribution a matter for lawyers to argue over, which they have done for years without end. The result is that now, seventeen years after the decree was first issued, the agrarian problem is still largely to be solved. If the land program has been merely for the purpose of temporary pacification, of just giving the more rebellious communities enough land to keep them quiet for the time, then perhaps the law has justified itself. But no member of the Mexican revolutionary family would admit that to have been the purpose of the Revolution, and if it was not, then the agrarian program requires a broader base than it has even at present, and a more active and more honest administration than it has had to date.

Even in its narrow scope, the Carranza decree found but little application till after his régime was overthrown in 1920. This law, among other things, gave the state governors the right to make provisional grants to villages to be later confirmed by the national government. Within a year, in September, 1916, Carranza took this power from the local authorities, practically bringing land distribution to a standstill. Not until four years later (November, 1920), was the original power of the governors to grant provisional holdings restored. During the years, therefore, when the agitation among the peasants was most vocal and insistent, when the country was torn in conflict over this issue, land distribution was prevented by the law's very authors who had converted a popular and unorganized urge into a national movement resting upon a legal base.

In addition to this change of heart on the part of Carranza, the law of 1915 made restitution the basis of a solution of the land problem. This alone reveals that the reformers had no notion of destroying the *latifundia* or of establishing the principle of a right to land either by individuals or villages. Restitution made implicit the assumption that only those villages that could prove previous title and unjustified deprivation of their lands were entitled to legal recourse. In fact, as we have already indicated, such proof was frequently difficult, if not impossible. The little Indian and *mestizo* villages had neither the tradition, nor a sense of the importance, or even a knowledge of the nature of legal title. With minor exceptions, possession and use were for them the only basis of ownership. It was not until December, 1920, that the provision for restitution was modified to the point of declaring that every demand for restitution which could not easily be satisfied might be converted into a demand for donation. After five years of trial, therefore, the law moved somewhat nearer to a recognition of a right to land rather than of a right to have legal justice done only if proof of despoliation could first be established.

Another serious limitation was the declaration that only villages which had *categoría política* (political status) had a right under the law. It enumerated such villages as *pueblos*, *rancherías, congregaciones* and *comunidades*. These names did not represent a definite type of community. There are states where these names are rare and almost nonexistent, and a classification of the type of inhabited places reveals over a hundred different characterizations. A large number of communities, having equal or even greater population, having similar origin, and only by accident having a different classification, were denied the benefit of the law. The majority of communities in Mexico do not have *categoría política* and as long as the right to land was limited to this classification, land distribution was sharply confined. Individual communities frequently demanded from the state legislatures a changed classification, and when they got it, the courts often interfered on the grounds that it was an improper extension of that right in view of its consequences. This limitation in the early law became a serious impediment to the development of the agrarian movement, and was a source of wide and persistent conflict.

The handicap of *categoría política* was not removed till April, 1927. After twelve years of internal conflict the law was broadened to include villages in general rather than certain very specific and comparatively few villages in the country. The law of 1927 declared instead that all villages having twenty-five agrarian families were qualified to ask for land. This, in itself, is a serious limitation (it has since been changed to twenty families) but the law shifted the basis of land distribution from what it was in the beginning, the rectification of an injustice, to the recognition of a right to land as a matter of social policy. It excluded, however, the *acasillados* (resident plantation laborers) from the prerogative, and thus, in effect, continued the older limitation.

Finally, the law of 1915 made it possible for the landowner to resort to the courts against the actions of all the officials involved in the process of land distribution; even the final action of the president could be held up by an *amparo* (injunction) so that a definite land restitution by the president became subject to review by the courts. Given the poverty of the villages, and the innumerable legal requisites of the law, land reform became a long-drawn-out matter, frequently lasting for years, with continued and persistent friction. The agrarian movement was planned as something that could be carried out within the existing legal framework, despite the social revolution that had been fought to change it. It was not until February, 1932, that the Mexican Supreme Court declared itself incompetent to intervene by injunction (*amparo*) in the distribution of land under the *ejido* legislation.

This step, taken seventeen years after the Carranza decree was issued, finally removed the last serious obstacle to the process of land distribution. In the meantime, the existence of this obstacle had delayed the movement and made the Revolution less effective than it would otherwise have been. It came, too, at a time when the original impulse had quieted down. In effect, it simplified the legal problem and made land distribution much less cumbersome, much less expensive, and much more rapid. Legally, the proposal to break up the large estates and to satisfy the needs of the villages for land is better today than it has been so far. But, politically, there is much less pressure to carry the program forward. It would, however, be a mistake to assume that the process of land distribution is drawing to an end. It is clear from the evidence that unless the Mexican central government were to declare itself opposed to land distribution, a declaration that no Mexican government is likely to make for a considerable period, the process will continue as it has in the past, incidentally, in response to local pressure and in response to the local political belief of the governor of the state. It should be remembered that just as the original impulse has died down, so has the violent opposition to reform. There is now a wider sense of the political and social necessity for the program of land distribution. The younger political elements take it as a fact, a matter of course. It seems possible to argue that even without any further impact the agrarian reform will continue for another generation at least.

The process, as can be seen, has from the beginning gradually acquired a broader base. It has moved from a remedy to a right; it has moved from a limitation to a few villages possessing *categoría política* to the inclusion of all villages having a certain number of families, and finally, it has moved to a point where the courts have decided that they cannot interfere in the program of land distribution and have left the landowner the recourse of asking through the courts for compensation, but not for the return of his lands. The law as it stands at present, therefore, establishes a right to land by all villages (excepting cities, ports, mining towns, industrial and resident plantation communities) that have twenty agrarian families. The right to land within each village is limited to certain persons. These must not be professionals, governmental employees, or have an amount of land equal to what they would be entitled to under the law. Those entitled to land are members of communities who have resided there for one year, have no other means of support, and are agriculturists by profession. The men must be over eighteen years of age, the women must be widows with children, and there are certain other limitations that need not be discussed.

We have said enough about the law to indicate that the demand for twenty agrarian families means that a village having a hundred people may still be outside its reach. There is, therefore, even for free villages, no general right to land. The Revolution, it must be clear, has not to date recognized the right of the Mexican peon, Indian, or landless peasant to land, except under certain specified limitations.

The census of 1921 reveals that the great majority of the rural villages were and are excluded from the right to benefit by land distribution. In 1921 there were 46,381 resident plantation communities and 13,388 agricultural villages. The average population of the resident plantation community was 84 people, the average size of the rural village was 495. Taking these figures as they stand and leaving the present

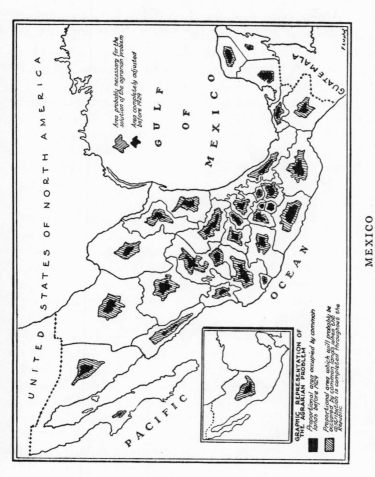

MEXICO

Map showing lands distributed and those still required to satisfy present agrarian laws.

law with its denial to resident plantation communities of a right to land, and the agrarian Revolution, even if it affected all of the other villages, would still leave the greater part of the rural communities outside of the benefit of the law. The law automatically excludes over 46,000 out of a possible 60,000 rural communities.

We may look at this program from another angle and consider the material recently collected by the National Agrarian Commission. There are, according to this study (disregarding the differentiation between the resident plantation community and the free village) 35,595 communities that have fewer than twenty families. More than half of the communities in Mexico, therefore, are excluded from the benefit of the law. Twelve states have more than a thousand communities, each with fewer than twenty agrarian families. It is useless to talk of a solution of the Mexican agrarian problem until these small communities are taken care of. And it has come to a point where plantation owners are burning down the villages that have more than that 'number of families—as I can witness from personal knowledge in the state of Nayarit, and as is testified by the National Agrarian Commission when it states in a recent publication,

The National Agrarian Commission has records of numerous cases where the proprietors have ordered the burning of houses of peasants and their forcible ejection from the estates. This has been especially true in recent years.

Clearly enough, half of the problem remains untouched.

We may now consider the other half of the problem. The National Agrarian Commission estimates that to June 30, 1930 only 8,995 of the 25,854 villages with more than 20 agrarian families made any attempt to take advantage of this right. Fewer than 35 per cent, therefore, of the villages that come within the law have so far made use of the privilege. In part, this is because villages which fulfill the requisite of the law as to size do not do so for other reasons, or are ignorant, intimidated, or discouraged from seeking to affect the neighboring plantation. The larger villages alone seem to have had the courage to apply for land.

If we divide the 25,854 communities which come within the present law into three groups having from 20 to 125 families, from 126 to 250 families, and from 251 to 500 families each, then 45.9 per cent of the last, 34 per cent of the second, and 10 per cent of the first group have asked for land. As things stand, the more important rural community with a population of 1,000 or more has most frequently benefited from the law. The smaller the community the less benefit it has received from the Revolution. In those states where the plantation system was most fully developed, like Guanajuato, Jalisco, Michoacán and Querétaro, the population groups are small, land hunger is at its height, and the Revolution has been least effective. Up to the end of June, 1930, only 3,877 villages had received definite land grants.

At the present rate of land distribution to approximately six hundred villages a year, it will require some ten years to provide land even for one-fourth of those communities that are entitled to it under the law. Ten years from now the agrarian problem will remain largely unsolved, in large areas the plantation system will be left intact, thousands of villages that still come within the law will be without land, and the position of the greater part of the rural population will not have materially improved as a result of the Revolution.

The present program of the agrarian movement is, therefore, clearly insufficient. When, and if, completed within another generation there will remain the 35,000 population groups with 100 or fewer souls who will not have received land. In addition, there will be, according to the estimates of the National Agrarian Commission, 12,000 out of 25,000 villages that come within the law, but that, because of stringent interpretation, will have been excluded from receiving any land.

This development, unlooked for as it is, becomes still more important from the increasing division of the country into two types of rural organization that will follow the application of the law in its present form. In the states where the villages existed the law will have had its most important effects. The villages in the states of Guerrero, Morelos, Oaxaca, Veracruz, Puebla, Tlaxcala, Mexico, and Hidalgo will have received the most benefit. In these states the plantation will have largely disappeared, the villages will have increased in power and in the size of their land holdings, in well-being, in the possession of political influence, and in the freedom and coherence that come from common possession and a sense of security.

In the rest of the country where the plantation dominated in the past, and where the majority of the population groups are too small to come within the present law, the villages will have gained little or nothing from the upheaval. They will be as they are now and as they were in 1910—subject to the capricious will of the landowner. How important this matter is may be seen from the thirteen states, nearly half of all the states in the Republic, each of which have more than a thousand communities that fall outside the law because they have less than twenty agrarian families in one place. When one recalls that it has long been a practice of the *haciendas* to scatter their resident populations in small groups, in *rancherías*, for the purpose of preventing large groupings, which, under Spanish rule would have given communities above a certain size the status of villages with their own *fundo legal*, it becomes clear that the present law is favoring the plantation in the continuance of an age-old practice and punishing the rural population upon the *haciendas*. This situation explains the burning of villages that still takes place in states such as Nayarit.

Of the thirteen states, Jalisco has 5,136 such resident groups, Michoacán and Chiapas, nearly three thousand each (the first, 2,927, the second, 2,948); Nuevo León and Ta-maulipas a little more than 2,000 each (the first, 2,188, the second, 2,009). The others—Baja California, Chihuahua, Guanajuato, Sinaloa, Sonora, Tabasco, Veracruz and Zacatecas—each have more than 1,000 population groups that fall outside of the law, which will be left without any land grants, and which, if the present system of land distribution continues, will be left without any direct benefit from the Revolution. In these thirteen states there are 25,-475 villages that retain a position comparable to that before the Revolution. It is to be noted that, with the exception of Veracruz, not a single one of the states surrounding the Valley of Mexico has as many as a thousand communities beyond possible benefit of the agrarian law. It is, I am convinced, idle to assume that Mexico can look forward to internal peace with such an inequitable and purely artificial system of land distribution among the rural communities, especially as there is such wide variation between the states. No such sectionalism can be conducive to internal peace—at least not in terms of Mexican history.

This impression of the inadequateness of land distribution to date is strengthened by analyzing the recent material compiled by the National Agrarian Commission. Up to 1930, out of a total of 61,566 communities in the country, only 3,877 have been definitely granted their lands; 1,176 had their petitions denied. The villages benefited have received a total of 6,743,904 hectares or 3.4 per cent of the area of the Republic, taken from 6,993 properties, which were affected to the extent of 13.4 per cent of their total area. As things stand at present, and if the general movement now under way continues at approximately the same rate of land distribution per individual until all of the approximately 13,-000 villages that the commission estimates will ultimately benefit by the law have been given their lands, an additional 9,400,996 hectares will have been distributed. Unless the law is changed to include the communities not now allowed to benefit by the land distribution, the movement will, therefore, have been satisfied by the distribution of 16,144,900 hectares, or 8.2 per cent of the area of the Republic.

To the end of June 30, 1930, land had been given to 773,-819 families. At the present rate of land distribution to the villages within the scope of the law, when 1,209,824 more families will receive *ejidos*, the total number when completed will embrace fewer than 2,000,000 families. The large number of families in so small a number of villages is accounted for by noting that the larger communities are securing land.

The 6,993 plantations so far affected had a total of 44,696,-417 hectares divided into tillage, bush, pasture, and mountain. The villages received 19 per cent of the tillage, 36.7 per cent of the bush, 12.6 per cent of the pasture, and 5.1 per cent of the mountain. By every count, therefore, the agrarian movement has to date given land only to a small percentage of the inhabited places of the Republic, and has left to the plantations, even where affected, the greater part of their lands, both as to quantity and quality. The meagerness of the agrarian policy is further revealed by a view of the area given to each family. Although the average, up to 1930, was 8.8 hectares, this average is misleading. In states like Chihuahua and Zacatecas, Sonora and Sinaloa, where land distribution has been unimportant, the average has been high because of poor land. In Chihuahua it was 40 hectares, in Zacatecas 20, in Sonora 26, in Sinaloa 21.

On the other hand, in the states where land distribution has been more general, the average given to each family was much lower—too low in fact for any basis of livelihood. In the Federal District the area per family was less than one and one-half hectares, in Mexico and Tlaxacala less than three hectares, in Oaxaca less than five hectares, and in Veracruz a little over five hectares. In fact, the land given away has been so niggardly in many places and the quality of the land has frequently been so poor that much complaint and criticism have arisen even from official sources. On July 2, 1931, the Secretary of Agriculture made the following statement:

Experience derived from the activities of the National Agrarian Commission indicates that many of the villages that have received *ejidos* have not solved their economic problem because the land given to them does not justify the effort put into it. The purpose of the agrarian movement to satisfy the needs of the peasant is defeated, because the peasant does not achieve a better economic position and becomes subject in addition to losses and risks. The agrarian authorities should attempt within each region to give the villages lands of the first grade, as is the purpose of the law. If possible, these should be irrigated lands, so as to place the village beyond the risks of cultivation. The area granted should be large enough. There are many cases in which the land awarded to a family is not sufficient to cover its needs. The parcel of land ought to be carefully estimated, and not so small as to be ridiculous in view of the purposes of the movement.

The agrarian Revolution, it is true, has expressed itself in other ways, and its effects are broader than would be indicated by a mere tabulation of the amount of land distributed or the number of villages benefited. Certainly, wages in the rural districts have increased; in some places they have more than doubled, and along the American border perhaps tripled, since 1910. But so have prices. On the whole the standard of living of the rural population has improved. It should be remembered that there are still places in Guerrero, Oaxaca, Hidalgo and other states where the traditional wage of 25 *centavos* persists.

More significant is the practical disappearance of the debt system. This change in the position of the plantation peon freed at one stroke approximately half of the rural population of Mexico. In importance it is comparable to our own abolition of slavery. It was, in some respects, more important in the Mexican scene than the abolition of slavery was in the

United States, because the Mexican plantation peon constituted a larger proportion of the total population than did our Negro at the time of the Civil War.

To the freeing of the peon from inherited debt should be added the abolition of the *tienda de raya*. It definitely improved the economic status of the plantation laborer. It gave him access to free and competitive markets, generally abolished payment in kind, especially in pulque, corn and candles, and freed him from the token coin with a limited circulation. The system of both token coin and payment in kind, as well as the *tienda de raya*, is still to be found, but it is confined to isolated places instead of being in general use as it was before 1910.

The Revolution has also given rise to an elaborate system of agricultural labor law. It would be over-estimating its importance, however, to assume that this law will have any large or immediate significance in governing the life of the agricultural laborer. Isolated cases of application can undoubtedly be found, but it is unlikely to have general applicability for a very long time to come. The reasons for the failure of law to find application involves the whole scheme of Mexican political and economic life. In so far as the plantation has escaped destruction it has conserved its influence. The *hacendado* who was able to preserve his land against the village is also able to prevent the enforcement of the law governing his resident plantation labor. Rather than have the labor law applied, it would probably be cheaper for the planter to lose some of his land. The enforcement of the law in all of its details would make the present economic organization of the *hacienda* untenable. The economy of the plantation system is not geared to operate with organized and protected agricultural labor, with a limitation of hours, accident insurance, profit sharing, collective bargaining, legal right to house and pasture, sickness and death benefits. The application of the labor law would as quickly force the liquidation of the plantation as would the application of the agrarian law, except that the Mexican peon is by tradition in the habit of working the land under communal ownership (the *ejido*), and is not accustomed to the management of a labor union, especially under isolated agricultural conditions. The first is possible; the second is not. In the long run it may provide a promise and a threat for the future—for the present it is largely a futile exercise in good intentions.

Even these details do not fully describe the consequences to the rural areas of the social upheaval in Mexico. One of the results of the Revolution has been to reverse the tendency of the free villages to disappear. This reflects itself first in the increase of non-plantation communities. Although the figures for the period 1921–1930 are not available, it is clear that the tendency that revealed itself between the years 1910–1921 has continued. In that period the free villages increased from 11,117 to 13,388. In 1910 the free village had an average population of 576, whereas the plantation had an average of only 97. In spite of the decline in population and in the number of communities between 1910 and 1921, the population in free villages had grown by nearly 150,000, but the plantation communities had declined in numbers as well as size. The plantation community had shrunk from 97 persons in 1910 to 84 in 1921. Even this is not a complete detailing of the situation. The law as embodied in the Constitution of 1917 gives the state legislatures the right to create free villages out of the resident plantation communities. Few of the states have taken general advantage of this power. Here and there during the last fifteen years individual villages have been raised to the status of *categoría política*, with a right to an expropriated *fundo legal* and later to *ejidos*. This was especially notable before 1927, when the *categoría política* was an essential in securing an *ejido*. The movement was not of great significance. The power, however, exists, and at least one state has taken advantage of it.

The tendency to make a free village out of a resident plantation community manifested itself early in the Revolution. As far back as 1913, when Pastor Rouaix, the provisional governor of Durango, passed the first agrarian law, he included in it a provision that

The government may erect new villages within the State in those places it judges to be convenient by taking [expropriating after valuation and the issuing of bonds payable with interest in ten years] 2,000 hectares, part of which land shall be set aside for the *Fundo Legal* of the new village.

This law was enforced within a month for the erection of the first village to be carved out of a *hacienda*. It was the first application of a law such as has been repeated many times since. The first village created under the legislation occupied the area around the railway station of San Gabriel. It was a railroad center and marketing community for many surrounding villages and was located within the confines of the *hacienda* San Gabriel. A hundred hectares were taken from this *hacienda* for the village proper, and the *ejidos* of the village were taken from the adjoining plantation of *La Tapona*. The possibility inherent in this constitutional prerogative may be seen from the recent law upon the matter of *fundo legal* in the state of Guerrero.

A plantation community located upon private property has no municipal rights and is liable to dispossession by the owner at his own whim. Workers living upon such a plantation are usually expected to pay a rental in kind, in work, or in money in addition to the labor which they regularly do for the landowner. This lack of legal tenure has made possible the forced removal of workers from place to place on the same plantation or tract.

To give the plantation laborer a sense of permanence has been, therefore, an objective of the Revolution. The undertaking has been carried out haphazardly by different state legislatures. Some inhabited places have been declared villages with a *fundo legal*, a municipal ground, a community with legal organization, and rights to ownership. How important this is in the life of the people is to be gathered from the capital investments and improvements they have made over years and generations. "They have built houses, constructed fences, dug wells, elevated fences of stone, planted fruit trees, bridged rivers and developed many other community services." The need or caprice of the landowner has frequently led him to destroy all of this capital investment of the inhabitants without compensation or recourse. To prevent this in the future, and to give stability at least to the larger plantation communities, the state of Guerrero, under Governor Castrejón, has declared every inhabited place in the state having more than thirty families (in 1921 there were 257 communities or plantations of over 100 people) a village with a right of each resident to his house, to the land upon which it is located, and to the community benefits that have been developed. The law itself falls within the general legislation based upon Article 27 of the Constitution of 1917, which makes it possible to expropriate private property for public utility. It does not, therefore, establish a new principle in law, but it does, through its general application, establish a new principle in fact. Every occupied place in Guerrero having more than thirty families is now a community with internal legal organization, a part of the municipal structure of the state. That this is not the last of this legislation and that it may be copied in other states is indicated by the official organ of the National Agrarian Commission when it says in referring to the law

It is to be hoped that the isolated action of one or another governor will serve as a stimulus to all so that at an early date not one Mexican will lack a home.

The Law of *Fundo Legal* in Guerrero was issued on April 4, 1930, and is known as Law No. 156. It provides that each inhabited place in the state having more than thirty families located upon private property can ask and receive for each family free from all costs an area equal to 2,500 square meters of land for a house and its surroundings. In addition, an equal amount is to be added for streets, school, plaza, market, etc. This property, received by the resident free of any charge, may not be alienated or transferred for any reason whatsoever. It may, however, be inherited. The abandonment of the house for over a year may lead to its transfer to another resident in need of a home, but this may be done only with the previous consent of the governor of the state. Payment to the owners of the land is provided according to the provision for compensation set up in Article 27 of the Federal Constitution of 1917. This, as is well known, includes tax valuation plus ten per cent. A special bond issue is provided for and the payment is to be made by lot over a period of twenty years.

The Revolution in the rural districts has also stimulated organization among the villages in certain states, making them factors in the political equilibrium of the Republic. It would be difficult from a social and political point of view to over-estimate the long-run influence of the organized *Ligas de Comunidades Agrarias* in the states of Veracruz and San Luis Potosí, and to a minor degree in other states. For the first time in Mexican history a successful organization of the peasant in the rural villages has been achieved. These leagues at their annual conventions bring together the isolated villages, with their own elected leaders, with a sense of power and of an armed militia, and have in the states of Veracruz and San Luis Potosí, at least, become factors of not merely local but national influence.

As a part of the agrarian revolution is to be added the legal right of the states to break up the large *haciendas* by imposing a limit to the area that any one individual may hold, forcing the sale of the rest. These rights delegated to the states by Article 27 of the Constitution of 1917 have been written into law in a number of states, but have found application in very few. Up to July, 1930, the six states of Guanajuato, Durango, Zacatecas, Michoacán, Tlaxcala and Nayarit had applied the law to the extent of breaking up a million hectares into parcels. The enforcement of this law has been negligible.

The *hacienda* has resisted dismemberment. If the large landowners had been willing and ready, voluntarily, to break up their own plantations, conditions in Mexico would have made it difficult. There was no one to fill the gap between the *hacendado* and the peon, who had no tools, no credit, and no personal ambition. The large estates could not have been dismembered by sale before the Revolution because there were no purchasers, not even immigrants in sufficiently large numbers and with sufficient capital, and there are, generally speaking, none today. The few small landowners who did exist could purchase but little additional land because they had difficulty in maintaining their own land, because credit was not available for them, and because they were forced to bear a greater measure of taxation than the large estates, for they, in proportion to their weakness, were more subject to all the handicaps of poor roads, distant markets and insecurity. The only way out, if these estates were to be dismembered, was a forceful break-up of the *haciendas* and their distribution by gifts of small parcels to the Indian village. If Mexico had had a large agricultural middle class, the agrarian reform would have taken a different direction. It had, however, only peons and villages of Indians, and they did not have the resources to purchase lands that were in the hands of the large estates. Escape from serfdom was possible only by a sudden break in the crust that encased them. State legislation for the forcible break-up of the large estates has failed. Expropriation seems the only possible method.

CHAPTER 18

FEUDALISM AND DEMOCRACY

I F WE review the history of the agrarian movement since 1915, we see clearly that the scene is set for the complete dismemberment of the plantation system, which, it is true, has not happened and possibly may not happen at present. But for the first time since the Spanish Conquest, the Mexican *hacienda* is on the defensive. For the first time in four hundred years the plantation system has lost its prestige and power at a time of social upheaval. Until now it has always gained during a time of crisis; at present it has lost, and it may never recover its hold. Certainly, from a legal point of view, the *hacienda* system is in very bad shape. Article 27 of the Constitution of 1917 gives the Federal and state governments the power to ultimately destroy it, and unless Article 27 is amended, or removed from the Constitution, such an outcome will be inevitable.

From another angle, that of persisting in the exploitation of a semi-enslaved peon labor, the plantation is also threatened. Although labor legislation may prove ineffectual, the whole atmosphere of rural life has changed. The plantation can no longer live by the same kind of exploitation that served it so well for so long a time. It must now deal with free labor rather than with peon labor. It must now pay its wages in money rather than in kind, it must now meet the competition of thousands of little villages that have grown independent of it. Its labor supply is not so assured, its wages must now be higher than before. Economically the plantation is perhaps even worse off than it is politically. It may be able to stave off dismemberment by bribery, by the use of "white guards," by burning the houses of the small communities settled upon it, but it cannot at present and for a long time to come, establish the conditions of an adequate credit system. As long as the laws making possible the dismemberment of the plantation system are on the books, and as long as the possibility of a change in the law for the giving of *ejidos* to plantation laborers exists, and as long as each governor may, when the spirit so moves him, at one swoop declare every plantation community a free *municipio*, or as the governor of Jalisco has recently done declare that all *tierras ociosas* [idle lands] may be tilled by propertyless peons, the credit of the plantation is bound to be practically nonexistent. It is true, of course, that the Mexican plantation was never served by a very good credit system—at least not since the independence and the destruction of the power of the Church. But then the plantation had other resources—it had a dependable labor supply, it was more immune from outside interference, it was not subject to the competition from the thousands of *ejidos*, and it was practically free from taxation. In all of these measures, except the last, the plantation has suffered a profound change of position, and even in the last there is considerable evidence that with the increasing political power of the *ejido* it will insist that the large plantation shall carry its fair share of the tax burden. Such an imposition would so materially affect the fortunes of the plantation that, under present conditions, it could escape only through sale. There is, however, as we have already pointed out, no individual purchaser in Mexico. The only possible purchasers on any considerable scale will be the villages that have *ejidos*, which already have some land. By purchase or otherwise the village *ejido* will overflow its present boundaries since the land that it received is clearly insufficient for an increasing population, or a rising standard of living.

The assumption seems to have been that the amount of land given to a village ought to be enough for each family, to maintain that family in its present standard of living, using its present tools and remaining perpetually as backward as it was for the period when its life was dominated by the plantation. In fact, in many places the villages that have received *ejidos* have had to resort to labor supplied by the neighboring plantations to eke out an existence for which the *ejido* was insufficient. That might have been a complete answer to the problem if other factors had not interfered. But in addition to the *ejido* has come a school, with its insistence upon a better technique, upon the use of better implements, upon a broader horizon, upon a greater utilization of resources and the living of a fuller life. Given this change and the increase in population that a better health program, better care for children, and better food habits (which come with the school) will make possible, the need for land to satisfy these newer needs and possibilities becomes inevitable. The answer is, either the purchase of the remaining lands from the plantations (which suffer in proportion as the villages prosper), or a continuation of the process that has already taken place—a greater and more rapid expropriation under the laws now on the statute books. That the second process will prove of greater appeal in the long run is to be expected. Every tradition of the villages as well as personal interest would make such an outcome more consistent with their history and psychology.

From this point of view the agrarian movement must be described as having proved itself halting, inadequate, meager and contrary to the best interests of peace and prosperity in the country. It would have been better and easier and more economical to have solved this problem rapidly and adequately. The failure to do so merely reflected that the leaders of the movement were not themselves children of the villages that needed land, that in fact many of them were large landowners (Madero and Carranza are good examples), and that others have become large landowners in the process. We need not impute any motives to them except to say that they have not intellectually repudiated the *hacienda* as an economic institution, whereas the villages have, and in time to come more certainly even than in the past the villages will shape the policy of the country and drive the leaders to other moorings.

Just as during the Díaz régime the end of the villages seemed to be in sight, so now the end of the plantation system seems to be in sight. It may still be a long way off, but at least there is the dream of its disappearance from the Mexican scene. Saturnino Cedillo, when Secretary of Agriculture, declared:

If ever the large plantations become a matter of the past and rural properties are equitably divided, our agriculture will probably within ten years not merely satisfy our own needs, but will make possible exportation abroad.

This is a complete contrast to the dominant philosophy at the end of the Díaz régime. And Cedillo is a person of great weight in comparison with the Governor of Querétero, who, a few months ago, declared that the land problem in his state was solved, only to have the organized communities soon after not merely repudiate his policy and demand from the President that the decree which declared that policy be abolished, but also to have them elect an *agrarista* as governor of the state, for the first time since the Revolution. The conflict is still on. Both Portes Gil, former President of Mexico, and Dr. Puig Casauranc, recent Mexican Ambassador to the United States, said recently that the agrarian movement must continue until every Mexican peon who needs land has his need satisfied. The landowners, in convention, on the other hand, have asked that the government return to them the *ejidos* taken away from them. On January 20, 1931, one of the leading newspapers took the position that

Not for a moment do we think that it would be desirable to take a step backward. Not even from a distance does it occur to us that the *ejidos* ought to be given back to their original owners. . . . In effect, neither we nor anyone with half a spirit of foresight, wishes a new agrarian revolution in the country, new violences by armed peasants. But if we do not wish to go backward, we still less wish to go forward in the erroneous path.

And so the battle keeps going. General Calles, in a recent speech in Guadalajara at the inauguration of the newly elected governor of the state of Jalisco, emphasized the fact that "at the earliest possible moment it is necessary that the *campesinos* have their need for land satisfied." Fifty villages in the region of Quitupan in the state of Michoacán complained to General Calles that the landowners were making their lives miserable, destroying the crops of the villages; they asked for relief and threatened vengeance. So bitter was the complaint that the official organ of the party in power refused to print it because of its possible effect. The conflict of opinion and of fact is still on. The plantation is fighting for its life and doing so with considerable resources; but if the tendencies that are implicit in the present social movement, and which have made themselves felt through the *ejido*, the school, the *Ligas de Communidades Agrarias*, the *Defensa Social*, persist, then the future success of the *hacienda* as an economic or political system is dubious at best.

Another aspect of this problem is in the kind of community that is being created as a substitute for the plantation. In so far as this community is represented by the *ejido* as it now exists, it is at least in harmony with the tradition of the rural village. Eighty per cent of the villages that have retained some land have done so in communal form, at least for their pasture and wood lands. The community replacing the plantation is coöperative, semicommunal, with a high degree of internal organization, with the possibilities for an internal unity which seem to have existed generally before the Spanish Conquest and which are still to be found in those communities which have succeeded in retaining their older *mores*. In so far as the plantation has been replaced by the *ejido* it has been replaced by this semi-communal, as against the older feudal, pattern. It is a conflict of two ways of life: domination and paternalism on one side, freedom and coöperation on the other. The first implies great wealth and great poverty. The second demands no great wealth and avoids the poverty, at least in the sense that there is a sharing of the goods of the earth as they are produced. True enough, each system has its virtues and its faults. However, the problem is here being considered from a historian's point of view and the present historical fact is that after a trial of four hundred years the first system is being replaced by the second. The older tradition has reasserted itself and is apparently winning the battle. If it wins, Mexico will become characterized by thousands of little communities owning their lands in semi-communal form, tilling them collectively, with a school in the center, with a high degree of community coöperation for many activities, with a basis for democratic government resting upon a unified community. That is the ideal. If the village should again be defeated, then continued convulsion for another trial of strength is the inevitable answer. It has been so for four centuries, and there is no reason to assume that any other outcome is possible. In one direction lies the promise of peace; in the other, lies the certainty of continued violence. The leaders of Mexico are making their choice naltingly, blindly. The people are making theirs instinctively and directly, although without any broad ends except land, except freedom, except internal peace.

THE ULTIMATE VICTOR IN ANY BATTLE

CHAPTER 19

FOREIGN CAPITAL AND NATIVE WORKERS

LIKE all profound social upheavals, the Mexican Revolution has given rise to some strange and unexpected results. Of these the new labor philosophy and organization is the most interesting and significant. In 1910 Mexico had neither the background nor the social organization to suggest the emergence of an elaborate labor philosophy, organization and policy. This makes the subsequent growth of the labor movement in Mexico of exceeding interest to the student of social policy and politics.

Mexico was not an industrial country in 1910. It is not an industrial nation today. All, or nearly all of Mexico's industry was artificial, a hothouse product, foreign to its history, interest and practice. The proportion of the population engaged in industry in 1910 was of minor significance. Mexican industry was incidental to the economy of the nation. It played an important rôle in the eyes of the industrialists, of the city population and of the government. But it was incidental in the lives of the mass of the people that drew their living from a semifeudal agriculture untouched by the newly developed capitalism, and one might say, unconscious of it. It is interesting, therefore, that a revolution of the back country against the city, of the indigenous population against a feudal social and economic structure should have given the urban workers a place within the new scheme of law, politics and social institutions far beyond any they could have acquired for themselves and far beyond that of labor groups in more industrialized nations.

It is interesting to note that the legal and political achievements of the Mexican worker antedated the Russian revolution. The labor revolution, and it deserves that name, was more reflective of a native urge than it might have been had it followed the Russian upheaval. Instead of attempting, as have the Russians, to exclude foreign capitalistic enterprise, Mexico has sought to share in its benefits. Much of this labor development is a by-product, an afterthought. This, however, only makes it consistent with other trends in the Mexican Revolution.

Mexican industry was of recent origin, mainly in foreign hands, and dependent upon governmental favor. It proved to be important in the development of labor policy that practically all of Mexican mining, commerce, and industry was foreign owned and foreign managed. Foreign ownership was to be found not merely in the larger industries requiring heavy initial investment but in the small industries and commercial enterprises as well. At the end of the Díaz régime the large mines were all American, English or French. They belonged mainly to the first two and were managed by foreigners resident in Mexico, while the head offices were in the countries where the capital originated. The railroads were foreign (English and American), managed by foreign staffs, and the skilled labor on the railroads was foreign until after the fall of the Díaz régime.

The textile industry, which next to the mines and railroads represented the largest investment in the country, was foreign (chiefly French). Again it was not merely foreign owned but foreign managed. In a lesser degree this was true of all the other basic industries. The oil industry which was soon to flourish, also proved to be of foreign ownership and control. Foreigners owned and managed the public utilities. The street cars, the electric lights, the water systems, each in their turn were developed by foreign capital, and managed by foreign representatives of this capital, employing foreign technical staffs, and as nearly as possible under the circumstances, located within the country but not of it.

What was true of industry was true of commerce. Virtually

all of the important commerce was foreign (German, French and Spanish). Spanish capital was to be found both in wholesale and retail trade. Most of the retail business in the larger cities, however, was in the hands of Turks, Armenians and Chinese. Even many of the restaurants on the railroads, for example, were in the hands of Chinese. In addition to controlling most of the commerce and industry, the foreigners also owned much land. Among them, the Spaniards, the Americans and the English owned the greater portion of the best lands in the Republic.

At every turn in the economy of Mexico, therefore, some foreign agency regulated, organized, directed and ministered to the industrial and commercial needs of the nation. In part this was due to recent growth of industrial and commercial activity. Except for mining, most of the industrial enterprise of Mexico followed the peace and quiet, the order and rule of the Díaz régime. Until then the earlier Spanish tradition of opposition to foreigners on one hand and the persistent turmoil on the other had kept foreigners out and had kept Mexico immune from the commerce and industry developing in other parts of the world. The coming of peace and with it the infiltration of foreign notions of progress had laid the foundation for a welcoming of the foreigner and his industrial and commercial establishments.

The nation as a whole was little changed by this sudden incursion. Not merely was the life of the country folk practically untouched by the development in the large cities and about the mines, but even in the smaller cities, with poor internal communication, and the persistent tradition of four hundred years of non-industrial life, the Mexicans left the new ways to the foreigners who brought them. They played a minor rôle except as laborers, except as consumers in so far as their means made them purchasers of the things that were being manufactured by machinery rather than by hand as had been done for centuries.

The foreign control and recent origin made this growth dependent upon a degree of governmental favor that industry in other countries does not ordinarily enjoy. Apart from mining, the industrial and commercial development of Mexico was fostered by a high tariff. The theory was that Mexico ought to become an industrial nation; the fact was that with inadequate industrial equipment, lack of capital, the absence of managerial experience, untrained labor and poor resources, the few industries that developed protected by the government by means of tariffs, concessions and prerogatives, were built upon a basic price level higher than that obtaining in industrial countries. The industrial development of Mexico was, and still is, largely a special tax in favor of the foreign investor-manager at the expense of the consumer who must pays a higher price for the articles that they used and use. The chief benefit to Mexico was the wage a few laborers received from the industry thus fostered.

Other results might have followed this artificial stimulation of industry if the process had created a Mexican middle, or managerial, class. But native tradition and foreign interest worked against this. The activity and interest that business required were outside the ordinary ken of the Mexican. The only Mexicans who really benefited were the lawyers who helped the foreigners to circumvent, fit into, manipulate the Mexican law, and the politicians who found in this flow of investment a ready source of profit and emoluments which replaced the funds which they at one time systematically abstracted from the Catholic Church. The prosperity which the politician derived from the funds of the foreign investor and business man explains in part the peace which Díaz found it possible to maintain during so long a time. But no Mexican middle class was being created. The conflict between Mexican labor and the representatives of foreign-owned capitalism stirred to resistance by the Revolution found no native middle class to step into the breach.

The attack against the capitalistic elements proved to be largely an attack against the foreigner, and found little disfavor even among those Mexicans who were capitalistically minded, as they looked to discover in such an attack an opening for themselves.

The ownership of so much of the best lands of Mexico by the elements that controlled the industrial life of the nation complicated the issue for both the foreigners and the Mexicans. The agrarian problem was made more difficult by the great holdings of some of the oil, mining and timber companies that were at the same time connected with railroads or other industries. Under those conditions an attack upon the land problem in Mexico stirred the foreign industrial elements into opposition, and they came to be counted among the opponents of the agrarian movement, and in turn roused against themselves the hatred that raged against the *latifundista*.

It was characteristic of Mexican capitalism that it developed within, and adjusted itself to, a feudal social and political order. It did of course stimulate change which contributed to the destruction of the feudalism. These influences (greater literacy, greater freedom of movement), however, were incidental, inevitable by-products of industrialism. As a matter of policy the foreign capitalistic incursion utilized the feudal structure of Mexican society for its own ends. It did not hesitate to use forced labor in the *monterías* of Chiapas, Tabasco and Quintana Roo; also in the tobacco plantations in Valle Nacional, Oaxaca; and in the coffee plantations in Chiapas. Under the promise of colonization it fomented the forced migration of the Yaquis from their native habitat, and for the benefit of a foreign-owned sugar industry in Morelos (Spanish-owned mainly) to foment the destruction of villages and the absorption of the lands of the natives.

If we are to explain why Mexico, with an inconsequential industrial development, evolved a revolutionary Labor code

229

on the heels of an agrarian movement, we must see that it was in part due to the foreign control of industry that utilized a willing and feudal government to serve its own ends without either understanding or scrupling the damage done to the native populations. It is not suggested that the industrialism carried no good features with it. That is beside the point. In the process it left a rancor of discontent that later strengthened the revolutionary movement. Had there been a native middle class, then an internal struggle between it and the feudal landlordism might have developed and there might have been an agrarian revolution in Mexico without seriously affecting industrial interests. In fact the native industrialists and capitalists might themselves have made the agrarian revolution for their own ends. But foreign industrial influence tended to perpetuate and increase the very type of feudal structure which in western Europe had been destroyed or weakened by growing capitalism during the hundred years preceding the outbreak of the Mexican social movement.

To the politicians the foreign-controlled capitalism was a great boon. In favoring it they were serving both their country and themselves. Concessions could always be sold to foreigners at a good price, and politicians could always secure concessions. The *compañías deslindadoras* are good examples. Concessions for railroads, harbors, oil lands, mines, city water systems and public utilities could be disposed of similarly. The politicians lined their pockets, sold these prerogatives to outsiders, advanced foreign influence in Mexico, alienated increasing portions of the national resources into foreign hands, and helped their country to become "the catspaw, the tail of a foreign capitalistic kite." It was like a new invasion, again by foreigners, but with money instead of soldiers, who now took not merely the land, but the remaining resources of the country. The foreigner in addition to enjoying his hold over so much of the Mexican political machinery had at the same time the aid and comfort of his country's diplomatic representatives, who furthered and supported their nationals in the development of their investments and who stood as an additional bulwark against the Mexican. The foreigner enjoyed both Mexican and home governmental support. It is from such facts as these that the nationalism and antiforeign character of the Mexican Revolution took its inspiration and its lesson.

We thus have in the hands of foreigners a rapid capitalistic development accommodated to a feudal economic structure, accepting and sharpening its social and racial distinctions, utilizing the prevailing philosophy of racial superiority for its own ends, and adding to it the notions of individualism, of competition, of the survival of the fit. The foreign capitalist strengthened these class and race distinctions further by bringing to them a theory of economics which justified the semi-slavery of the peon and his low wage on the grounds that he received only what he produced, and that he produced so little because he was an inferior being. It was on this basis that the feudalism inherited from Spain and the capitalism of large-scale mineral exploitation and smaller-scale industrial enterprise found a common meeting ground. It was on this basis that industry was given the special governmental favors that the *hacienda* had for so long a time enjoyed; it was on this basis that progress was to be achieved by the rapid alienation of the resources of the country into capable hands; and it was on this basis that a great nation was to be built by special privilege and prerogative at the expense of the mass of the common people who had no voice, who if they had had one would not have known how to express their grievance in any language which their masters could have understood. To the colonial landlordism was now added a more subtle, but equally colonial, industrialism.

This industrial development went on for over thirty years without any protest from the common people. They were so far down the scale that they had no voice. The turbulence of industrial labor in other parts of the world had no echoes in Mexico. There were no labor organizations; they were forbidden by law. Any attempt to force wages above their "natural level" was punished as a conspiracy against the State, with a fine and sentence to prison, or not uncommonly by forced labor in unhealthy climes, by the forced levy in the army, or by the *ley fuga* (death while attempting to escape). It was not till 1907 that labor troubles made themselves felt in the mining region of Cannanea and the textile mills of Rio Blanca; they were suppressed by the unhesitating use of the Federal army and the killing of hundreds of laborers.

The growing industrialism had, however, led to the seeping in of ideas from abroad, particularly from Spain, anarchistic and socialistic ideas which found a voice especially in the brothers Magón. This initial labor movement made itself felt even before the agrarian problem had attracted national attention. The scene was thus laid for labor's participation in the social revolution. When the Revolution did come in 1910, labor found that it could play a rôle in shaping government policy and in wielding political power far beyond what the numerical strength of the workers would have led one to expect. The foreign ownership of industry and the traditional dominance of the city played into the hands of the labor leaders and gave them for a time at least an important place in the development of the social movement of the country.

The outbreak of the Revolution, therefore, found an incipient labor movement. It had fought its first battles, had paid a heavy price for its daring, and was stirred by ideas of industrial revolution, socialism, anarchism and syndicalism. But it would be a mistake to attribute much significance to it as a leaven in the mass. It was a small movement scattered in a few industrial cities, and it embraced a fraction of even the factory labor. In Mexico City there grew up the *Casa del Obrero Mundial*, which became a gathering center for leaders and intellectuals interested in the social problem.

In the early days this small organization drew together the most diverse intellectual elements. It was not a movement. It was rather a propaganda center where all sorts of ideas were discussed. From this center many of the most active intellectual spirits of the Revolution developed, which were later to play more or less significant rôles.

Madero's revolution when it came to power looked with little favor upon this group. His was not a social but a political movement, and when the occasion offered he suppressed the *Casa del Obrero Mundial,* expelled the foreign labor agitators, and in general utilized the powers of the government to discourage labor propaganda and labor organization. The low fortune of the labor movement under Madero fell still lower under Huerta, who hesitated at nothing in an effort to destroy opposition to himself and to suppress the activities of either the labor or the agrarian movement.

It was not, therefore, until Huerta was overthrown and the conflict developed between Carranza on one side and Villa and Zapata on the other that labor found any favor in government circles. The hard pressed Carranza, driven from Mexico City and seeking support from whatever source, turned to the incipient labor movement and entered into an agreement with it, literally signing a treaty with the *Casa del Obrero Mundial.* The workers agreed to, and did, organize "Red Battalions" which went into the trenches against Villa. For that the workers received all the favors that a weak and nearly defeated government could give, the right to organize behind the lines. In the signing of this agreement, Obregón played an important rôle, and it was from this contact that he later received much of the support he needed to achieve the presidency. It was also from this contact that he received needed support in the early days of his administration to pacify the country and to win for himself public support at home and favor abroad through the influence of the American Federation of Labor.

233

But the alliance between Carranza and the labor movement, important as it was for the movement, and significant as a historical fact, because it gave the labor leaders an inside track upon governmental favor and support which served them well for a number of years, was so far as Carranza was concerned short-lived. No sooner was he in power, with Villa defeated, than he found that the labor movement's activities and pretensions were inconsistent with his own prerogatives and conveniences. He did not hesitate to suppress a strike to call up an early law of Juárez against public disorder, dating from 1864, and to shoot workers on strike as traitors. This happened in 1916, while the convention that drew up the 1917 constitution was in session. Under these circumstances it is an interesting question as to why the Constitution of 1917 included as it did one of the most elaborate and comprehensive labor codes extant anywhere in a basic public document. Clearly enough, it was not the doing of Carranza himself; the only thing he asked was that the Federal government be given the right in Article 73 of the proposed constitution to pass labor laws for the entire country. When the constitution was completed, however, it contained not what Carranza had asked for, but a complete and detailed labor code that has given the Mexican Revolution a new and unexpected significance both at home and abroad.

How this came about cannot be told, for the threads of the story are not clear. The debates upon the article in the Constitutional Convention were insignificant. The discussions within the committee that elaborated Article 123 were not recorded and so are not available to the historian. If one looks for influences that made this article feasible they are not readily discernible. Clearly enough the labor code was not the work of the labor movement. Its influence was insignificant in comparison to the magnitude of the achievement represented by Article 123. In the Constitutional Convention itself there were only two representatives who had trade-union experience; these were Nicolás Cano and Carlos L. Gracidas. The latter still occupies a place in the trade-union movement of Mexico. But in the Convention itself these two men were of minor importance, and the name of neither is on the report of the committee that brought Article 123 to the Convention floor. We have, therefore, a basic labor program being accepted by a Constitutional Convention that was largely made up of military men and lawyers. It seems clear that it would never have happened if the attack upon industry had not been an attack upon the foreigner in Mexico and a declaration of national emancipation from foreign tutelage. The labor code was devised as a means of defending Mexico and the Mexican from too much foreign exploitation, as a means of bridling the foreign capitalist in Mexico.

CHAPTER 20

THE CONSTITUTIONAL CODE

THE ideas in Article 123 are of foreign origin. During the early days of Carranza many ideas were propagated for the "Constitutional Movement" as a justification of his side of the battle. One of these ideas concerned the elaboration of a labor program. In the search for support a project for a labor law was elaborated, signed and published in April, 1915 by Rafael Zubáran Capmany, Carranza's Secretary of the Interior. The difference between the labor and the agrarian law was that Carranza issued the agrarian law as an official decree while the labor code merely remained a *proyecto* (project), which received no official sanction. As we have already seen, Carranza made no demand for such a body of laws in his projected constitution submitted to the Constitutional Convention. But a number of the men in the Convention knew of this labor project, had participated in its formulation, and were restive under the neglect of the labor problem. Gracidas and Cano, the only two trade-union representatives, made themselves heard in their demand for labor protection, and General Mujica, as chairman of the Committee on the Constitution, brought Article 123 before the Convention. The influence of General Mujica upon the development of the program of the Revolution in the convention is one that can hardly be overestimated. His ability, energy and persistence made him a leading figure in shaping both the agrarian and the labor code. If one examines Article 123 and the *proyecto* issued in Vera Cruz two years earlier, it is clear that a large part of the program of Article 123 is an elaboration of the basic ideas in the earlier document.

Where did the ideas come from? They were certainly not Mexican, nor derived from Mexican experience. The earlier document itself says that many of the ideas suggested and the institutions favored are new to the law of the country (*una verdadera novedad*). The answer to this question is embodied in the preface to the project. The ideas were drawn from abroad, from civilized nations (*paises cultos*) like Holland, Belgium, France, Germany, Switzerland, Spain, Italy, Australia, New Zealand, and certain states of the United States. Specifically the project mentioned a number of individuals whose ideas were drawn upon. Among these are Justice Brandeis, Father John A. Ryan, and Justice Higgins of Australia. The project of a law laid before the French parliament by Gaston Doumergue, and another by M. Viviani in 1910 are also mentioned. In other words, what was done in the formation of the original project was to cull the best labor laws in those countries which had modern social legislation and bring them together in a single code.

In essence the laws are not new. Their being brought together into a single code and embodied in the Constitution made them, in fact, a completely new labor code, both for Mexico and for other parts of the world. In those days no code was so elaborate, or so comprehensive. It was the boast of the Constitutional Convention that it "freed labor," just as the French Revolution of an earlier day had boasted of freeing "man." It was called "the nicest page in the Constitution."

Even with these ideas, and the opposition to foreign capital, it might still have been impossible to embody so broad a statement of doctrine into the Constitution had it not been for the influences of the Great War and the rising power of labor all over the world. The War had set in motion a series of influences in the shaping of labor legislation, the participation of labor in government, and the socializing of natural resources that in part culminated in the Russian Revolution, in part in the establishment of the Labor Office in the League of Nations, and in part (it must be counted as one of its influences) in the development of Article 123 of the Mexican Constitution of 1917.

The introductory paragraph of Article 123 is an enabling act, providing that the state legislatures

shall make laws relative to labor with due regard for the needs of each region of the Republic and in conformity with the following principles, and these principles and laws shall govern the labor of skilled and unskilled workmen, employees, domestic servants, and artisans, and in general every contract of labor.

The agricultural laborer is specifically mentioned in an early paragraph as one of the classes of labor for which a minimum wage is to be established.

The article provides for an eight-hour day and a seven-hour limit on night work; overtime work is limited to three hours in any one day, and may not be repeated for more than three successive days. Women and children under 16 are barred from engaging in any overtime work. One day's rest for every six days' work is mandatory, and working mothers must be allowed two half-hour rest periods during the day to nurse their children. Children under twelve cannot become subject to a contract, and those between twelve and sixteen may work only six hours per day.

Employers, whether engaged in agricultural, industrial, mining or other work, must provide their laborers with sanitary dwellings at a rental not exceeding "one-half of one per cent per month of the assessed value of the properties." They must do this even within inhabited places, if they employ more than 100 persons. They are, in addition, responsible for the establishment of schools, dispensaries, and other community services. Every labor community having a population in excess of 200 must be provided with a "space of land not less than 5,000 square meters" for public markets, municipal buildings, places of amusement, and "no saloons or gambling houses shall be permitted in such labor centers." Houses "designed to be acquired in ownership by workmen" through workmen's coöperatives by their construction shall be considered as "social utility" and therefore entitled to such help and assistance as the state and communities may provide to undertakings so designated.

The principle of the minimum wage is clearly embodied in the Constitution although there is no attempt to equalize the minimum for all sections of the country. On the contrary, "the minimum wage . . . shall be made by special commissions to be appointed in each municipality and to be subordinated to the central board of conciliation to be established in each state," and shall be considered sufficient, according to the conditions prevailing in the respective regions of the country, "to satisfy the normal needs of the life of the workman, his education, and his lawful pleasures, considering him as the head of a family." These two provisions, therefore, in addition to providing for a minimum wage, create a local machinery for the determination of a minimum family income according to the needs of the varying local conditions, and set up a central agency in each state to which these local boards are to be "subordinated."

These same two paragraphs that set up the minimum wage also provide that "workmen shall have the right to participate in the profits . . . in all agricultural, commercial, manufacturing, or mining enterprises." The machinery created for the establishment of the minimum wage is also charged with the responsibility of determining the rate of profit-sharing "provided in the law."

The minimum established by law is protected from "attachment, set-off, or discount." This hedging about of the minimum and exempting it from legal attachment is carried a step further by the declaration that "the law shall decide what property constituted the family patrimony. These goods shall be inalienable and shall not be mortgaged nor attached." All wages must be paid in legal tender and not in "substitute money." Overtime work must be paid double and for the same work there shall be no discrimination in payment because of sex or nationality. All labor contracts which are to be fulfilled in foreign countries must be viséd before the local consul of the country to which the laborer is to go, and must include provision for "repatriation." Nor can any private agency or public office exact a fee for finding employment for workmen. In case of bankruptcy or "composition," the claims of workers for wages and salaries shall take preference above all other claims.

The income of the worker is further protected by the provision that debts contracted by workmen in favor of their employers may be charged only against the workman himself, and under no circumstances against the members of his family. Nor can such debts be paid by the taking of more than the entire wage of the workman for any one month. This is a very important provision. It is aimed at the abolition of the system of debts which for so many generations governed the relations of workmen to their masters, not merely in agriculture, but in practically all employments.

This question of the debts of the peons is one that has played an important part in the labor legislation of Mexico both present and past, as well as in the discussion of the relations existing between the agricultural laborers and their masters. The Constitutional Convention felt it was satisfying an important need when it decreed that "all debts contracted by workingmen on account of work up to the date of this Constitution with Masters, their subordinates, or agents are hereby declared wholly and entirely discharged."

This general body of standards and limitations, protection, and privileges which is thrown about the financial position of the worker also includes a provision for the encouragement of "institutions of popular insurance, for old age, sickness, life, unemployment, accidents, and others of a similar character." These institutions are declared of "social utility" and are to receive all help which the law provides for such institutions.

The law provides not only for the right to organize on the part of workers and employers, but also recognizes strikes and boycotts as legal under certain conditions. The strike is considered a legal weapon when peaceful and when it tries to "harmonize the rights of capital and labor." In the case of public services, the workers are to give ten days' advance notice to the boards of conciliation and arbitration. Strikes are unlawful when the majority of workers resort to violence, or in case of war in industries under government direction, or in the case of military establishments that make supplies for the army. Lockouts are lawful when they are declared with the consent of the boards of conciliation and arbitration and are for the purpose of maintaining a reasonable price "above the cost of production."

Differences between capital and labor shall be submitted to a board of conciliation and arbitration to consist of an equal number of representatives for each party and one representative of the government. Refusal on the part of the employer to submit, or refusal on his part to accept the award subjects him to the penalty of having to pay three months' wages to all of the employees in the dispute, in addition to any liability incurred during the dispute, as well as to the termination of any contract that he may have had with his employees. On the part of the worker, a refusal to accept an award places him in the position of having his contract terminated. The discharge of a worker because of union affiliation, for having taken part in a legal strike, or without "proper cause" makes the employer liable for three months' payment, and at the option of the worker, to reinstatement for the performance of the contract. If the worker abandons his work because of mistreatment, or because of the misuse of any member of his family, the employer remains liable for the payment of a three months' wage, even if the injury was inflicted by subordinates and agents, provided they were acting with his knowledge.

Employers are made liable for accidents and occupational disease "arising from work" and responsibility for "proper indemnity" even if they "contracted" their work "through an agent." There is also under the general law a very broad provision for regulation and supervision of work places in regard to sanitation and machinery protection.

In addition to the provisions outlined and described above, Article 123 contains a series of "stipulations" which cannot be made subject to contract and which are void even if embodied in a contract. Any contract is declared null and void that provides for "an inhuman day's work," for a wage which is not remunerative in the "judgment of the board of arbitration and conciliation," for a span of "more than one week before wage payment," for the use of places of amusement, cafes, saloons, or shops as places for the payment of wages, or any "obligation" to buy in "specified" places, for deduction from wages as payment for fines, for any waiver of indemnities that may arise from disease, accident, breach of contract, or discharge, and finally any "stipulation" waiving any right derived from labor legislation. It is interesting to observe the large proportion of these limitations of the contract that center about the protection of the wages of the worker and strive to make impossible the reappearance of payment by "substitutes" for "legal tender," or that open the way to a reëstablishment of the *tienda de raya* and its consequent debt relationships.

CHAPTER 21

POLITICS AND LABOR ORGANIZATION

THE promulgation of the Constitution by Carranza on February 5, 1917 marks a revolution in the history of labor in Mexico more sudden and drastic than any that we can record except that of the Russian Revolution, which had not then taken place. The workers of Mexico achieved at one stroke a legal position which gave them rights, powers and prerogatives for which the workers in other parts of the world had been struggling a hundred years. The industrial conflicts of England, Germany, France, and the United States had all gone to shape and influence the ends achieved by the Mexican workers. It was a victory which the Mexican laborer had a few years earlier neither aspired to nor dreamt of and for which he was inadequately prepared—for which the nation possibly was not prepared industrially. It was a full-blown labor code in an agricultural country, and the code had its major justification in its bearing upon the defense of the Mexican laborer against foreign exploitation. The code, too, was revolutionary in the sense that it set out a definite and legally prescribed program for an incipient labor movement. This distinguished the Mexican trade-union movement from similar movements in the world.

The Mexican labor movement now had a definite goal, the enforcement of the specific provisions so fortuitously written into the constitution. It became clear that instead of being in opposition to the government or seeking to overthrow the existing order the most obvious policy for Mexican labor was to be conservative, to be legal, to support the government, to insist that the law be applied. Here is one reason why the alliance between labor and the government has been so close. Here too is a reason why, comparatively speaking, the labor movement has been conservative, why it has been so little influenced by the more radical projects derived from foreign experience.

It became clear that for at least fifty years the Mexican trade-union movement would have all it could do to develop the kind of organization, the kind of social *milieu* that would make possible a full and general application of the labor code embodied in the law. This I know from my contacts and conversations with Mexican labor leaders. They ceased to follow the will-of-the-wisp of a social revolution in the European sense and became dreamers of a practical way of achieving in fact the promise of the law as embodied in Article 123.

They felt that if they but had the organized power, Article 123 could be made to serve all of their needs and make them in fact participants in the industrial process. The way towards the ideal, even the ultimate ideal of a socialized state, could in their judgment now be followed gradually by the paths marked out within the law. The law was broad and flexible enough to make the end possible as experience and power dictated, without a convulsion. It was their main objective now to support the government, because it was the government, with the support of labor, that would have to enforce the law. That, perhaps more than anything, explains the political activity of the Mexican labor movement of the days of Obregón and Calles. It made the participants in the labor movement for a time the most consistent, the most loyal supporters of a constitutional order in Mexico. It also brought into the political arena a group that had never played any rôle whatsoever. It made the worker a power in the government, and gave him a political consciousness that in the long run is bound to be highly significant in the process of government in Mexico.

The continuance of the internal military conflict and the counter revolutions which were always being plotted and attempted gave the government in turn a very strong motive for accepting the loyalty and support of a movement that seemed to have great powers of growth, discipline and organization. Nor was this inconsistent with the position of a government come to power on a revolutionary program and after a Revolution of broad consequence in the social structure. Although the government never became a labor government it did depend largely upon labor for support. Mexico has never had a unified government, not even under Calles. There were conflicting elements in the situation and there was no general philosophy or program. This strengthened the position of labor, it had a philosophy and a program, and both were in the Constitution. It only needed an instrumentality to enforce it. Part of this instrumentality was the government; but the major part had to be trade-union organization.

And as things stood, this organization was something that had to be created after the labor code was on the statute books. It is clear that if the law had not been on the statute books it would have proved impossible to create the movement so easily or so effectively. The right to keep other workers from the establishment, the assurance that the Board of Conciliation would generally vote the labor point of view in any conflict, were strong aids in a struggle to achieve organization and power. It may be said here that the support of the government became, and has remained, the one major policy for the labor movement. The boards of conciliation and arbitration, which became in the early days the arbiters of the fortunes of labor in the daily detailed conflict, would have whittled away the rights and prerogatives of the law by interpretations. The support of the boards of conciliation and arbitration was essential in the early days, and could only be assured if the government representative was of labor's choosing, or at least, one that was acceptable and friendly to labor. Support by the government was a matter of life and death for Mexican Trade Unionism, and it still is, in a measure.

With all such support even the organizing and the disciplining into trade unions, of a large host of workers, workers who had until recently had no rights, no power, no place, no voice, no experience—the organizing into unions of people who had never been organized into anything before, who were illiterate and inexperienced, the converting of the peon, the Mexican industrial laborer, who had earned less than fifty centavos a day, and who depended upon his *amo* (master) in a way which is hardly to be compared with any industrial labor that we know, was an undertaking of great magnitude. It would, it seems to me, be difficult to overestimate the value and the greatness of the work in organization, education and discipline that was performed by the early trade-union leaders. The change in spirit, in self-respect, in sense of power and place that was achieved by the labor leaders of the C.R.O.M. (Confederación regional obrera mexicana) which came into existence as an organization in 1918, is worthy of comparison with the best spiritual by-products of the Mexican Revolution.

It has always seemed to me that the work of Luis N. Morones, in its general and specific influence upon the place of labor in the scheme of Mexican life and labor, of Mexican politics and policy, in the bringing of the worker into the arena where he is both counted and counts, compares with that of Zapata in the agrarian field. Morones created through the C.R.O.M. and through the *Grupo acción* a group that stood together over long periods of time and that supported one another loyally under the most diverse fates of fortune. It is true that for the moment the labor movement in Mexico and even the leadership has declined, as so often everything seems to decline in Mexico, sacrificed to political ends and personal fortune. The leaders of labor may be censured, but no group in Mexico has been more loyal to its broader aims than the labor group that collected about Morones.

Neither Calles nor Obregón can boast of having had as

much loyalty and consistent support from their immediate followers as can Morones; and neither can boast of having given to Mexico so permanent and, in the long run, so effective an institution for broad democratic ends as is to be had in the trade-union movement regardless of what happens to the personal fortunes of Morones or of the *Grupo acción*. Few things can withstand the political *mores* of Mexico, and the fact that the trade unionists withstood it so long speaks volumes for them. We have discussed this situation at length because there has developed a tendency both in Mexico and abroad to over-censure the shortcomings of both the trade-union movement and of its leadership. Admitting all of the criticisms, it still remains true that most of the power, most of the feeling of strength and place that has come to the Mexican labor movement, and the sense of right and dignity that has been acquired by it, is derived from the dramatic history of the C.R.O.M. and that fact is of major consequence in the present and future influence of the Mexican Revolution.

The first opportunity of labor came during the split in the revolutionary forces of Carranza, Villa and Zapata. The second came in the split between Obregón and Carranza before the election of 1920. The attempt of Carranza to keep Obregón from office gave the labor movement an opportunity to render Obregón a real service. And when he came to be President the trade-union movement achieved its first real success. The leaders of the movement were rewarded with government positions, were elected to public office and to the national legislature. Their position in the government strengthened their cause enormously. They used the powers of the government in their work of organization. Labor organizers were given government jobs and permitted to continue their work as organizers. The government gave labor delegates to conventions free passes over the railroads; in a thousand ways the trade-union leaders utilized their position with the government to carry on the work of organization. Labor leaders as officers of the government came to enforce the labor law. This change of fortune had its dangers as well as its merits; the dangers were serious, as is evidenced by much of the present internal conflict within the trade-union movement. But it also made possible the first real emergence of labor as a power in the social and political arena in Mexico, with a promise for the future that is possibly more important than the wreckage of personal character and personal idealism along the way.

Under these early influences the C.R.O.M. grew rapidly in power and prestige. With the election of Calles the movement came to such a head as was not dreamed of a few years earlier. It seemed for a while as if labor was the most important influence in the State, and certainly Morones was perhaps next to Calles the most important member of the government. But such sudden rise to power led to opposition and jealousy. Obregón, who was aspiring to office again, began an attack upon the C.R.O.M., and utilizing the *agraristas*, especially Soto y Gama and Manrique, forced a division between the labor and agrarian movements that for a time endangered the very Revolution itself.

According to General Mujica the attack upon the labor movement made in 1923 at the first unified convention between labor and agrarian elements was directly inspired by Obregón. Then too there were dissenting movements. The railroad brotherhoods antedating the C.R.O.M. refused to become absorbed, and the labor leaders used their power in the government to force them into a general movement or to destroy them. The C.R.O.M. failed in this. It also failed in its attempt to suppress the C.G.T., a more radical trade union movement. In fact, after the death of Obregón, Portes Gil as president utilized the C.G.T. and other movements, including the communist, to undermine and destroy the C.R.O.M. He failed to destroy it, but succeeded in weaken-

GENERAL ALVARO OBREGÓN

ing it. At present, however, trade unionism itself is probably stronger than it was. The first work of the trade union movement was so well done that even a destruction of a central powerful organization has still left the labor organizations with a degree of power and influence, of prerogative and right, that makes labor a matter of great significance within the industrial and political milieu of Mexico.

The reason for labor's present power lies in part in that at last the nation has succeeded in passing a general labor law "regulating" the constitutional principle embodied in Article 123. The Article had remained undeveloped in administrative law and found but partial application, mainly in the Federal District, less so in the states. The extent of enforcement depended upon the strength of the local labor organization. In each state the extent of organization depended upon whether or not the local governor was on political grounds favorable to the trade-union movement and the trade-union leaders. The conflict, for instance, in Jalisco between Zuno and Morones is a good example of many situations that prevailed even in days when labor had maximum power.

A general law became essential. In the years since the enactment of Article 123 the workers entered into collective contracts where they could, and were successful in most of the larger industries. These contracts embodied the basic principles of Article 123, and utilized the boards of conciliation and arbitration. The first of these boards was created in 1917 in the Federal District, and provided much in the way of experience, tradition and modes of procedure. Both the industries and labor discovered what could and could not be easily enforced. The rights of the workers as embodied in the collective contract were a detailing of the principles of Article 123. In the early days the courts whittled away the powers of the boards of conciliation and arbitration. But in 1926 the Supreme Court took the position that the decisions of the boards were not subject to review. This made the boards courts creating industrial law enforcible by the State. Under these circumstances districts that had powerful labor unions and friendly governors were maintaining one type of industrial standard, while industries and states that had no such influence were maintaining others.

All these differences required standardization. The provisions of Article 123 required detailing and elucidating. State laws were not complete. An effort was therefore made to create a national law. This effort was opposed by the industries, large and small, the large industries because they were afraid of the ultimate and permanent sanction and universalization that such a law could give, and the small ones because they would become subject to a law with which, because of the absence of an "administrative" application, they had largely avoided complying. In the early days of both Obregón and Calles general labor laws were devised and placed before the Legislature, but they were not passed. Before Portes Gil became President he presided over a convention that drafted a labor law. This convention represented both labor and capital, and its debates received very wide public discussion. It was, however, not until Ortiz Rubio became President that a law regulating Article 123 was finally passed on the eighteenth of August, 1931.

CHAPTER 22

NATIONAL LABOR LEGISLATION

THE Federal labor law passed 14 years after the adoption of Article 123 embodies the experience gained in the attempt to enforce and apply the latter during those years. It also represents a crystallization of the ideas and attitudes that the years of revolutionary activity provided. The code must therefore be considered the underlying judgment of the Mexican government, especially as it was not passed by a labor government, nor by a government that had any strong labor influence. In fact there was not a single member of the labor party or of the trade-union movement in the Congress or Senate that passed this law, which shows how pervasive the ideas have become with the general revolutionary elements in control of the government. The law is an elaborate and detailed document having approximately 700 specific articles and covering 175 closely printed pages. It attempts to be a complete labor code for the whole country, not merely embracing industrial labor, but having special chapters devoted to railroad labor, domestic labor, agricultural labor, and home industries. So much for its scope. Its character is also inclusive. It deals with the various types of labor contracts, has separate chapters devoted to hours of labor, wages, minimum wage, the work of women and children, apprenticeship, strikes and lockouts, accidents and compensation. It develops long and detailed rules for the organization of municipal, state and federal boards of conciliation and arbitration. It establishes special commissions upon the minimum wage and sets up a body of labor inspectors and agents. In short, the law seeks to regulate every type of industrial organization.

For our purpose it is not necessary to give here a minute

description of the law or of its specific enactments, it will be sufficient to indicate its general scope.

1. *Universality.*—The law is national. It attempts to cover every type of employment in all parts of the country, and provides both for central and local administration according to the spread of the industry, and sets up through boards of conciliation and arbitration a legal machinery which becomes a law-making and law-enforcing body. The trade-union movement has specific legal sanction, and with it becomes subject to control and guidance by the State. The law makes the trade-union movement in a sense one of the organs of the State in applying the administrative labor law. The worker who had no rights nor prerogatives before the Revolution has thus moved to a position of special privilege, power and protection at the hands of the State, and is vested through his organization and through his collective contract with the power of the State itself. This is especially true as long as he controls the boards of conciliation and arbitration. The present position of trade unionism is dependent upon the assumption that the influence of labor in the government will continue to be significant. Should the employers secure control of the State and through it of the boards of conciliation and arbitration, the body of rights and prerogatives elaborated in the law could be whittled away.

2. *Minimum wage.*—This principle is derived from Article 123 and made to apply to the entire country. In response to the great variety of conditions in a country of such sharp contrasts in climate and industrial character as Mexico, the minimum is made to vary with the needs of the separate *municipios*. But the determination of a minimum becomes mandatory upon the agencies created by the law, and once established is enforcible against the employers. In practice the meaning of the law will, in the long run, depend upon the slow process of education and habituation to a new type of relationship between labor and its employers. When one re-

flects that wages differ very widely in Mexico, and that the older practices of payment in kind still persist in places, it becomes clear that any general enforcement of the law will be slow. It will be a long time before the law reaches beyond the larger industrial and mining centers; it will be longer still before it reaches from the small commercial communities into the rural districts. But as it stands, it is a declaration of policy that all labor must receive a wage that in each specific area is considered sufficient to permit a man to bring up his family consistent with the prevailing standards of living and the prevailing notions of right and justice. Unregulated competition as a theory of labor employment has disappeared. The worker can now claim a minimum wage determined by a public body upon which he is represented; this minimum becomes enforcible in law.

3. *Compulsory trade unionism.*—Equally important and perhaps of greater significance both in theory and in fact is the trend toward compulsory trade unionism. Indicative of this trend are such rules as the following: All workers have a right to organize. All organized workers having registered their union with the boards of conciliation and arbitration acquire a legal character, and no one may decline to have dealings with them. All employers employing organized labor must, if they are so requested, enter into a collective contract with the organization. The contract must be with the majority group, but cannot be less favorable than the one already in existence with any other group. If various trades are represented in the industry, then a contract must be signed to include all after a common agreement between them or with each group separately.

The collective agreement must be in writing and a copy must be placed in the hands of the boards of conciliation and arbitration before it can become enforcible in law. The contract applies even to those workers who are not members of a union. The employer must collect the dues if he is so requested. The union has a right to demand that an employer shall in the future hire only members of the organization. The contract remains in force even if the union is disbanded and during periods of negotiations for its renewal and during strikes and lockouts. A collective agreement made between two-thirds of the employers and employees in any industry becomes enforcible upon all the other employers and workers in the same region. The trade union has a right to demand the dismissal of any worker who is either expelled from, or resigns from, the organization.

A sufficient number of rules and regulations made enforcible in law by the boards of conciliation and arbitration have been indicated to show that if enforced they must result in a general organization of workers, in at least the larger industrial units. It is not too much to say that we have here, as a matter of public policy, a general declaration of compulsory trade unionism. True, no workers are compelled to organize. But the advantages for organization are so obvious that the general development of trade unionism as an instrument of public policy may be considered as a declared objective of the government. In practice, the labor contract embodies the basic industrial law of the Nation and is enforcible through the special agencies created for that purpose.

4. *The right of a worker in his job.*—The law further carries out in practice the implication that the worker has a right to the job he holds. In fact, a property right in the job seems to be created and protected. The major provisions indicating this purpose include the following: The law declares all labor free except that which interferes with a third person, or is inimical to public interest, and then defines as an interference with a third person the substitution of a discharged worker before the case has been settled by the boards of conciliation and arbitration; and defines as inimical to social interests the substitution of strikers by other laborers before the conflict has been settled.

It also declares it to be against public policy for the minority to continue at work after the majority has declared a strike. The strike does not extinguish the labor contract; and if the strike is declared legal and the employer found in the wrong, then the employer must pay the workers for the time lost during the strike. Suspension of plant requires legal sanction from the board of conciliation and arbitration, and if the plant reopens the former employees have a preference to their former jobs within thirty days. In case of legal foreclosure the employees are entitled to one month's pay; and if the firm reopens it must reëmploy them or give them three months' salary at their own choice. If the establishment is forced to close by an act of God then the workers have the first lien upon the insurance of the concern to the extent of three months' pay. The rule covering three months' compensation for unfair discharge is another item in the same general principle, as is the assertion that a contract continues in force until, and unless, a new contract is signed.

These general principles covering a great multitude of special limitations and rights, such as the prohibition of child labor, limitation of women's labor, the assertion of a right of free ingress and egress to the property of the industry, to a right to free commerce, to a right to a school if the industry is located in communities below a certain size, and many other specific details, make industrial labor a special and highly protected class in the community. It is true of course that the law has no universal enforcement at present. It is also true that it will be a long time before such enforcement is possible. It is also true that under the pressure of economic necessity the workers bargain away one or another detail of the rights to which they are entitled under the law. Clearly enough, however, the workers in Mexico have a position very different from that which they occupied before the Revolution.

In 1907 when General Díaz attempted to settle the strike

in Rio Blanco, one of his chief provisions was that each worker should be given a little book in which the manager would write down, "in justice and without prejudice," the character and attainments of the bearer. The worker would recive this little book free the first time and pay 50 centavos for it if he lost it. It would be signed by the manager hiring or dispensing with the laborer. It was a sort of blacklist under official sanction. That was in 1908. In 1917, within nine years the workers were given Article 123, and now fourteen years later they have a general labor law which if fully enforced would make Mexican labor the best protected labor group in the world, with the possible exception of Russia.

Certainly there is no code of labor quite so elaborate or so fully favoring the interests of labor as the one now in existence in Mexico. It can be said that although the agrarian revolution has been partial, the labor revolution has been comprehensive and sweeping within the scheme of the capitalistic system. Whether current business enterprise can support such a system of industrial law as we have described remains to be seen. It is too early, perhaps, to attempt to describe its effect upon the development of industry in Mexico, but we may venture to suggest the type of broad influence which the law may be expected to have.

CHAPTER 23

IMPERIALISM AND LABOR LEGISLATION

THE Federal Labor Law will tend to restrict the rapid development of industry in Mexico. It will require great inducements and unusual promises of a secured profit to lead foreign capitalists to venture their investments into a market where labor prerogatives are so firmly established in law and where labor agencies can impose what amounts to a supervising hand over management. On the other hand this system of law is bound to give a security to capital that is invested which it could not count on before. The mere existence of an elaborate body of law reducible to a written contract and subject to adjudication before a judicial body upon which the entrepreneur is represented tends to the avoidance of strikes, rebellions and undue and unexpected upheavals. Moreover the existence of such an organized body of labor tends to assure the continuance of government with a greater certainty than could be counted on in Mexico before this.

The effect of the law upon the profitable operations of the industry will probably tend to the rapid adoption of modern labor-saving machinery. The general cost of labor will be high in proportion to similar industrial establishments under similar economic conditions, and to reduce that labor cost the employers will have a very real inducement to utilize every new device that comes to hand. The law will tend to restrict industrial development in Mexico to those industries that have a great natural advantage in available resources or market, or in special aptitude of its labor. Taking the situation as a whole, the law will tend to favor the large-scale industrialist as against the small one, since cost per unit is bound to be higher for the small manufacturer because of his inability to provide, under the circumstances, the high initial investment in new machinery required for profitable operation. The law will tend to enlist labor on the side of a high tariff to exclude foreign goods produced under lower cost because of poorer labor conditions. Better machinery will in part compensate for this, but it must be clear that it will tend to keep both labor and industry in a privileged position as against the rest of the population, a position long occupied by the industrialists, and now shared by the workers as well. It will raise the cost of living for all of the people for the sake of keeping the prerogatives of the small proportion represented by the laboring and industrial elements. It will favor the continuance and the increase in local handicrafts. Just because the large establishment is subject to the elaborate control we have indicated, the production by hand of the things that can be so produced in a market protected by a high tariff, but unavailable to the manufacturer because of high cost of elaborate machinery and high labor, will probably in the long run result in a resurgence of that quality of workmanship which is so distinctive a feature of the more rural and primitive economy of the mass of the people.

The industrial development of Mexico, therefore, will tend to both the continuance and the increase of the handicraft industries. In that respect the incidence of industrialism will probably prove markedly different from what experience has taught us to expect. In England, for example, industrialism marked the death knell of handicrafts. In Mexico the opposite may well take place, and it seems sufficiently important to deserve comment. There is no good economic reason why Mexico should, for instance, exchange her rather meager resources for the doubtful privilege of importing cheap, machine-made cooking utensils when its own population can produce a rich variety of colorful and individualistic pottery that will serve the same ends, without sacrificing Mexico's limited ability to maintain her international balance of payments.

Two things stand out: first, the high tariffs and the high protection of Mexican labor against foreign employers constitute species of nationalism; second, and most significant, the indiscriminate exploitation of both native labor and native resources have come to an end so far as Mexico is concerned. The laws concerning land, mineral, oil, and similar legislation set distinctive limitations upon the unrestricted exploitation of land and resources. The labor code, if enforced, would set real limits upon exploitation of labor. Taken together the laws set a limitation upon the reach of imperialism and establish a new mode for the world in its relationships with undeveloped areas possessing raw materials.

This outcome, unexpected as it was from a purely Mexican point of view, has an even greater significance when viewed from an international view point. It isn't merely that specific legislation, rules and regulations, concepts and institutions which have been devised have already had a repercussion in other lands and have therefore overflowed the boundaries of Mexico itself, which is not strange in a world so closely bound by communication as ours, but what could not be foreseen, and what is of greater significance than even the Mexicans may have dreamed, is that it has set a norm for the control of the difficulties that arise between the industrial and non-industrial nations. The meaning of the Mexican labor development for what is known as economic imperialism is a matter of profound significance. These laws set up a new way of dealing with a problem that has torn and disturbed world opinion and politics since the beginning of the industrial era.

The position of an undeveloped country possessing natural resources has been peculiarly weak and indefensible against the power of modern nations bent upon exploiting the natural resources of the less developed areas. The demand for gold and silver, for iron, oils and coal has been so insistent, the gains of private investors seemed to fit in so well with the broader national interest of the industrial and capital exporting countries, as to place at the disposal of the investor the enhanced military power of the industrial nations against the practically unarmed and untutored people who by a freak of fortune were possessed of those things like rubber and tungsten, oil and tin, which the industrial nations needed.

Under these circumstances, the misfortune of the undeveloped areas was almost proportionate to the availability of their natural resources. Up until the Mexican Revolution it has seemed that the only defense against the sudden and devastating incursion of such foreign influence had to be devised within the industrial nation. The battle against the evils of imperialism, it seemed, had to be financed and carried by the liberal and humane elements in the imperial areas themselves. This was especially true where the great wealth and power of the private organizations engaged in such imperialistic enterprises made them almost invulnerable against the weak powers of defense of the backward communities.

Such a condition has been well illustrated, for instance, in the *Monterías* in southern Mexico. The wealth of the private concerns made a virtue out of cupidity, dishonesty and bribery. The local governors found means to wealth and well-being, to power and influence through the agency and support of the foreign concerns whose cats-paws they were willing to become for a consideration—not necessarily a large one either. Under such conditions, it seemed that the only defense of the interest of the mass of common people, Indian or Negro, in unindustrialized areas had to be found among the more disinterested elements in the investing country who could establish some control through pressure at home. That was the situation before 1910. If there were protests from the people in backward countries themselves they were either disregarded or suppressed.

The white man's burden became one that the common people in the backward areas had to bear, and the whole philosophy of international politics was tinctured with a doctrine of racial superiority and moral purpose that served the exploiting countries well, natural perhaps, but unsavory in any objective consideration. The prerogative of the industrial nations had found favor in the religion, the morals, the politics and the public policy of these nations, and the strange and curious, but insidious, fact was that not infrequently the governing elements in the backward areas were cajoled, flattered and bribed into accepting the belief that the best thing for them as a people was to give the foreign investing and exploiting elements a free rein in the use, not merely of the resources, but of the people whose labor made the exploitation of the resources possible.

The Mexican Revolution is distinguished in that it proved to be not merely a revolution for the reform of the internal social and economic pattern, but came to be an attempt to set a limit to the foreign control of the internal politics and economic affairs of the people. The Revolution was not merely national—it was in this sense international—for it set in force a series of influences that, continuing, must still in the future modulate the activities of foreign investing elements within the national area. From this point of view the development of labor in Mexico has a political and theoretical significance that far outstrips the national interest of Mexico itself. The Mexican Revolution through its labor movement has set up a series of institutions, rules and regulations that give the Mexicans the major rôle in setting limits to the reach and character of foreign imperialism within their borders. It has thus shown that the undeveloped nations, at least certain types of them, are not entirely incapable of self-defense. More than that it has shown that the native races can, under proper guidance, not merely set limits to and devise modulations for the influx of modern industrialism, to the damage of the native population, but that they can strive to become a participant in the fruits of the exploitation of the natural resources that invite foreign capital.

If the law continues on the statute books long enough to become the norm, the habit of a nation, and if in time labor is sufficiently organized to become truly participants in the benefits and rights that the law implies, then the workers of Mexico will be one of the best protected and, within their sphere, one of the most powerful labor groups among those in the less-industrial countries. Clearly, again, this law and procedure, if continued, will develop a distinctly Mexican type of labor relationship. The old slavery is dead. The more recent capitalism of the Díaz régime is nearly dead, and a new type, more native, more Mexican, has come on the horizon and is replacing the previous forms. Here the Revolution has created something new and challenging.

CHAPTER 24

EXPERIENCE AND PHILOSOPHY IN EDUCATION

N o outcome of the Mexican Revolution is more significant than the rural educational movement that
has grown from it. The educational undertaking is
profoundly creative, broader in scope and more deeply
touched with a sense of emergence of a new spirit than either
the agrarian or the labor movements. It attempts to reach
deep into the spirit of the people and open the modern world
to them without withering the culture they possess and have
preserved. It is the most modern, yet the most delicate and
sensitive, large-scale movement of cultural stimulus and social awakening that can be recorded in America, and perhaps
in the world.

The educational movement is the broadest effort of the
Revolution. Its aim is to reach even the most isolated communities and bring to them the values imbedded in the rural
school. I have seen schools among the fire-worshipping Hui-
choles in the Sierra de Nayarit, among the sturdy and stubborn Chamula Indians in Chiapas, among the Maya Indians
in the tropical forests of Southern Yucatan, and among the
Trique Indians in Oaxaca. Everywhere in mountain and dale,
in the tropics and in the wind-blown Sierras, one may find
a little school. It may be poor, it may be inadequate, it may
be an incomplete sampling of the deal, but it is there. The
impulse traveling from Mexico City has successfully reached
into all the highways and byways—from desert to forested
tropics, from the cold mountains to the hot climates of
Tabasco with its overflown rivers, and its schools half filled
with water, as I have seen them in the rainy season, the inspector and visitor wading with bare feet inside the school
room. But the school was there, the children were there, and

so was the teacher. The rural school now reaches into every state of the country, into virtually every county. Counting only the Federal rural schools, including those of *"escuelas de circuito,"* there were in 1931 as many as 6,401 schools, served by 7,454 teachers. These 7,454 teachers are the link between the city and the country, between the present and the past in Mexico. It cannot be repeated too often in discussing Mexico that the gap between the city, which is of today, and the country, which is of yesterday, is so vast that the effort to bridge it, which is in essence the deeper meaning of the educational movement, is a Herculean task, one which cannot be realized in a day, a year, or perhaps even in a generation. The school is the visible sign of the attempt to bring the two Mexicos, that of the past and that of the present, into a common focus. This going out into the primitive, the rural world, so different from the city, is the clearest evidence of the newer nationalism of Mexico, of a recognition that Mexico is a unified people and not merely a unified government.

The educational development came after the Revolution had achieved a certain maturity, a certain success. The demand for land was one of the initial impulses that made the Revolution possible. The cry for social justice embodied in the labor conflicts even before the fall of the Díaz régime gave a moral justification to the later urging of a labor code. But the demand for education was stillborn in the first days of the Revolution and for ten years after it got under way. It is true that in the last days of Díaz an attempt was made to develop rural education on a national scale. But nothing came of it, and it was a mere afterthought to preserve the Díaz régime. Under Madero, and later even under Huerta, there was some talk and some legislative effort at education, but the country was not ready for the undertaking. It was still too early. The direction of the Revolution had not been marked out, passions were too generally at a boiling point, and the battle for dominance between groups was still the major concern of those driven by public purpose. Carranza brought but little peace—his task was gigantic enough without embarking upon a new effort—and the turmoil persisted for another four years. In fact he reduced the participation of the Federal government in the education of the people and abolished even the narrow-scoped department of *instrucción y bellas artes*. Responsibility for education, even in the Federal District and Federal territories, was left to the local officials. It was only after the overthrow of Carranza, when Obregón came to office, that an educational awakening made itself felt.

Obregón took office in 1920. The Federal department of education was created in 1921. It was therefore more than ten years after the Revolution had begun that the Federal government assumed responsibility for the education of the rural population.

In those years an imperceptible, but real, change had occurred in Mexico. The Revolution had slowly become clothed with a social program and a philosophy. It had taken the movement ten years to triumph against its military enemies. In that time a popular consciousness among the masses had been stirred sufficiently to make Obregón feel secure in the support of the common people even against his own military supporters. It had taken the Revolution ten years for the agrarian and labor codes to become accepted as definite and defined objectives, at least among the more self-conscious elements. It had also taken Mexico ten years to shake off the burden of the foreign spiritual tutelage to which it was subject. The isolation of Mexico during the Revolution, due to lack of recognition by foreign governments and to the Great War, forced it to a self-reliance, to a self-consciousness it lacked before. Conflict with American interests and controversy with the United States made this self-consciousness more poignant. More important still, in those ten years the forgotten Indian had proved the most stubborn, the most persistent, and the most genuine of the Mexican revolutionists.

The symbolism now attached to Zapata is true at least in the sense that he forced upon the people of Mexico, by the unbending simplicity of his demands, the belief in the redemption of the Indian. Zapata was only one of the rural leaders, the most stubborn, the most effective; the Cedillo brothers in San Luis Potosí, and many others in isolated places, in their struggle for land, unconsciously fought the greater battle for acceptance upon a footing of equality by the other elements of the nation. In a deeper sense, the agrarian revolution was a spiritual one, a battle for social and cultural equality. The Indian came to be valued and to be highly valued. In fact, the Indian came to be considered perhaps the most important element in the nation. The pendulum had swung back again after four centuries. The educational movement, which emerged as the Revolution found a center of equilibrium when the scattered forces struggling against injustice found relief from battle, faced a new Mexico. The rural Mexico, the primitive, the Indian, the *peon* world, which had lain hidden and obscure for so long a time, was now suddenly confronting a city civilization and demanding cognizance. The rural districts had emerged with Obregón. They became for the time the major force in the make-up of the nation. The educational program of the Revolution now came to be a program that would reach into the mountain crevices and the hidden forests of the tropics. The Revolution came to express itself in an attempt to identify the Indian and the rest of Mexico as a common people. These changes had made but one route possible, the effort to forge a nation out of a divergence of race, one culture out of many cultures. The educational movement was the formal recognition of the new Mexico. It was not an artificial attempt to construct. It was an acceptance of a change that had already occurred.

VENUSTIANO CARRANZA

The philosophy of the movement, therefore, when it got under way, was a rationalization, a recognition of the new values that had come out of the conflict: the passion, the ruthlessness, and the unyielding character of the underlying population, especially of the Indian when once stirred into action. Whereas the course of the Revolution was frequently determined by accident and incident, by unplanned and unformulated impulse, by a wandering host of unconnected groups, the educational program, when it came to accept the change that had thus been wrought, found therein its program. The program of the educational movement was ready made by the Revolution, and consisted in taking a newly discovered people of Mexico into the sphere of the culture making activities of the government. The program was broadened later by a recognition of the scope, and deepened by insight into the complexity, of the problem. A philosophy had to be discovered that would embrace not merely a new nation but a nation of sharply divergent peoples, culture patterns, and economic needs and possibilities. It is, however, important to remember that the educational movement had direction forced on it even before it attempted to formulate that direction into words.

It was the special genius of Vasconcelos to dramatize and vocalize this change in Mexico. For this, Mexico owes Vasconcelos an incalculable debt. The present educational movement still lives by the faith that he generated. He converted the educated classes in Mexico to the belief in education for the common people, for the Indian. His service was in a large measure the service of a prophet to a cause, and it remains true that even those who deplore his more recent activities credit him with giving Mexican education the original impetus from which it still draws much of its drive. Vasconcelos' program, as he expressed it in the days when he was battling for the establishment of a Federal Department of Education, was to "redeem the Indian, educate the masses."

That is still the program, and is bound to remain so for a long time to come—for the completion of the task is still in the far future.

This change in attitude has grown into both a general and particular philosophy of education. The theory holds that the Indian is as good as the white man, if not better. The Indian, therefore, must not be separated from the white man; he must be taken in, accepted, given a place and a rôle equal to his strength in numbers and ability. It is a complete revolution in the attitude towards the Indian race. The theory proclaimed by the early Spaniards, that the Indian was a child, has been replaced. The theory that he was an inferior being, generated in more recent times, has been repudiated. The assumption that the Indian is and must remain the pariah of Mexico has been denied, figuratively and literally, by the Revolution. But such a change in attitude was not sufficient in itself. A more specific program of education, a program that would make possible the adoption of the newly discovered values to the problems of creating a nation out of nationalities, was essential. Here something of importance happened.

If it is true that the Indian is as good and worthy as the members of other races in Mexico, then his cultural patterns, which have persisted for centuries, are equally good. These, too, must be preserved. Education must not destroy and substitute, it must cultivate and develop the existing values. It may add; it may enrich; it may stimulate, but it must not deprive and deny what there is of value in their way of life and culture, that which is native and genuine. Education, therefore, becomes something very sensitive—it becomes a ministration, rather than a teaching. It becomes, too, a dealing with the adult and not merely with the child, for it is among the adults that the pattern is to be seen, the culture to be found, and the source of a future development to be sought. Education in Mexico tends to become education for the community rather than for the individual. The concern is for the cultivation of values imbedded in the group, the community.

The program of the Department of Education, therefore, when it got under way, was profoundly enriched by revolutionary experience and modified from what might have been its objective. The notion of redeeming the Indian had become, in the process, one of enriching the total Mexican scene by the cultivation of the unique culture of the groups that make the Mexican pattern. Education had moved from teaching to cultivation, stimulus, awakening of hidden springs of power and beauty; it had moved from teaching children to working with adults in their tasks of living; it had moved from the individual to the community. The program of education became a task—an enormous task of developing and providing leadership from some common fountain, with some common purpose that would bind the thousands of little communities together into a mutually understandable and participating people. Its task became primarily to make a conscious nation out of the thousands of isolated, little, self-sufficient corners, each different, each individual, each self-contained, content and stubborn and suspicious of the outside. This is a task for leadership, imagination, understanding and inventiveness. Children may be content to learn, communities must, and do, carry on and grow. Outside sources of coöperation can help in the process of growth. The school, of necessity, had little to give unless it could give a great deal. What it might impart to the children in the hidden mountain villages would be little remembered and of small purpose. In a world where there are no books, no newspapers, no contemporary mechanism that requires literacy, where the age-old pattern goes on from generation to generation because it is so well adapted to the environment, and where prejudices matter so much, reading, writing and arithmetic are matters of minor import. What the community needs is not reading, except as an incident. It requires something to evoke the spirit of the unity which lies imbedded in the little integrated community, and in the process to make it an agency of a better life, here and now, as part of the process of education and as part of the business of living. Unless the school could bring something to vitalize the sum of life in the little village it would be comparatively insignificant.

This program of ideas and ideals came to the fore more or less consciously, more or less rapidly, as the project of building schools, finding teachers, developing a school organization, began to be undertaken seriously. The ideal was clear enough. I remember Vasconcelos once saying to me, "we have all the ideas we need, more than we can use. What we need is money, resources, people, details, persistence." The ideas have grown with the years. So has the inventiveness, so have the concrete projects and plans, and so, one might add, have the people. But the ideal and real were far apart. It was no easy task to give Mexico an educational system, no easy task to undertake to do in a few years what had been neglected for four centuries. Not even the enthusiasm of the Revolution and the missionary zeal it left in its wake have been sufficient to consummate that task—and it remains an ideal, the fulfillment of which will require more than one generation of self-sacrifice and enthusiasm and faith.

Any one who has read the previous chapters of this book will have some notion of the difficulties that bestrew the path of an educational movement in Mexico. The country is very broken—*barrancas*, mountains, desert and tropics isolate one part of Mexico from another. There are few roads and heavy rains make such roads as exist impassable. There are schools now that are weeks by mule-back travel from any city. A system of education in a country so varied had to be flexible, it had to be resourceful. The school had to be adapted to its environment. The tropics, where it was hot, where it rained six months out of twelve, required a different school from the desert of Chihuahua, or the *sierra* of Puebla, where it was cold. Every detail had to be different, from architecture to the school season. The mere problem of supervision has seemed at times almost insurmountable. Inspectors—living on mule-back, traveling long, broken trails over mountains through rainy seasons, sometimes tumbling down hillsides and breaking their legs—in order to carry on had to be young enthusiastic missionaries filled with an ideal. Many a school district embraces regions having great variations in climate and physical character. The elements that make a school possible and easy in one place make it difficult in another. But the task of physical adaptation is mere child's play compared to the task of cultural adaptation. There are some forty races, and as many, or more, languages and dialects, some of them embracing hundreds of thousands of human beings, others only a few thousand. But the difficulty is not merely due to difference in race; but also a difference in culture. Here is a stubborn resistance to mixed schools, here early child marriages, here a deliberate hostility to the outsider, here a definite fear that the government is still, as it used to be, trying to do evil. "This government is different," said one Indian to me. "It is trying to be good to us." Here the children are expected to work with their parents in the field; there the community lies scattered for many miles, little houses dotting the steep mountains, with only a temporary community for festive days. Sometimes the children must be enticed away from the house and kept in the schoolhouse (as the teacher in Copala kept them), where meals are served them and sleeping quarters provided, because the homes are so far away that it requires a day's walk to get to school, and if they go home they can not come back again the next day. In some places the family moves to the *milpa* for the planting season and takes the children along. To build a school, a school with permanence and continuity of activity

271

is difficult under such conditions—in some places impossible.

Aside from these difficulties there has been the language barrier. To secure teachers who could make themselves understood (there are forty different dialects), who could leave behind them an impression sufficiently strong for the early training to continue—that has been a task too Herculean for even the best Department of Education. In addition, there is what we have already noted, a scattered population. There are some 70,000 little community groups, some of fewer than a hundred inhabitants, only a small number with a population of as many as four thousand. The more primitive the community, the more inaccessible it is likely to be.

These difficulties are sharpened by social conflict. Strife between the Indian and the *mestizo* has not disappeared, and in more than one region there is open hostility against the school because it is educating the Indian. In some places the conflict has even involved the teacher's life. Such conflict has occurred in Oaxaca, in Chiapas, in Chihuahua and in Michoacán: The *mestizo* and the white, near an Indian center, do not look kindly upon the education of the Indian, and cultural, linguistic and physical difficulties are made worse by a social attrition that even the Revolution has not destroyed. In addition there has existed, to a lesser extent at present, but certainly all through the years up to 1928, a considerable hostility that arose out of the conflict between the Church and the State. The common folk in the remote communities, stirred to opposition, made the attempt to organize schools difficult and sometimes hazardous. During the conflict in Jalisco and Durango, many schools were closed and the teachers concentrated in the larger centers, and occasionally Federal troops had to be called in to protect the teachers and the schools from an irate community that considered the school an outpost against the Church.

Added to these obstacles was the poverty of the Mexican government. The Revolution had drained the resources of the nation, and the tasks confronting the new government were so stupendous that finances for education commensurate with both the needs and the program were out of the question. Nor could the government fall back upon the states or the states upon the counties. If the income of the government was small, the income of the states was still smaller, and the counties were out of the running for a real educational effort. This poverty, great handicap though it was in the beginning, proved a blessing in disguise. It forced both the Federal government and the communities to discover ways and means of performing the task ahead with the little resources available. In a measure, the fruitfulness of the educational effort may be ascribed to the inventiveness that poverty imposed.

Another obstacle, and one deeply imbedded in all of Mexican social policy, is the persistent disillusionment and distrust. In the smaller communities, especially where there is racial division, or where *mestizos* are dominant, experience has taught the Indian to distrust the good intentions of outsiders, and the suspicion of the community against outsiders is frequently intensified by internal dissensions and passion that have made unity most difficult. The task of the early teacher became one of delicate adjustment to the mood and temper of a community. One had to be able to win his way slowly, to convert a community to the genuine honesty of the project. Here was something that really sought to be of service and that asked for nothing but an opportunity to be helpful. It might be said that although the movement has won, during the years, a large measure of support and confidence, the difficulties persist and make the task of the teacher much more burdensome.

In the more integrated Indian community this has been an easier task. There, at least, the basic faith of the Indians could still be counted upon. They were frequently suspicious and hostile, dubious and resentful, but at bottom there was still a remnant of faith, internal leadership and unity, and if confidence could be won, if the teacher had the skill and the knack to ingratiate himself in the community and gain its leadership, he had the assurance of complete coöperation. The teacher became the new spokesman of the community, its new spiritual leader. In a measure, the teacher has replaced the priest in the affections, loyalty and coöperation of the people. Where the teacher succeeds with an Indian community, there is nothing its inhabitants will not do for the school; no sacrifice is too great. They show a childish belief in the school and its teacher. But it requires a special type of leadership, a teacher with the genius of winning a place for himself in a community that is closed and stubborn to the outsider.

These various traits of conflict and prejudice, of poverty and doubt, describe the background for the school system. In passing judgment upon the failures and successes of a project that has had some ten years to grow and develop, one must do so with this background in mind.

CHAPTER 25

DIFFICULTY AND ACHIEVEMENT IN EDUCATION

IN A country where rural education is non-existent, the primary effort, must be to discover the teachers who will carry the task forward under conditions of poverty and insufficient support, who will be able and willing to go into the mountains and live in a primitive environment, sleep on the floor, eat the food of the common people, and live with folk that do not understand their language; these teachers must carry on lacking outside stimulus, where there is no one to talk with, where there are no books, no newspapers, where isolation is as complete as it would be on an island in mid-ocean. Weeks and months may pass without contact with the world abroad, without an opportunity to exchange in any common language such gossip and information as may be had. Any one who has seen the school teacher in the Mesa de Nayar in Nayarit will understand the possibility for isolation that being a teacher may involve. It required an exceptional teacher to make the task feasible at all in its early days, and it was only made feasible as a result of the Revolution.

Just as the Revolution provided the impulse for the movement, so it provided the instrumentalities. The students in the higher educational institutions, the *preparatoria*, the university, and the city normal school, were deeply stirred by the Revolution. The conflict provided them with a field for action and the promise of a social program that converted many of them to the service of their fellows in a way that was new in Mexico. When the Revolution broke like a flood, many of them joined the rebel forces to wander as soldiers in its armies. Vasconcelos found these young students, who had tasted hardship and bitterness in camp and battle-field, ready to hand, and enlisted them in the service of redeeming the Indian. The first task of Vasconcelos was to survey the field, to stir the rural communities of Mexico to the need of education, to work out some program, to locate the communities that would be receptive to the new venture. The students who had become soldiers now turned missionaries (as they were called), and with a pittance for a salary, with a mule under them, began to wander over *barranca* and mountain, in tropics and desert, to seek out rural communities and awaken them to the need for a school. The missionary became the outpost, the vanguard of a new army that was to invade and settle in the country. The arrival of a missionary led to the calling of the town together, the holding of meetings, the process of persuasion and conversion. The community was offered the service of a teacher if it could provide a school, a piece of land, and coöperation. The missionary made a census of the community, enumerated the children of school age that were available, signed a species of contract with the elders of the community, and informed the Department of Education that such and such a village, in such and such a place, of such a race and language, had so many children and was willing to receive a teacher, willing to provide a school building, willing to take part in the effort of education. That was the first step.

The Department then set about to find the teachers for the rural schools. That was no easy task. The effort to develop such teachers has been, and still is, one of the major responsibilities of the Department. The ordinary, normal-school teacher, city born and city bred, was hardly fit for the task. Here again the Revolution served its end. The years of struggle had drawn into the conflict many who later became teachers. They had been poorly trained as teachers, but they had qualities of leadership, of initiative, of character born of the years of strife, and they were stirred by an ideal.

Anyone who had the privilege of knowing the earlier enthusiasm of the educational movement and the zeal with which the first teachers went to their tasks, will have realized that what these teachers lacked in equipment they made up in enthusiasm, in loyalty, in leadership. The teachers, men and women, were taken in hand by the missionary, brought to the little community and received in all solemnity, with a *fiesta*, with music, with faith.

The teacher was located in a community. The missionary, now become inspector, departed to other sections of his zone and the teacher was left to his own resources. His first duty was to secure a school. The task was sometimes easy. The unused buildings next to the church were cleaned up and scrubbed, the church yard was cleared, the church bell came to life, the children sat on the floor or on stumps or on mats, a home-made blackboard was improvised, the teacher brought a few pieces of chalk with him and a book or two. The Department of Education began printing reading material and sending it out. The school was started. If an annex to a church was not available, then the *municipio* might be used, the town hall, or part of it, or the town jail was converted into a school, or a little chapel that was in sight might, after much deliberation, thought taking, and heartburning, be turned over to secular use. If these were not available, some *vecino* might donate his house. If the worst came to the worst, the school could be held under a tree, as it was in many a place. The teacher was paid and supervised by the Federal government; all else was in the hands of the community. A school, once started, in time acquired a building. It took money, it took labor, it took ingenuity. The community was always poor in money; it was also almost always poor in technique. There was usually no carpenter, no mason, no blacksmith, no tools. To build a school under the circumstances was a measure of large endeavor, but it has been done in thousands of communities. By 1931 nearly 3,000 communities had set up their own school buildings. The Federal government has, apart from the schools in empty buildings attached to churches, provided no school housing, which has been done entirely by the community. The communities are frequently ambitious. The school is often the best building in town, the newest, the cleanest, the most modern, and frequently, the largest. And it has been built as a community enterprise. There is always a school committee of elders. The school committee, the town government, the villagers, the children, with the teacher as architect and engineer, get the building under way. They decide on a piece of land after much discussion, they fix upon a plan, then they begin to collect material. It may be stone; if so, the children and the elders, the men and the women, go out and gather stones and pile them up. Then there is lime to be made. Then there is flooring to be purchased, and roofing, and windows and doors. A carpenter or a mason may have to be hired. Money must be secured. For this purpose the community will set aside a piece of land and till it, using the proceeds of the crop for the school financing. It will make a special collection of a few cents a week. It will sell a pig or a burro. The teacher will organize a *fiesta* and collect money.

Then the building will commence. On Saturdays, on Sundays, on holidays, the whole village will be there. Old men, bent over, will carry small stones from the big pile to the place where they are needed. The children will do their share—they will carry water. The younger men, under the direction of the teacher or of a mason, will place the stones. If the work cannot all be done during the holidays, then the community will work on the school by turns, each member giving a day or more a week, depending upon the season of the year. During the planting and the harvesting seasons the work may have to be suspended, and then taken up again. The building of the school may take a year, or even more. I have seen schools all built except for the roof, the doors and the windows. There was no money.

"After the *zafra*, if we have a good crop this year, we will finish our school."

"I hope I will live to see the school finished," one aged Indian in VeraCruz said to me.

"Why?"

"Because I want to be able to say to God that I came with Him that far."

When the school is finished it is inaugurated with a great *fiesta*. Other towns are invited, the inspector of schools, the director, the Governor of the state—it is a great day. The important thing is that the school belongs to the community in a spiritual as well as a physical sense. Much of the enthusiasm and the aspiration of the year have been entwined about it.

If one asks why the school in rural Mexico has succeeded in socializing its activities, in incorporating the community, the answer is that it began as a community effort—a genuine process of social endeavor. The schools constructed in this fashion in the last few years have been valued at 2,000,000 pesos. This is an impressive amount to come from communities that have little or no money income. But the larger value has been in the by-product of the activity. The school has reënforced the older community *mores*, has brought forth again the older powers of leadership and activity that have been dormant for so long a time. Examples can be given by the hundreds of the spirit and effort involved. Here is one from a letter written in 1931 that will typify the rest:

The school committee of this village of Pozo Grande, to fulfill its duty, renders the following report to the *pueblo:*

The fifty-five citizens who live in this community were invited by Compañero Martín Angeles to construct a house for the school. Being all in agreement, we immediately elected a committee.

With the help of the Governor of the state and the Presidente Municipal, we acquired the land from the Señora Margarita Zamora, the widow of Herrera. As we are all poor we agreed that on Sundays, when we do not work in the field, we will each do our task under the direction of the educational committee. In this we were aided even by the children. To buy certain materials we taxed ourselves in proportion to our earnings and we gave our share very willingly because we understand the benefit that our children and even we ourselves will receive.

The work began last year and was finished in a period of thirteen months. It has been evaluated at 1,400 pesos, but the greater part of this is represented by the work which was done by the whole community. The Governor of the state had the kindness to present us with a dozen beams, ten sacks of cement, and two sacks of gypsum. The cultural mission was kind enough to help us by paying for the carpenter who made the windows and the doors, we supplying the material. This help we are very grateful for. We hope that the village will approve what we have done and will continue assisting us.

This tapping of the community spirit made possible by the type of leadership produced by the Revolution and by the nature of the community itself, determined the character of the school. The school became the center of the community's activities, and these activities grew to be the program of the school, the program of the department, the philosophy of education. The ideal and the practical were being fused in the process of developing a program. In a sense, therefore, the program of social activity and community betterment grew, not from the top, but from the bottom. The need and the activities of the communities and the intuitive sense of the teachers made possible the absorption of this aspiration as a program; the school accepted it as its main end. Reading and writing and arithmetic were useful, and important in their place, but what was more significant was the opening through the schools of channels for the kind of social coöperation which is the special genius and tradition of the small Mexican rural community; and the more unified in race, the greater the strength and power of common endeavor that these communities display. It was the special genius of leaders like Moisés Sáenz, like Rafael Ramírez, to be receptive to this need, to become conscious of this spirit, to take it on as an objective after it had become apparent as a possibility, and to project it as a philosophy and program of the Department of Education. The burden of interest shifted from schooling to living. The question that was asked of the teacher ceased to be how well can your children read, but how much is the school the center of activity in the community? How much has the school done for the community during the last year?

A good school became a school with multiple activities, with something going on all of the time. The school, the good school, has no rest period, It is open from early dawn till late at night. I asked one teacher when school stopped. She reflected a moment and then said, "It never stops. When I get tired I go and rest."

The school, like the community itself, is always alive. An ideal school has many things in it. The list we give here may not be duplicated in any one school, but there are many schools that have very nearly all of these things, and some have more. The community, having built a school, tends gradually to acquire these other features.

There is, first of all, the school building; a special house for the teacher, built the same way; school furniture, constructed by the community; a flower garden; a vegetable garden; a plot of agricultural land, frequently as large as $12\frac{1}{2}$ acres, worked by the community for the benefit of the school, known as the *ejido* of the school; a carpenter shop; a leather working, a weaving, a pottery, or other shop adjusted to the needs of the community; a medicine chest; a barber shop (the children have their hair cut in school); a small library; a small regional museum; a basket-ball field; volley ball, baseball and other games; an open-air theater; a chicken coop; a bee hive; a piggery; a rabbit house; a dove cote; a shower bath; outhouses (great innovations in the rural community); a sewing machine and a community stove.

Not only does the school have all of these *anexos*, but it

tends to become an agency for all sorts of general community activities. The open-air theater becomes the meeting place of the community; the school provides weekly affairs, night courses for adults, afternoon courses for the women, cultural activities for Sundays and holidays. It organizes inter-community athletic meets, it has carried on a campaign (as I have seen it), with a banner and band, in favor of the census which was soon to be taken. It organizes regional fairs, it gathers the community together and digs a well, or brings the water into town. It stimulates the building of a road. In places like Oaxaca, I have seen the Indians carry the wire on their backs over the mountains for days to install a telephone. They placed the poles, the Department of Education providing the technical skill, the teacher acting as telephone operator, and the school being the receiving center. It organizes post offices for communities where they do not exist, it builds baths for the community, ir organizes parent-teacher associations, it establishes coöperatives for children and elders, it carries on a campaign in favor of saving the lives of little children.

These are but a few of the more obvious activities that the schools undertake. I have seen others—such as straightening the streets of the community, numbering the houses, whitewashing the houses, and planting, as an experiment, new crops unknown to the village; organizing orchestras and bands; providing musical training (if the teacher is competent); teaching new crafts. The teacher frequently acts as the representative of the community in its disputes and problems, and on more than one occasion has become the agrarian leader of the community.

We have here an indication of the task of the school and of the teacher. It may, perhaps, be worth giving an official listing of the kinds of activities and the number of schools that participated in them during 1930.

Of the 6,032 schools under Federal control at the time the

FRANCISCO I. MADERO ENTERING MEXICO CITY

record was made, the following distribution of activities is recorded:

Number of Schools	Per cent	Activity
6,032	100.0	Total under Federal control
3,197	53.0	Course for adults
644	10.7	Course on Saturday and Sunday
3,744	62.1	Social gatherings
4,047	67.1	Cleanliness campaigns
4,115	68.2	Anti-alcoholic campaign
2,408	40.0	Did vaccinating
3,251	53.9	Organized expositions and fairs
515	8.5	Built roads
296	4.5	Brought water into the community
384	6.4	Established post-office
156	2.6	Established telegraph lines
156	2.6	Installed telephones
1,503	25.0	Organized libraries
780	12.9	Installed baths for the community
3,962	65.7	Organized educational committees
3,223	53.4	Organized anti-alcoholic committees
678	11.2	Organized committees for the protection of children
1,597	26.5	Organized adult cultural societies
1,899	31.5	Organized adult athletic societies
2,363	40.0	Established small instructive industries
1,310	21.7	Had small skilled crafts
4,561	75.6	Had either children, adult or neighborhood coöperatives
3,120	51.7	Cultivated fields
2,229	37.0	Kept chickens
1,169	19.4	Kept doves
806	13.4	Kept rabbits
588	9.7	Kept bees
463	7.7	Kept pigs
288	4.8	Kept other animals
197	3.3	Children's playgrounds
2,815	46.7	Athletic fields
1,409	23.4	Open-air theaters

Number of Schools	Per cent	Activity
575	9.5	Regional museums
1,426	23.6	Had outhouses
2,884	47.8	Had their own schools
11		Built special houses for their teachers

A few reports from villages and from teachers and inspectors of schools, will indicate that this list of activities is more than a mere cataloguing of form and program. The small primitive communities in their poverty and simplicity make every effort expressive of an aspiration. The little town of Comaltepec, in Oaxaca, held a solemn meeting on the twenty third of January, 1928, to transfer to the new educational committee the responsibilities that had been exercized by the one elected the previous year. The report of the chairman of the old committee to the new one is as follows:

The village authorities and the educational committee that I was honored in presiding over, and which I surrender today, have brought their grain of sand to the civilizing work of the Federal school in this village in the following manner:

In December, 1926, we secured the gift of land for a school garden.

In January, 1927, this garden was fenced in.

A new school was commenced on the 9th of March.

Sills for the windows of the new school were constructed.

The new school was completed on the 29th of May, 1927. The materials of construction were adobe, clay, and it still needs roofing, flooring, and doors.

On June 7 there were planted for the school two *almudes* of maize.

On June 26 two bee hives were bought for the school.

On June first the school was presented with chicks and on June 28th the maize patch was hoed.

In August, 1927 the chicken coop was built.

On September 12th a half dozen benches and desks were secured for the school and on the 17th a plot of land was set aside for the school and its own maize.

A spinning wheel and a comb were bought for the school.

In November we planted four *maquilas* of wheat for the school.

A lamp was bought for the night school.

The corn, a poor crop, was picked, amounting to one *fanega*, which the new committee received on the 23rd of January, 1928.

The new committee was given $3.75, which is the remaining fund in the cooperative.

Members of the new committee, in undertaking the sacred task of the Federal school, my humble co-workers and I hold the hope that you will outdo us in enthusiasm and in effective acts. We beg of you to neglect no effort or resources for the good of the children of our village; if you act that way the nation will honor you. If not, it will blame you.

This report from the educational committee is one way of detailing the activities that are organized about the school. Here is another, a different one, from a little poverty-stricken community among the Otomí Indians in Hidalgo who undertook to support an *escuela de circuito*. The inability of the government, for budgetary reasons, to assume responsibility for all the schools forced it to attempt to develop schools which were, in part at least, self-supporting, and the following is a contract with the educational authorities that tells its own story:

We, the neighbors of Boxaxni, belonging to the Municipality of San Salvador, in the state of Hidalgo, assembled together near the chapel of our village, solemnly promise in the presence of Professor José del Carmen Solís, the representative of the Department of Public Education, to establish and maintain our own school, in accordance with the following conditions:

I. Every one of us will pay the teacher one cent daily; we, being fifty-three in number, will pay consequently, 53 cents daily; this amount will be collected by the treasurer of the School Committee and delivered to the teacher precisely on the last day of every month.

II. We will, by turns, give the teacher meals of the quality which our poor economic circumstances will permit, promising to deliver these to him in such a way as not to interfere with his school work.

III. We promise to give the teacher a house which he may use as his residence. We will give a locality for the school, and little by little, we shall erect the annexes which it may require later on.

IV. We promise to send to the said school all our children of school age, boys and girls, and we, the adults, will also go to the school in so far as our work permits us. Professor Solis solemnly promises on his part that the teacher appointed by him will Comply with his duties as a good teacher, teaching the children and the adults and advising all the neighbors in all the affairs of vital importance. He also promises to visit the school frequently for the purpose of ascertaining whether it is running with regularity without encountering any difficulty on its way. As security for constancy of our obligation we enter into this agreement on Saturday, the 9th of February, in the year 1929, at 5 o'clock in the afternoon, and it is signed by those who know how to sign and the names of those who do not know how to sign.

These reports of committees and communities may be supplemented by similar reports from teachers, and from inspectors as well as from Federal directors of education. Space will not permit many such records. But it is difficult to resist including a few. The inspector of schools reports for the village of Miahuatlán, Oaxaca, the following activities:

The school building has been whitewashed, a donation of five hectares of land for the agriculture of the school has been secured, we have secured school furniture, the house for the teacher has been constructed, we succeeded in getting the community to purchase a gasoline lamp for the night school, a school seal was purchased, a chicken coop, a dove house, an athletic field and a garden have been constructed, a flag has been secured for the school. We are asking from the National Telegraph the installation of the telegraph-telephone apparatus, we secured through the cooperation of the community the fixing of the road, a new educational committee has been named, a committee on health has been installed, all of the children and most of the members of the community have been vaccinated, an anti-alcoholic committee has been named, the open air theater is under construction, and intense campaigns for personal cleanliness of the children and adults is under way, a school shower bath has been constructed. I taught the children some new games and the adults some setting-up exercises. We made efforts to improve the attendance at school and asked the village authorities for a *quota* to varnish the school furniture; we secured some agricultural implements; the dress-making shop in the school has been organized, the school has a sewing machine; we organized a social the evening I was there; the school census has been improved; we asked for the final completion of the school building; outhouses are now under construction; we tried to interest the village authorities in cleaning up the streets; I gave a talk to the community of the meaning of the Federal rural school. The school has, in addition to the Federal teacher, an assistant paid by the community; various socials have been held to increase the interest of the community in the school; a school clock has been purchased; there is a school cooperative with 102 pesos and 8 centavos; there is a flower and vegetable garden; water has been brought to the village; there is a carpenter shop; there is a school theater; there is a school store; the children planted twenty trees. We are trying to get the flooring placed in the school. The school has ten hectares in coffee and three in cocoanuts. There is a post office.

No mere cataloguing of events is sufficient. The spirit of the venture and its difficulties are more clearly revealed in letters. Here is one from an inspector to Mr. Rafael Ramírez, the head of the Rural School Department:

Colotlán, Jalisco
October 15, 1931

My dear *Maestro*,

After wishing you all that is good I take the liberty with a hasty pen to send these lines and present some matters connected with our work. Mounted on a horse, I have spent the last two weeks traveling over this isolated region of my state and have visited 11 schools. Yesterday, my *mozo* deserted me with beast and all and has left me desolate, because I wished to visit at least two more schools in the remaining part of this week. You may not believe it, but I tired the peasant of my own age, and am mighty pleased with this proof of my endurance.

I wish to know all of my schools, to appreciate their present position and to have an idea of the problem in general. I arrive early, get off my horse, and work with the children and teacher all day long. At night I watch the night courses, gather the neighbors, with whom I talk and discuss until eleven or twelve at night. I read something to them, we work over the pressing problems, they tax themselves for the construction of the school, or of the furniture, because most of the precious schools (precious by the spirit of the children and the teachers) have neither an adequate school building nor adequate school furniture. The children are still seated on the ground, on stones, or on pieces of logs and are still crowded in narrow, dark and dirty quarters where one can neither see nor breathe. I say still, because some of these schools have been under way for eight years. *Maestro*, I believe that without neglecting the task that the Department under your control entrusts to us with so much earnestness and affection, that I should concentrate this year upon solving this problem of school housing and school furniture. If I succeed this year in solving this problem then I will feel that I have taken a definite step in the right direction. The *campesinos* are enthusiastic but wish that we would understand them and enter into their spirit. I have called all of the neighbors together and only those that were away from the community failed to come. It was moving to see even the women with little children in their arms listening with the greatest interest and stimulating the men. When I see this I wish that I were a great teacher so that I could inspire them with a vision of the better world which they barely envision.

Maestro, I wish to beg of you that you put your attention mainly for the present upon this region. We need schools, there are now only 18 and we need 40. Certainly I understand the difficulty of our government finances, but I am in hopes that in some other state there might be a re-adjustment, because they may not be indispensable there; in such a case favor this region, so much in need and from so many different points of view. Not one of my schools has a library and there are agrarian communities that beg for them. I asked the library section of the Department for four libraries, and I beg of you to use your influence to see to it that they are sent to us. Perhaps the *Misiones culturales* could send us some material. I have talked to the *campesinos* about libraries and about sports. They are anxious to have athletic fields, and we are going to construct some. I shall have good news for you soon. I only ask that you, if possible, send me basket and volley balls, and if possible a complete equipment for baseball as that is the game most desired here.

Clearly enough, if the school is to take on, and carry through, the burdens that have come to it, then the character of the teaching staff becomes crucial in the program. The limitations under which the educational program operated circumscribed the opportunities for selection and training. The Department, to fill the need for teachers, had to accept what it could lay its hands on. Limitations of time and money have made adequate teacher training (adequate in view of the need) out of the question. The program had to be carried through by compromise. There was no time to train the teachers in the beginning, there has been no money with which to do it properly, since then.

The need, however, has been imperative, and there has been a compromise—a happy compromise under the circumstances. The government could not send the teachers to a training school; it therefore sent the training school to the teacher. That proved simpler and cheaper. It could not give its teachers a minimum of two or three years preparation, it therefore attempted to continue in short periods, year after year, the improvement of the teachers already on the field. It could not develop a highly paid staff of experts, so it drew from the teachers themselves, and from their experience, such light and knowledge as could be obtained for mutual improvement. The traveling Cultural Missions, first tried out in 1923, and of which there are now 12, are the agencies designed for the training of the teachers in service. It is in fact a species of seasonal teachers' institute for rural teachers, organized at low cost, but equipped to impart the kind of knowledge most essential if the rural school teacher is to assume the ever-increasing responsibility which comes to him as the sole representative of the outside world in the isolated hamlets where he functions.

The plan of organization of these cultural missions is simple. Each is composed of seven members; a nurse, a social worker, a teacher of music, a teacher of physical education, an expert in arts and crafts, an agriculturist, and an experienced teacher. These missions are allocated to regions, and settled for a month at a time in a centrally located community. To the village are brought all the teachers from the surrounding country, sometimes as many as one hundred. For the period of a month these rural teachers live in close coöperation, exchange experiences, and acquire as much as can be abosrbed in that time from the teaching staff.

They are divided up into sections and each is given the specialized training the staff can impart. The physical director puts the teachers through an intensive daily course in setting up exercises and games which the teacher, upon returning to his school, is expected to impart to the children. The nurse teaches the advantages of vaccination, simple preventive medicine, first aid, the handling of the little *botiquin* (medicine chest), sanitation. The social worker concentrates upon home life, community organization, domestic arts, and the special needs of children and women. The agriculturist gives simple instructions in gardening, planting, soil, seed selection, special adaptation of crops to peculiarities of climate and soil, and so forth. All the teachers are put through the same training. A special and valuable feature is the utilization of the community where the cultural mission is located for the month as an experimental ground, as raw material.

The entire community is drawn into the activities of the mission, and an attempt is made to do for that community, by collective effort on the part of the teacher and his associates, that which each teacher is expected to do over a period of time and by himself in his own community. The traveling mission permits an exchange of experience among the teachers, and gives the isolated individual a periodic opportunity to refresh his spirit and reinforce his enthusiasm. It also serves the end of making teacher training a process repeated year after year. What the teacher learns in this improvised training school he may give out in his community, and what he learns in his community he may share with the other members of the cultural mission. It, therefore, combines learning and doing, and gives that continuity to professional training which is so essential if the daily routine is not to weaken the initial vigor and enthusiasm.

But it is clear that this process of teacher training is not sufficient for the problem in hand. It has served its purpose in increasing the sense of complexity of the problem among many members of its educational staff, and it has also provided stimulus, ideas and enthusiasm. But it is entirely too temporary as a teacher-training method. It gives the staff of the mission insufficient time to become thoroughly familiar with the problem of a region, and it takes on something of the spirit of an excursion and a holiday. This is said not in criticism of the performance of the cultural mission, but in an attempt to indicate its limitations. Under the circumstances it has servied a useful function and has had a good influence. It merits the highest praise as a technique, but clearly it is not sufficient for the ends in view—the incorporation of the rural community.

A further effort at teacher training, initiated in 1926, has been through rural normal schools, of which there are twenty at present. These are located in special areas and attempt to develop teachers for the country surrounding them. Into the rural normal schools are drawn the more promising students of the rural schools themselves, selected with the aid of the inspectors. They are given a two- or three-year course in preparation for the career of rural school teacher. Just as the first teachers were taken from the urban centers, these are drawn from the rural environment. Experience has shown that the city-bred teachers adjust themselves to a rural environment with great difficulty. The gap between them and the rural population is too great. In the rural normal school therefore a studied effort is made to increase the knowledge and aptitude of the students without taking them out of their *milieu*. The rural normal school attempts to prepare the rural school teacher for the tasks ahead by requiring him to carry out these tasks in school as a matter of daily routine. The school has its own farm and farm animals, small industries, all of those activities which can be developed within it and around it with the tools and equipment ordinarily available or which may be devised in a small community. The rural school teacher is, therefore, much better trained for his special task than were the earlier teachers from the city. These teachers go back to their own villages, or to villages like theirs, and fit more easily into the environment; they know the language and the habits of their communities, are steeped in its traditions, are known to and are accepted by the rural village with less friction.

The rural normal school opens a wider horizon and a greater opportunity to the children of the isolated communities; it stimulates internal leadership and taps the spiritual resources of the villages for their own needs and aspirations. The rural normal school is closer to the soil and avoids difficulties that come from a stranger's incursion as teacher and leader, because the city-bred person is essentially a stranger in the rural environment. Recently twelve Federal Agricultural Schools have been turned over to the Department of Education as part of its equipment for teacher training.

But, clearly enough, even if the rural normal school develops so that it can ultimately supply all the teachers needed by the rural communities in Mexico, it leaves an essential problem unsolved—the problem of extending to the rural community the varied and manifold services and contacts it requires for growth and fusion with the rest of Mexico.

In addition to the rural normal school, another agency is needed, and the cultural mission has been made to serve that purpose by localizing it and making it permanent. This is still an experiment, but even as such it has been, I think, largely successful, and has indicated the kind of institution that can be developed and that might serve the larger aim of both continued professional training for the teacher in the field and the development of activities and services within the communities themselves.

The Permanent Cultural Mission at Actopan, Hidalgo, has certainly served to show that this is possible, even in an environment of greatest poverty, with a group of Indians (the Otomi) who are not only very poor, but among the least developed of Indian groups in Mexico, living in an arid and unkindly environment and having few of the resources that make for easy economic betterment. Certainly anyone who has seen these communities respond to the stimulus and guidance provided by the permanent cultural mission must recognize its great possibilities for usefulness. This mission, composed of a staff that consists of a physician who is in charge, a midwife, a nurse, a social worker, a musician, a teacher of handicrafts, a mason, and a carpenter, permanently housed, and possessed of a truck to carry the staff from Actopan to the different villages, has served effectively the double purpose of teacher training and community development.

The permanent mission sought to utilize the school as the social center in each village, and through the agencies developed about the school, endeavored to raise the social and economic level of the community—each craftsman working on his own specialty, but all coördinating their work, through meetings and discussions. The doctor, in addition to developing a sanitarium in Actopan, where the mission was housed, worked toward building small first-aid units in the surrounding communities. With the help of the nurse he successfully attempted to develop among the young women in a number of villages *comisiones* (committees) that could do vaccinating, bandaging and simple nursing. The staff was bent on developing self-help and self motivating agencies within the community. In two of the villages the communities built small hospitals.

What was done by the doctor and nurse was done in turn by the midwife, who, working with the local midwife in each community, by demonstration, by regular meetings of the midwives from the different villages on a specified day during the week, attempted to improve the crude and primitive practices to which they were bound by tradition. The social worker, in her turn, worked to develop leadership among the women, and to pass on to them the varied techniques that would improve both the home and the social life within it.

The importance of the effort lay in its constant search for the development of local leadership, the building up of local initiative, the development of local institutions that would of themselves become agencies for spreading the newer knowledge. Such a simple thing as fruit conservation became useful, not merely because it led to the organization of a *comisión*, the development of leadership, the improvement of food, but also because it led to the teaching of such simple things as weights and measures, the use of a clock, the importance of cleanliness.

The agriculturist became active in the organization of coöperatives, in the development of new crops, in the teaching of animal husbandry, in the utilization of soils. The instructor of handicrafts occupied himself in similar fashion, in developing coöperative tanneries, in developing new uses for the fibre, in the weaving of hammocks, and in many other activities.

Mason and carpenter were loaned to the villages, as they were needed, in the building of schools, in construction of open-air theaters, in the making of school furniture.

In the small truck, the group used to visit certain villages on specified days; the coming of the truck would lead to the ringing of the church bells and the gathering of the people. The *comisión*, with special interest, gathered in a group about the instructor who was showing them some special technique. Those studying music went off with the musician, the farmers formed a circle around the agriculturist, the young women around the social worker, the expectant mothers grouped themselves close to the midwife, the ailing and the *comisión* of health gathered near the doctor and nurse. That is, the problems of an entire community were being treated and handled, with persistent emphasis upon the immediacy of the problems and the possibility of developing initiative and leadership for their solution within the small community.

This emphasis upon the development of internal initiative, this constant search for the bringing of leadership to the front, and the effort to build up institutions within the little village is of profoundly greater importance than the specific help that the communities receive from the mission. It is stimulating the growth of institutions within the rim of the political machinery of the *municipio*, inside the political organization of the counties and independent of them. Until this time every new project had first to come from the outside, every little thing that a community wanted was to be had by going to some one in authority and asking for it as a favor and waiting for its satisfaction, a satisfaction often long delayed and frequently never fulfilled. The development of the habits of internal motivation and leadership within the rural village, not merely for the maintenace of the old (they have, through persistent use, learned to keep that with sufficient tenacity) but to develop the kind of effort and attitude that would make possible the solution of new difficulties by the assumption of responsibility for community reconstruction internally, is very important indeed.

This type of institution, working with the school and the school teachers, using the school as a center, gathering the community about it, organizing inter-community coöperation, as was often done in Actopan, stimulating internal leadership, attacking all of the manifold problems within the community, is essential, it seems to me, if the program of rural reconstruction is to have its full development. The institution must not be too large, nor must it attempt to serve so large a district or so many villages as to make it impossible to develop personal contacts, friendships and loyalties, between the members of the mission, the teachers and the people of the villages. One of the most interesting and valuable aspects of the development in Actopan was the friendly relationship that developed between the people in the communities and the members of the mission.

In addition to the traveling cultural missions, the rural normal schools, and the permanent cultural missions, there was, until recently, also a school for Indians located in Mexico City, which admitted only pure-blooded Indian boys from the mountains, provided them a three-year course and prepared them to be teachers. The school was interesting and valuable as a manifestation of the changed spirit in Mexico toward the Indian, and was a symbol that the Indian had come into his own. It stood also as a proof to the City of Mexico, which has for so many centuries been the Indian's greatest enemy, that the imputation of the Indian's inferiority came out of a prejudice originating with the Conquest. For the fact seemed patent that these children, taken from the most backward areas of Mexico, showed within a very short time an aptitude and ability that gave them a scholastic status in the regular schools equal to, and not infrequently superior to, the children of the city. In fact, so striking was this manifestation of scholastic aptitude that it caused no little comment and helped to strengthen the conviction that the ancient imputation of inferiority is unjustified. This school was recently closed because it was too expensive and because it had served its purpose.

In numerical terms, the result of the educational undertaking can be summarized in a few words. At the end of 1929 the total number of schools in the Republic was 19,412, according to *Estadística nacional*. These included all schools, Federal, state, county and private, as well as kindergartens, rural schools, primary schools, normal schools, preparatory schools, professional schools, schools of technology and fine arts. Of these, 6,106 were rural Federal schools (including *escuelas de circuito*), 4,574 were rural schools maintained by the states, and 1,799 were private rural schools. These last are really schools maintained by large estates, industrial or mining companies, in compliance with requirements of Article 123 of the Constitution of 1917, and supervised by the states.

There were, therefore, at the end of 1929, 12,479 rural schools. This number has increased somewhat since, and the lastest figure for the Federal schools is 6,689.[1] The teachers in Federal rural schools were largely teachers who had no normal school training. The 3,459 Federal rural schools (not counting *escuelas de circuito*) were served by 4,527 teachers, 4,162 of whom had no normal school training. Most (2,439) of these schools met in a single room. The total registration in rural schools, including *escuelas de circuito*, was 467,137 and the average attendance was 273,253. There was also an attendance of 95,449 adults.

The total enrollment in all the rural schools in the Republic at the end of 1929 was 1,662,371, and of these the registration in Federal, state and private rural schools amounted to 1,560,786. The amount set aside by the Federal and state governments for rural education is something above 7,000,000 pesos.

[1] There are now, (July, 1933) 6,850 Federal rural schools.

CHAPTER 26

THE VILLAGE AND THE SCHOOL

I N SPITE of the magnitude of the present achievement, the
problem of educating the rural population of Mexico remains largely a matter for the future. The mere size of
the problem is staggering. If it were only possible to shift the
burden upon the country, the *municipio*, but that is clearly
out of the question. Every bit of evidence available, historical and contemporary, shows clearly that the *municipio*
is not a competent agency for dealing with education. It is too
poor; it is too ignorant; it is subject to the whim of local
political passions and local politics. It has neither the character, the resources, the ideals nor the standards for the rural
reconstruction—in the sense in which the school assumes
that problem. What is true of the county is true in a lesser
degree of the state. Although there are states like Oaxaca,
Hidalgo, Mexico, Tamaulipas and VeraCruz, where the attack upon the educational problem has been extensive and
intensive, it is still true, unfortunately, that so far as rural
education is concerned the state schools are poorer in every
way and by every test when compared with the Federal
schools. They have less imagination and enthusiasm behind
them. They are more poorly equipped. They have poorer supervision, are more subject to political consideration and influence, are less responsible institutions.

It would be a good thing for Mexican education if the
whole rural school program were placed under Federal control. It is true, even today, that the best work done in the
rural schools in the states copies the work of the Federal
rural schools, and follows the same trends—but it requires
no great insight to see that they shine with a reflected light.
Politics becomes more intense in Mexico as the unit in which

it operates becomes smaller. State politics are more intense than Federal, and local politics are more intense than state politics. For this reason it is better to have the state, rather than the county, administer the rural schools, and still better to have the Federal government, rather than the state, exercise authority over them. The problem is one of rural incorporation—not merely Indian incorporation.

If the rural community is to be made to feel the impact of the modern world, made to absorb something of the modern civilization that the cities in Mexico enjoy; if some sense of national unity is to be achieved; if the rural districts are to become a part of Mexico in more than a merely physical sense, then the sooner the rural-school program achieves unification under the auspices of the Federal government, the better for the program and for the people. Left to the counties, the problem is hopeless. Left to the states, the problem is very nearly so. It will be a long time, indeed, before the states, with a few honorable exceptions, take their responsibilities seriously.

But for the Federal government to take the task in hand is a matter of gigantic proportions, something which will tax not merely the economic, but the spiritual, resources of the country. It is clear enough that the country cannot afford the program financially, and spiritually it cannot afford to neglect it. The task must be done and it will have to be done largely without money, largely through the enthusiasm and the faith that has made so much of the present program possible. In dealing with this problem, Mexico will have to prove its genius in an even greater measure than it has so far done.

There are at present, as we said before, counting all of the rural schools in the country—state, Federal and municipal, 12,479 schools served by teachers. But that, after all, is but a fraction of Mexico's need. There are, by whatever count, between sixty-five and seventy thousand communities in Mexico. If we take the study made recently by the

National Agrarian Commission, there are 35,595 communities of less than a hundred people each, and 25,854 communities of a hundred and more. Mexico should have at least 30,000 more rural schools to serve the population. Even then, it would still be true that a number of the more isolated, more primitive, and less stable population groups would not be served by schools. But 30,000 additional schools means developing five times as many schools as the Federal government is supporting at present; training five times as many teachers; providing for five times as much general overhead. And it is clear that, mighty as is the present effort, it must be considered a minimum, an experimental minimum. The school must become more embracing, must be served by larger resources from outside, must generally assume responsibility for many of the things for which it has assumed responsibility only in special and isolated places. Clearly enough, so large an undertaking cannot be supported by the present administration and the present political set-up. It will have to be done without money—and with the use of the ingenuity and enthusiasm that have already been displayed.

The school building can be provided by the community. Schools have been provided so often in the past that there is a very real technique developed, and even the poorest community can and does contribute its own housing. The land can be given by the community, especially if it has its own *ejidos* and if it hasn't, then the Federal rural school as it exists has little place or opportunity in that community.

Land, not only for the school and the school garden, but also an *ejido* for the school (a piece of land of at least twelve and one half acres) can be provided, and with the community effort for tilling this school land it can be made, as it has been made in many communities, to serve many needs of the school. I have seen schools where a school lamp, school furniture, tools, and many other essentials have been secured from the income from the school land. This income is not sufficient for all the school needs, but under the circumstances it can be made to serve many of them. The school furniture, if there is to be any, must be homemade. The reading material is best supplied from the daily, or still better, the Sunday, newspapers. One of the most interesting things I have seen in Mexico is men and women, sitting under a gasoline lamp or the light of homemade candles, listening to a story read from the Sunday paper (some very old Sunday paper) by the teacher, and I have seen this in the remotest sections of Mexico, in the tropical forests of Yucatan and Tabasco, in the mountains of Nayarit. Everything about the Sunday paper becomes useful. The stories, the news, the pictures, the funny sheet, the games, the designs for dresses, the cooking recipes. In fact, I have seen the teacher cut out the separate sections and sew them together as a sort of book for future reference.

Either this type of material, or a specially printed weekly magazine, especially adapted to the needs of the rural school, but alive with the currents of the present world, will have to be provided. The purchase of books on a large scale for the children and adults is out of the question—there is no money for such a project at present, and unless the government can forego its army there will not be any for a long time to come.

In addition to the land, the services in the form of labor and the equipment that can be improvised, there is still the question of pay for the teacher. If the Federal government undertook to pay the rural teachers all over the country (at least fifty thousand) even at a minimum of a peso a day, this would mean for the country as a whole fifty thousand pesos per day, or more than 18,000,000 pesos a year for salary alone. Under present circumstances that is not within the reach of the government.

An attempt to face this difficulty has been made in Mexico

before, when the *escuelas de circuito* were started. Here the government developed under Federal supervision some three thousand new schools with a minimum of expense. The teachers were largely, though not completely, paid by the communities. A teacher received his income from the contribution of one *centavo* a day by members of the little community with the food for the teacher provided in succession by the families, each in turn giving food for a day. That is but a partial solution of the problem.

An additional solution of greater permanence is the recent suggestion that in each community there should be set aside an *ejido del maestro*, a piece of land set aside for the teacher. The community could by the traditional method of community effort till this land, and from it the teacher might draw, if the land was sufficient, a considerable part of his needs for livelihood. This land might also serve as a sort of experimental ground, as the teacher will, of necessity, be more sophisticated and better trained in the use of his land than are the other members of the community. Here, then, is another and an essential step in the direction of the solution of the problem.

As things stand, the contribution by the rural community towards the solution of the basic aspiration of the Revolution must, therefore, include the following items: the community must build the school building; it must provide the basic essentials (the furniture and equipment of the school), in so far as they are provided at all, by making them; it must furnish a piece of land for the school, from the resources of which the basic school needs can be slowly satisfied; it must provide keep and maintenance for the teacher through the tilling of the plot of land set aside for the teacher's income. *The rural community must support the school in the future the way it supported the Church in the past.* It must do this if the present and future generations in Mexico are to have the schools that they need, and the program is feasible, for it is consistent with the traditions and aspirations of the village communities.

If the communities can take these matters over, as they have in many places—and must, if it is to be done at all—then there is some hope for the extension of the school program generally in the rural districts. Otherwise, education will for many years to come be the privilege of a small proportion of the larger rural communities.

With such a program taken over by the village communities, the effort of the Federal government will become largely one of teacher training and supervision, with some supplemental financing of the teachers themselves in special instances. But such a program of education will depend for its feasibility, not to say success, upon the possession of lands by the communities, of the possession of *ejidos*. In other words, the fulfillment of the educational program of the Revolution will depend upon the fulfillment of its agrarian program. The first becomes impossible without the second, and the second becomes only half useful if it lacks a school. The rural community in Mexico cannot have a school unless it has an *ejido*—I mean a modern school of the type developed by the Federal Department of Education. And if it has an *ejido* the rural community requires a school of this type to make its *ejido* serve those broad ends which lie embedded in the Revolution itself. They are both parts of the same aspiration, the rejuvenation of the rural community.

When one reviews the sacrifices that the most primitive of Indian groups are making for the school, when one sees that nothing seems too great a task, that for the school nothing seems impossible, the question arises—why? Why this love for the school? Why this labor of building, carving, digging and carrying? Indians march through narrow mountain paths in single file for seven days, carrying on their backs tin for the roofing of a school. I have seen them loaded with empty boxes on a four days' march for chairs and desks for their school. They will turn out and till the soil (the *ejido* of the *escuela*) in turn or in groups, without remuneration and with a song; they will carry logs from great distances; tax themselves to buy lime; tax themselves to bring a band and parade to receive the inspector of schools or the director of education. It is not mere love of the school, surely. They, especially the poorer and more primitive Indians, can barely know what it is all about. They themselves do not read or write. They have never really felt the need for reading and writing. Their life has marched on in a perfect rhythm of dance, worship, play, work and sorrow, without books and without teachers. In their experience the occasional person who could read was a stranger and foreigner. No, there is something else in the love and affection which they lavish upon the school—something closer to their hearts and nearer to their beliefs and attitudes than mere reading and writing.

For one thing the school is for the children. It is there that the children gather, play and work, and there is a proverbial affection and respect for the children in many an Indian community. For example, in one Mije community I found that no sale could be made if any member of the family, even the smallest, objected to it. It is illustrated in another Indian community, Amatanango, where the children of early age were introduced into the village government by being incorporated as messengers of the village *cabildo*, and that is the first step in the process of passing through all of the steps of government and governing that the community provides until one becomes an *anciano*, an elder. It is illustrated in the religious dances, except where they have been formalized and standardized, in that the smallest of the children, both boys and girls, dance with their elders all through the fiesta. I recall one Huichol Indian who, with his little son by the hand, danced about a fire for hours, and when the little fellow tired he lifted him up, continuing the dance, and among these same Indians the women dance with their children on their backs or in their arms. The school, when it is for the children, is not merely an isolated affair for the children; the children are interwoven into the very fiber of the life of the community, as children in an urban, or even a rural, modern community are not. There seems to be no distinction. They are a part of the community itself. It is this, perhaps, that explains why one finds upon occasion an elder in the seat of a child in school. "I had no work today," said an elderly Indian among the Zapotecs, "so I came to school." I found similar illustrations in Tabasco and Yucatan.

There is another fact that explains this enthusiasm and activity. The school is not from the outside, but from the inside, so to speak. It has fitted into the village democracy and become a source of stimulus and strength to that democracy. It has been incorporated into the texture of the community activities to an extent that seems incredible to one who has not seen it. It is this that must be taken into consideration when one talks about the "living" school. It isn't something outside and foreign. It is something native and integrated. It may bring new elements of culture, but does so unconsciously with the consent and participation of the community. It has in many of the smaller villages become the very center of all activities, social, economic, cultural and political.

But in addition to all of this, there is something more. There is in the school something of the mysticism and love that were given previously to the Church. When one sees the immense churches which stand towering in many of even the smallest villages in Mexico, one wonders at the effort that went into them, one wonders at the sacrifice that was made for them. A little village of straw-thatched huts, or of adobe *casitas*, poverty stricken beyond measure, would find the means to build itself a church which in our world would do for a large and rich community. It is not enough to talk about forced and slave labor, which may have been used, but not all churches were built that way. When one sees the carvings and the paintings, the love lavished upon the saints and the altars, one realizes that it was not due to mere force, but to that mystic something which in older days built the pyramids of Teotihuacán, the cities of Chichen-Itzá, which strewed Mexico from one end to the other with untold numbers of stone cities raised to their gods, without tools, but with patience, and love, and faith, and fear. It is something of this that goes into the school; it is something of the "mystic attitude that leads the Indian to work for his school with the same affection with which he previously worked for the Church." These words are from a letter by the Director of Education in the state of Sonora, and they help to shed some light upon the problem here under discussion.

The church is now poor. The priest comes rarely (once a year, or once every few months), if at all. The church is still used and the people carry on their religious life in their own way. The school, however, is open all the time. The teacher is there all the week. The children play about the school. The teacher has become the guide, the counselor, the adviser. It is said that in many schools he serves not merely as the doctor, but also as the priest; he marries the villagers. He has become the source of most of their contact with the world, of most of their inspiration. He writes official letters, represents them before the state government, looks after their troubles, helps them in their needs, answers their questions. He is frequently the only contact with the outside world, the only representative of civilization in the community. It is this that explains his hold upon the village. In many villages which I have visited the teacher occupies a moral position, holds a place in the affections and enthusiastic support of the members of the community comparable to the place previously occupied by the priest. In comparison to him the priest is an outsider and a stranger who comes rarely and stays but a few days during the year.

The school is not merely replacing the church in the affections of the community, but is frequently closely identified with it physically. The school building may occupy the old church residence or convent, the basket-ball ground is often in the church yard, the very bells of the church are rung to call the children to school in the morning. The old mystic faith which made the Indian so good a church member makes him today an equally good supporter of the new school which has come to him.

One may, perhaps, summarize the changed philosophy of education in the following terms: give the rural villages the land which they occupy and till so that they may have the means of economic well-being; bring to them the benefits of modern civilization which to date have been enjoyed only by the white race and those associated with them; but in the process, make every effort to save the cultural content that survives among the Indians. In fact, provide means for the development and reinvigoration of the native culture. Make the new elements an addition to the old; an enrichment of the past heritage rather than a substitute for it. Bring the new, but let the new be absorbed slowly, voluntarily, adopted, modified, and incorporated. Education must not merely be a unilateral process of giving the Indians newer methods and newer ways of life. It must be a process of adoption of the white culture by the Indians and a reciprocal adoption of the Indian culture by the whites, each group absorbing and modifying, a process of mutual infiltration and fusion that will not involve sudden and violent destruction or denial. The process will be lengthy; it cannot be sudden. Culture is persistent and tenacious. It hangs on in spite of every difficulty. What must be sought is a method of mutual adaptability, and above all, freedom to choose, to take, to modify. There must be a conscious attempt at a mutual evolution of the various cultures, and not efforts at artificial imposition.

That, perhaps, is descriptive of the spirit that animates

the educational movement in Mexico; and it is for Mexico at least a complete repudiation of the theory and practice that prevailed for four centuries; it places its hope for the future upon a base that is broad enough to absorb, without destroying, all the variants of life and culture that make up the Mexico of today, a conscious appreciation of which is laying the foundation of the Mexico of tomorrow. The Spanish Conquest has been completely repudiated; the Mexico of tomorrow, which is envisioned by the educational leaders of today, has its roots in that racial and cultural base which was denied for four centuries, but which has again, as a result of the Revolution, become the main source of the Mexico of tomorrow.

AGRARISTA GUARDING HIS NEWLY WON LAND

BIBLIOGRAPHIC NOTE

Good bibliographies on Mexico may be found in George McCutchen McBride, *The Land Systems of Mexico*, "American Geographical Society Research Series," No. 12 (1923); Herbert Ingram Priestly, *The Mexican Nation* (1923); Ernest Gruening, *Mexico and Its Heritage* (1928); Vicente Lombardo Toledano, *La libertad sindical en México* (1926) and *Bibliografía del trabajo y de la previsión social en México* (1928); Juan B. Iguíniz, *Bibliografía de novelistas mexicanos* (1926) and *Bibliografía biográfica mexicana* (1930); Departamento del Petróleo, de la Secretaría de Industria, Comercio y Trabajo, *Bibliografía del petróleo en México* (1927).

For a bibliography of the Revolution up to 1916, see Ignacio B. del Castillo, *Bibliografía de la Revolución mexicana de 1910–1916*, also *Bibliografía de la imprenta de la Cámara de diputados*, in *Concurso de bibliografía y biblioteconomía, convocado por la Biblioteca Nacional, México* (1918). A more recent bibliography of the Mexican Revolution is *Bibliografía de la Revolución mexicana (hasta mayo de 1931)*, by Roberto Ramos. A really adequate bibliography of the Revolution would have to include the special articles that have appeared in the Mexican newspapers and magazines since 1910.

INDEX

INDEX

Méndez, Juan, 90
Menéndez, Luis, 156
Mestizo(s), 10, 12, 13, 14, 15, 17, 18, 19, 20, 21, 22, 23, 24, 25, 26, 29, 30, 33, 46, 52, 63, 69, 70, 75, 94, 102, 125, 141, 191, 198, 272, 273
Mexicano, language, 9
Mexico City, 10, 14, 23, 45, 80, 96, 117, 120, 122, 123, 124, 131, 132, 154, 155, 156, 157, 158, 159, 160, 161, 162, 163, 165, 177, 178, 183, 192, 193, 194, 195, 232, 233, 263, 296
Mexico, State of, 14, 54, 78, 140, 141, 178, 189, 193, 194, 197, 209, 211, 298
Miahuatlán, Oaxaca, 286
Michoacán, State of, 139, 192, 194, 208, 209, 218, 272
Migration to United States, 136–37
Miji, language, 9
Mijis (Indians), 7, 11, 69
Mining, 13, 15, 16, 25, 35, 36, 37, 68, 89, 146, 226, 227, 228, 230
Miramón, 104
Misiones culturales, 288, 289–91, 292, 293–95, 296
Missions, 8, 13, 42
Mixteco (Indians), 32
Molina Enríquez, Andrés, 6, 95, 118, 141
Moncaleano, Juan Francisco, 156
Morán, 81
Morelos, 47, 65
Morelos, State of, 10, 14, 76, 140, 157, 163, 178, 179, 193, 194, 197, 198, 209, 229
Morones, Luis N., 148, 246, 247, 248, 249
Morrow, Dwight M., 174
Mujíca, Francisco J., 150, 165, 167, 236, 248

National Agrarian Commission, 129, 202, 207, 208, 210, 212, 216, 300
Nayarit, Sierra de, 263
Nayarit, State of, 3, 13, 28, 30, 90, 192, 194, 207, 209, 218, 275, 301
Negrete, 81, 104
New Mexico, 69
New Spain, 8
New Zealand, 237

Nuevo León, State of, 77, 78, 192, 194, 210

Oaxaca, State of, 10, 14, 39, 77, 78, 80, 95, 193, 194, 197, 209, 211, 212, 229, 263, 272, 282, 298
Oaxaca, Valley of, 121, 122
Obregón, Alvaro, 105, 116, 120, 126, 137, 147, 154, 157, 158, 159, 160, 165, 166, 171, 176, 180, 233, 244, 246, 247, 248, 250, 265, 266
Oil, *see* Petroleum
Olvera, 90
Orizaba, 14, 162
Orozco, Pascual, 148
Orozco y Bara (quoted), 6
Ortiz Rubio, President, 250
Otomis (Indians), 11, 293

Pachuca, 14
Palafox, Juan de, 46
Palavacini, Felix, 153, 165
Parrés, Doctor, 180
Paso del Macho, Vera Cruz, 148
Patronato, 48, 49, 55
Pedraza, 81
Pérez Taylor, Rafael, 156, 157
Petroleum, 135–36, 226, 230
Philippines, 68
Pimentel (Francisco), 32, 144, 145
Plan of Guadalupe, 155
Plan of Vera Cruz, 77
Portes Gil (Emilio), 127, 222, 248, 250
Pozo Grande, 279
Priestley, Herbert Ingram, 309
Profit sharing, 239
Protestant Church, 35
Puebla, City of, 10, 14, 54, 77, 122
Puebla, State of, 10, 14, 90, 139, 152, 155, 178, 193, 194, 197, 198, 209, 271
Puebla (Indians), 26
Pueblo Nuevo, 28
Puerto Rico, 40, 68
Puig Casauranc, Doctor, 222

Querétaro, State of, 30, 77, 78, 90, 139, 192, 194, 208, 222
Quichés (Indians), 69
Quintanar, 81
Quintana Roo, 229
Quiroga, 37

315